ICE WORLD

ICE WORLD

TECHNIQUES AND EXPERIENCES OF MODERN ICE CLIMBING

JEFF LOWE

THE
MOUNTAINEERS

Published by
The Mountaineers
1001 SW Klickitat Way, Suite 201
Seattle, Washington 98134

9 8 7 6 5
5 4 3 2 1

Published simultaneously in Canada by Rocky Mountain Books, #4 Spruce Centre S.W., Calgary, Alberta T3C 3B3

Published simultaneously in Great Britain by Cordee, 3a DeMontfort Street, Leicester, England, LE1 7HD

Edited by Kathleen Larson Florio
Cover design by The Mountaineers Books
Book design and typography by The Mountaineers Books
Printed and bound in Hong Kong

Cover photographs: *Front:* The author climbing Octopussy, Vail, Colorado
Back: On Octopussy, Vail, Colorado *(Photos: Brad Johnson)*
Frontispiece: The author climbing Bridalveil Falls, January 1974 *(Photo: Mike Lowe)*

Library of Congress Cataloging-in-Publication Data
Lowe, Jeff.
    Ice World : techniques and experiences of modern ice climbing /
Jeff Lowe.
        p.   cm.
    Rev., expanded ed. of: The ice experience, c1979.
    Includes index.
    ISBN 0-89886-446-1 paper
        0-89886-471-2 cloth
    1. Snow and ice climbing. 2. Snow and ice climbing—United States. 3. Snow and ice climbing—Canada. I. Lowe, Jeff. Ice experience. II. Title.
GV200.3.L677 1996
796.9—dc20
                                                  95-31710
                                                  CIP

Because of liability concerns, at the time of publication there is no public access to Bridalveil Falls. The Access Fund, which represents the interests of American climbers, and the town of Telluride are working to find a remedy to the problem. Contact the Access Fund, (303) 545-6772, for current information.

▼ ▼ ▼

**The author on a serac, Mont
Blanc du Tacul**
(Photo: René Robert)

For Teri, Sonja, and Hunter—
teamed up for adventure in this cold, beautiful world

". . . my empire is made of the stuff of crystals,
its molecules arranged in a perfect pattern.
Amid the surge of the elements,
a splendid hard diamond takes shape,
an immense, faceted, transparent mountain."
—Italo Calvino, *Invisible Cities*

CONTENTS

FOREWORD

It was on a Russian peak in the Pamir range more than twenty years ago when I first realized that Jeff Lowe was destined to become one of the world's great mountaineers.

As we belayed and climbed up the steep snow and ice face of Peak Nineteen to the 19,423-foot summit, Jeff, even at the age of twenty-three, showed me he was one of the few athletes in any sport who could live up to his growing international reputation. His flawless ice-climbing technique and fluid, effortless motion were obvious skills few mountaineers could match. But it was his confidence and almost spiritual perception of the climb that moved us to the summit.

We separated after the Pamirs trip and followed separate trails and climbed with different partners to achieve our goals. Jeff went on to accomplish some of the world's great alpine climbs. My path led me to the Himalayas. I always hoped, though, that someday we would again share a rope.

Fifteen years later our trails finally merged. I teamed up with Jeff once more on a Nepalese peak named Tawoche, six miles from Everest. I knew from having trekked to the base of Tawoche's great Northeast Face in the spring of 1986 that success hinged on two factors: the route must be climbed in winter to avoid falling rock and ice debris and the team would have to include the world's best alpinist, Jeff Lowe.

Despite intense cold, nine bivouacs, my cerebral edema, Jeff's acute mountain sickness, and some incredibly difficult mixed climbing, we summited and made it down safely. Jeff proved to me on that climb that fifteen years had turned a superb climber into a genuine master of his craft.

After climbing with Jeff and knowing him for so many years, I've come to realize that it is not just physical movement in the cold and vertical world that he uses to overcome difficulties but also intense mental preparation and the often neglected sixth sense. As you will read, this sense is perhaps his most important asset.

It is an honor for me to be a part of Jeff's book. Rarely have I seen an author blend instruction and technique so well with their own actual experience and emotion. *Ice World* takes the sport of ice climbing to another frontier and challenges the next generation.

John Roskelley
July 1995

ACKNOWLEDGMENTS

This book is a labor of love that would have been stillborn without the involvement of the following consenting adults (and two great kids!).

Photographers: Greg Lowe, Mike Lowe, George Lowe III, Bill Belcourt, David Breashears, Brad Johnson, Chris Jones, Jon Krakauer, Dan Levison, Tom McCarthy, Mike Munger, Christie Northrop, Jean-Marc Porte, Thierry Renault, René Robert, François-Guy Thivierge, Lance Wilcox, Mark Wilford, and Willis Wood. I would especially like to thank Ian Tomlinson, who was a blind date when my wife, Teri, and I first met him in the Canadian Rockies for the alpine ice shoot. Ian, you went way beyond what was expected. Your photos are excellent, and your quiet competence and good Welsh sense of humor made the time we spent together extremely pleasant. The well-timed shots of single malt scotch never hurt either! Thank you, friend.

Richard Rossiter: Richard took time out from his own massive book project documenting climbs in Rocky Mountain National Park to create the topo drawings for this book. As always, Richard, your drawings are accurate and elegant. Thank you for sharing your artistry.

Special thanks to Rick Medrick, Jeff Long, Bill Roos, and Pat Ament for reading and improving portions of earlier versions of this work.

Correspondents/Informants: Todd Bibler, Barry Blanchard, François Damilano, Mal Duff, Joe Josephson, George Lowe III, Rob Newsom, Rick Wilcox, and others.

John Roskelley: A classic, no-nonsense American who is a giant in Himalayan history, John was one of the first climbers to push into serious class 6 ice twenty years ago. He was the perfect partner on one of my all-time favorite climbs, the East Face of Tawoche in Nepal. Thanks for agreeing to write the Foreword, pilgrim!

Students: Over the years I have been privileged to introduce over eight hundred highly motivated and interesting individuals to the secrets of the ice world. Each seminar had more than one instance in which the teacher became the student, and many of the techniques in this book originated from these exchanges. Thank you all.

Sponsors: I work as a design consultant with some of the top companies in the outdoor industry. Their individual and collective support of my projects keeps me and my family going. Thank you Lafuma (packs), Trango USA (climbing hardware), Marmot (technical outerwear), Terramar (Transport EC2 underwear), Charlet

Moser (ice tools), Edelweiss (ropes), La Sportiva (climbing shoes and boots), and Outdoor Research (gloves, hats, gaiters, and accessories).

Greg Lowe: Greg provided the original inspiration for waterfall ice climbing and helped with development of techniques and tools. Thanks for showing the way, bro.

Bird Lew: Who would have guessed that our student for the water ice shoot would turn out to be such a fast study? Although a top rock climber, Bird was a complete novice on waterfall ice, and after two weeks she was doing M7 climbs in Vail! Bird, your deft climbing style is inspirational.

The Mountaineers Books: Donna DeShazo was enthusiastic about the book from the outset and pushed me to complete it in the end. Cindy Bohn worked exceptionally hard to make sense of text and captions in the final layout, and Alice Merrill's artistic efforts are evident throughout the design of the book. The rest of The Mountaineers editorial, design, production, and promotions staff have also been great to work with. I'd like to thank each of you for your contribution to bringing this project together.

My kids: My seven-year-old daughter, Sonja, and nine-year-old stepson, Hunter, saw very little of me during the photographing and writing of this book, but they accepted the physical and emotional absence quite philosophically, alleviating some of my guilt. I promise to make it up to you guys. We *will* take that two-week camping trip this summer.

My wife and partner: This book is almost as much Teri Ebel's as my own. Being a hopeless computer illiterate (never seem to have time to learn how to operate the damn things), as well as a writer in severe need of an editor, I lucked out when I married a wordsmith with excellent computer skills. Teri's input at every stage of conception, photography, writing, and editing ensured that The Mountaineers at least received a workable manuscript. And she couldn't have been a more joyous student for the alpine ice photos. You're the best, Teri!

INTRODUCTION

The unencumbered rock climber moves freely over good rock, like an ape swinging through the forest. At first glance, the differences between the nearly naked rock climber and the bundled and spiked ice climber are glaring. To achieve a totally "pure" experience, the rock climber, if he or she so desires, might reject all tools—even clothing and shoes. One is obliged, though, to use tools to climb ice. Those who choose the pleasures and challenge of frozen waterfalls or alpine ice slopes must be equipped with specialized hardware and clothing that would seem to dictate a less direct encounter with the environment.

But humans have evolved beyond the simple joys of the ape, and today most of our knowledge of our world and universe comes to us indirectly, through extensions of mind and body—through tools. Just as a powerful hand glass allows us to see clearly that the flakes of falling snow are far more intricate and exquisite than they appear to the naked eye, an ice axe and crampons wielded with skill and concentration can magnify the climber's appreciation of existence. The ice climber's sensitivity is amplified by tools, and a new being is created that revels amidst awesome, seemingly impossible terrain.

The purity of the ice experience lies in learning to use the minimum number of aids in the most efficient manner possible. The first-ever climb of Canada's Takkakkaw Falls took six days, the climbers ascending by means of aid slings clipped to their ice axes and returning to base camp each night with the help of a long series of ropes fixed to their high point. In contrast, the second ascent was accomplished in seven hours by climbers who had pared their tools and attitudes to the essentials.

By carefully selecting simple, well-designed, versatile tools, combining them with the proper skills and experience, and matching all this to an appropriate climb, it is possible for the ice climber to drink deeply of a heady wine. The surreal beauty of a belay situated in a cave with translucent blue walls and a ceiling of a hundred icicles is more otherworldly than anything in the rock climber's experience. And ice climbing has always appealed to the person who loves adventure more than gymnastic exercise.

Yet there are similarities in the rewards offered by the two types of climbing. On a winter icefall, the weekend recreational rock climber who has made the transition to ice can find the same relief from the ennui of everyday life as can be found on a sunny crag. The extremist, in these times of vertical waterfalls and thinly iced mixed climbs, can push technical and physical limits as far as imagination and vision allow. Another benefit to the rock climber who learns ice technique is that some of the finest rock in the world—the great granite free climbs of Mont Blanc or the big walls of the Karakorum, for example—becomes accessible.

There *is* one main difference between rock and ice climbing, and that is the nature of the mediums themselves. While the quality of rock runs the entire spectrum from crumbling sandstone to iron-hard granite, given sections of rock usually do not change a great deal from week to week, or even from year to year. Ice, on the other hand, exhibits daily, even hourly, mutations. A ribbon of hardened water may exist only in the morning hours after a hard freeze; by late afternoon, the only remains might be a wet streak on the rock. An icy couloir can be scoured and pitted by the rockfall that starts as soon as the sun hits that side of the mountain. A serac could collapse just as you decide to cross beneath it. The ice climber, besides attaining a degree of technical proficiency, must also develop a "feel" for these ever-changing conditions.

Ice climbing is a craft that must be further subdivided to give a clear understanding of the modern scene. The traditional terrain for ice climbing is found only in the high mountains—on glaciers, ice fields, and couloirs. The ice types in these locales, including Scottish rime ice, vary widely, but all have one thing in common: the ice begins as some form of frozen precipitation and, through time, pressure, and heat, metamorphoses into something identified generically as *alpine ice*. In the last two decades, another kind of ice has grabbed the spotlight. *Water ice* can be found wherever water and freezing temperatures coincide. It is generally much more brittle than its alpine cousin, and often much steeper, providing a welcome challenge to today's climber. With greatly improved gear and without the psychological burden of the unknown—thanks to a wealth of guidebooks and greater general knowledge of ice conditions and techniques—modern ice climbers make light of all but a few of the hardest alpine routes.

This book is a personal celebration of the slippery game as it has evolved and is played throughout the world. It is a radically revised and greatly expanded version of *The Ice Experience* (Contemporary Books, 1979) and the ice chapters in *Climbing* (Bell and Hyman, 1986), both of which have long been out of print. The scope of this book is the entire ice world, from waterfalls to Himalayan ice faces. A selective history of alpine-style and waterfall ice climbing (Icy Roots, Crystal Blossoms) sets the stage for stories from my own experience (One Man's Frostbite). This is followed by a thorough discussion of clothing, equipment, and techniques (Accoutrement and The Cold Dance Review), illustrated with photos by Ian Tomlinson. Ian's photos were shot specially for this book in the Canadian Rockies (showing techniques for alpine ice, with my wife, Teri Ebel, as my student) and in Colorado (showing techniques for water ice, with Bird Lew as my student). Finally the book concludes with a general guide to the ice world (The Hard Water Guide), with sixteen outstanding climbs singled out for detailed treatment, accompanied by elegant topos drawn by Richard Rossiter.

A couple of notes: Newcomers to the basic methods of ascent should seek competent instruction from an experienced friend or professional before attempting to use the information in the technique chapters. In making the transition to ice, even climbers thoroughly familiar with rock techniques often discover a pitfall or two. The technique chapters were written with a certain amount of technical knowledge and experience assumed.

Throughout this book you will find gradings associated with the climbs described. In the interest of consistency, all grades are in accordance with the system proposed in the following section. Wherever I am not certain of a grade, I have included a question mark along with my estimate of the difficulty.

Although I have striven for historical objectivity and geographical diversity, you will be aware of my personal bias. I make no excuse for that. The value of the ice experience lies not in faceless absolutes, but rather in its effect on each individual.

The legendary British climber Joe Brown maintained that if a climb is easier with crampons than without, it could rightly be considered an ice climb. This is the only definition comprehensive enough to account for the entire spectrum of activities that are generally included under the heading of ice climbing. In the Alps and Canadian Rockies people are climbing the iced-up chimneys of winter and spring, as well as the classic faces of alpine ice. In Colorado they are venturing out onto steep faces and buttresses of verglassed rock. In places as diverse as Scotland, Vancouver Island, New Zealand, and Patagonia, the attraction is rime ice and snow-ice. Mount Kenya's Diamond Couloir has a frozen waterfall headwall that provides the African parallel of an experience that can be replicated in the Caucasus, Norway, Italy, Peru, Japan, Korea, the Tatra—in fact, anywhere in the world where cold temperatures, steep hillsides, and running water coincide. The ice world is fascinating, challenging, ever-changing, ethereal, bold, scary, fun, beautiful, elemental, varied, mind-opening, and, for me, totally captivating.

An ice cliff can be quite stable and reasonably safe to climb or unstable and dangerous, like this one. *(Photo: Jeff Lowe)*

GENERAL INFORMATION

Ice for climbing is variable stuff, with different qualities depending on how it was formed and where it is found. *Alpine ice* and *rime ice* are forms of frozen precipitation that have undergone metamorphosis under the influences of time, pressure, heat, and so on. *Water ice* has frozen from a liquid state, although it may have originated from snow or alpine ice just before it became liquid. The following comments should help you to better understand the medium.

Terrain, Features, and Types of Snow and Ice

The lists below include the main types of terrain and ice encountered in ice climbing. Of course, there are infinite variations on these themes.

ALPINE ICE TERRAIN

Glacier: a body of permanent ice slowly flowing downhill under the pull of gravity

Bergschrund: the crack that develops at the base of steeper slopes and that separates the moving glacier from the stationary ice higher up

Moat: the crack between permanent snow or ice and the containing rock walls

Serac: a tower or block of glacier ice that is separated from the mass

Icefall: the broken surface of a glacier where it flows over steep, rough underlying terrain—like a rapid in a river, but on a grand scale

Crevasse: a crack in the glacier; sometimes hidden by snow cover

Snowbridge: a formation that spans a crevasse

Hanging glacier: a glacier above a rock cliff

Ice cliff: the broken edge of a hanging glacier

Accumulation zone: the area that feeds the glacier, where each year's snowfall builds on that of previous years, accumulating faster than it can melt

Ablation zone: the elevation below which snow melts faster than it is deposited

Couloir: a natural concave groove between steeper walls of rock; usually wider than a gully

Ice face: a broad slope of ice

Cornice: a buildup of snow on ridge crests, overhanging the leeward side and created by wind

Flutings: arêtes between avalanche runnels on an ice face

Sun cups: scooplike formations on the surface of ice or old snow, created by direct exposure to the sun's rays

Névé penitentes: sun-created towers of ice larger than sun cups and often larger than a person

Ice cap: glacier-covered summit of a peak or broad plateau

Mixed rock and ice: self-explanatory

WATER ICE TERRAIN

Summits: self-explanatory

Feeder slopes: slopes of snow or ice that provide the meltwater that can be frozen into water ice formations

Avalanche slopes: see information on avalanches in the chapter The Cold Dance Review: The Basics of Climbing Ice

Ice gully: an ice-filled depression between rock walls too wide to stem

Above: **Alpine ice terrain:** (1) glacier (2) bergschrund (3) icefall (4) crevasse (5) hanging glacier (6) ice cliff (7) accumulation zone (8) ablation zone (9) ice face (10) cornice (11) flutings (12) mixed rock and ice (13) ice arête (*not shown:* moat, serac, snowbridge, couloir, ice cap, sun cups, névé penitentes) *(Photo: Jeff Lowe)*

Below: **Water ice terrain:** (1) summits (2) feeder slopes (3) avalanche slopes (4) ice gully (5) ice wall or frozen waterfall (6) mixed rock and ice (7) approach gully (8) approach slopes (9) tree-covered slopes (*not shown:* valley bottom, ice chimney, free-hanging curtain, supported curtain, free-standing pillar, icicle, cauliflower cone, hollow ice tube) *(Photo: Jeff Lowe)*

Ice wall or frozen waterfall: self-explanatory

Ice chimney: an ice-filled crack in the rock between one and five feet in width

Free-hanging curtain: self-explanatory

Supported curtain: a curtain of ice hanging free of a rock but supported by contact with a ledge or the ground

Free-standing pillar: column of ice that stands free of the rock, attached at top and bottom

Icicle: a "stalactite" of frozen water

Cauliflower cone: a "stalagmite" of frozen water, building from the ground up

Hollow ice tube: a hollow pillar formed by ice freezing around a running stream of water

Mixed rock and ice: self-explanatory

Approach gully: self-explanatory; avalanche danger often exists

Approach slopes: broad slopes that can be an avalanche hazard

Tree-covered slopes: less dangerous than approach slopes but not always 100 percent safe

Valley bottom or canyon floor: self-explanatory

In winter the west side of Wyoming's Grand Teton is sometimes coated with a thick veneer of rime ice more typical of Scotland or Patagonia. *(Photo: Greg Lowe)*

ALPINE ICE TYPES (SOFTEST TO HARDEST)

- Soft snow (any snow that takes a footprint one inch or deeper)
- Névé (like styrofoam)
- Corn snow (frozen ball bearings in the morning; slush in the afternoon)
- Windpack/wind crust (if thick enough to sustain weight, climbs like névé)
- Atmospheric icing (rime ice)
  - Frost feathers (collapse at a touch)
  - Snow-ice (more substantial wet, frozen snow or consolidated rime)
- Andean cheese ice (very steep, aerated snow-ice, wet or frozen)
- Packed cornice/serac/crevasse snow (hard snow that can be climbed with step-kicking or crampons, picks, or shafts)
- Granulated glacier ice (poorly bonded, ball bearing-like surface)
- Compact glacier ice (homogeneous and cold)
- Porcelain ice (névé polished and hardened by time and spindrift; squeaky and friable)
- Metamorphosed gully/ice face/black ice (old, hard, brittle)
- Winter alpine ice (cold and brittle)
- Alaskan green ice (old, cold, hard, brittle)

WATER ICE TYPES AND FEATURES

- Verglas (less than one-half inch thick)
- Frozen spray (instantly frozen to rock; usually very thin)
- Thin ice (one-half to six inches thick)
- Thin hollow ice (detached ice up to six inches thick)
- Laminated flow (successive freezing of thin layers)
- Solid pillar (well frozen, cohesive)
- Rotten pillar (melting, chandeliered, or cauliflowered)
- Cauliflower (resembles its namesake)
- Small pillar (less than one foot in diameter)

Left: **Alex Lowe on the first completely free ascent of Sky Pilot in the Canadian Rockies, a climb that exemplifies the attraction and challenge of free-standing pillars** *(Photo: Jeff Lowe)* Center: **A classic pillar and cauliflower cone of water ice** *(Photo: Jeff Lowe)* Right: **Verglas and thin ice ribs offer some of the most delicate ice-climbing terrain.** *(Photo: Brad Johnson)*

- Pencil chandeliers (early-season or warm-weather condition on pillars)
- Roof chandeliers (large icicles hanging from bosses of ice)
- Aerated water ice (lots of bubbles or melted interstices; whitish)
- Plastic ice (warm ice, but not rotten; doesn't shatter)
- Mineralized ice (often brown, orange, or yellow; brittle)
- Blue/green ice (usually well frozen; can be brittle)
- Old dry ice (very durable, stubborn)
- Mushrooms (like their namesakes)
- Exfoliation flakes (partly detached blades or fins)
- Lens over snow (a sheet of ice over snow; sometimes weight-bearing)

Rating Ice Climbs

Many climbers feel that rating ice climbs is an undesirable and even futile activity, given that a large part of the beauty of ice climbing lies in its appeal to the adventurous spirit, and that conditions, and therefore exact difficulties, vary constantly. But on well-known climbs the adventure of discovery is already gone, and after years of climbing all over the world, repeating climbs in the same and different seasons, I have found that rating a climb for the conditions under which it is normally climbed can provide a very good guideline as to what can be expected. This is especially useful for climbers with limited time who are traveling to a new area and who want to do climbs commensurate with their abilities. Most of the climbs in this book have been given a rating, which helps to compare them.

In *The Ice Experience* I introduced a rating system for ice climbing that has been widely adopted in America and is designed to describe climbs throughout the world. Basically this system uses a grading that was developed to describe the overall difficulties of rock climbs in Yosemite Valley. Length, continuity, and *commitment* (which includes such factors as objective hazards, possibility of escape from the route, availability and possibility of rescue, and so

The lower-angle crest of this hollow tube is too thin to climb, which has forced the climber onto the steeper—but thicker—vertical ice on its flank. (Photo: Mike Lowe)

forth) are all taken into account in a scale of Roman numerals from I to VI. A grade I climb has an easy approach, seldom has more than a few rope-lengths of actual climbing, and requires only two or three hours to complete. Most grade VIs require two or more days and 2,000 feet or more of hard climbing, although today's best climbers can sometimes complete such routes in one day. To this six-grade scale I have added a seventh, which is necessary to describe the biggest and hardest Himalayan alpine-style climbs, with their greater size, altitude, and commitment.

In addition to the overall grade, another rating, the technical classification, describes the hardest section of the route, thus helping to differentiate between long climbs of moderate difficulty and short climbs of great technical challenge that may merit the same overall grade. For technical classifications it is convenient to start with the Scottish grades of 1 to 6, which were originally intended only to convey a sense of overall difficulties similar to the Yosemite ratings, but for ice climbs. Over the years, however, the Scottish system has sometimes been misused to describe individual move and pitch difficulties. It is this bastardized version that I have found useful in describing the technical problems that one may expect on a given climb under "average" conditions. Once again, seventh and eighth classes have been added to the technical scale to accommodate today's hardest mixed climbs. A class 1 pitch is snow up to about 50° or ice up to about 35°, while a class 8 climb includes overhanging gymnastic moves comparable to 5.12 or 5.13 rock climbing.

A rough comparison of rock and ice technical classifications is included here. The type of ice to be found on a climb is designated by the letters *AI*, indicating alpine ice, or *WI*, indicating water ice, preceding the technical classification. When the primary difficulties of a climb are on mixed rock and ice climbed with crampons, the classification is preceded by an *M*. The relative technical challenge of climbs rated WI5, AI5, or M5, is the same; only the

climbing mediums differ slightly. If there is any aid involved on rock or ice, that is indicated with a classification of A0–5.

With this system it is possible to compare the overall challenge of climbs on both rock and ice throughout the world. The following table gives a rough (debatable) approximation of the relative difficulty of rock and ice free climbing.

Ice Classification (AI, WI, or M)		Rock Classification
1	Up to 50° snow or 35° ice	1st to 3rd class
2	Up to 60° snow or 40° ice	4th class
3	Up to 80° snow or 75° ice	5.0–5.7
4	Up to vertical snow or 85° ice	5.8–5.9
5	Overhanging cornices or 90° ice	5.10
6	Very thin or technical 90°+ ice	5.11
7	95° ice or overhanging mixed	5.12
8	Technical overhanging mixed	5.13

Free climbing on ice, as it has been defined in Colorado since about 1970 and has come to be accepted in Canada, France, and elsewhere by the leading climbers, means that no ice or rock protection is used either to pull up or stand on for progression or to rest. The common practice of hanging from tools by a daisy chain on a harness is considered aid (A0).

A final piece of information is necessary for some climbs that are difficult to protect adequately. If protection takes considerable skill to place and long run-outs are mandatory (fifteen to thirty feet above protection), then an S (for Serious) rating is added to the normal notations. If reliable protection is impossible to arrange even for a skilled climber and very long run-outs are required above questionable placements, then a VS (for Very Serious) is given. And if there is simply no protection possible at all and a fall would most likely result in death, an X rating is appropriate, meaning, "Cross this climb off your list."

A COMPARISON OF ICE CLIMBS AROUND THE WORLD

Technical Classification (preceded by ice-type designation: AI, WI, or M)

Overall Grade

	I	II	III	IV	V	VI	VII
1	Willey's Slide, Frankenstein Cliff, Crawford Notch, New Hampshire	Standard Route, Mont Blanc du Tacul, France	Guide's Route via Camp Muir, Mount Rainier, Washington				
2	Comb Gully, Ben Nevis, Scotland	Skyladder, Mount Andromeda, Canadian Rockies	Gervasutti Couloir, Mont Blanc du Tacul, France	Liberty Ridge, Mount Rainier, Washington	West Rib, Denali, Alaska		
3	Spiral Staircase, Vail, Colorado	Green Gully, Ben Nevis, Scotland	Cascade Waterfall, Banff, Canadian Rockies	North Face, Triolet, France	West Ridge, Mount Hunter, Alaska		
4	Dracula, Frankenstein Cliff, Crawford Notch, New Hampshire	Louise Falls, near Lake Louise, Canadian Rockies	Hadrian's Wall, Ben Nevis, Scotland	Orion Face Direct, Ben Nevis, Scotland	Cornau/ Devaille, Les Droites, France	Northwest Spur, Mount Hunter, Alaska	West Face, Gasherbrum IV, Karakoram, Pakistan
5	Dropline, Frankenstein Cliff, Crawford Notch, New Hampshire	Glacenost, Haute Maurienne, France	Repentance, Cathedral Ledge, North Conway, New Hampshire	Slipstream, Snow Dome, Columbia Icefields, Canadian Rockies	Bouchard Route, Chacraraju, Peru	South Face, Ama Dablam, Nepal	Northeast Face, Ama Dablam, Nepal
6	The Fang, Vail, Colorado	Shiva Lingham, Argentière Glacier, France	Bridalveil Falls, Telluride, Colorado	Weeping Pillar, near Columbia Icefields, Canadian Rockies	Super Couloir Direct, Mont Blanc du Tacul, France	Direct North Buttress, Mount Hunter, Alaska	Hungo Face, Kwangde, Nepal
7	Secret Probation, Vail, Colorado	L'Aventure C'est L'Aventure, near L'Argentière La Besée, France	Sea of Vapors, Mount Rundle, Canadian Rockies	Riptide, Mount Patterson, Canadian Rockies	Blind Faith, Tête de Gramusat, France		
8		Octopussy, Vail, Colorado					

A climber on the crux of the Balfour Face of Mount Tasman, New Zealand. The Balfour Face, climbed in 1971, is comparable to the Orion Face Direct on Ben Nevis, Scotland, which had its first ascent in 1960. (Photo: George Lowe III)

Icy Roots, Crystal Blossoms

▼ ▼ ▼ ▼ ▼

A BRIEF HISTORY OF ICE

Ancient peasant myths held that there were snow dragons lurking among the summits. *(Drawing by H. G. Willink, originally published in Dent's Mountaineering)*

A BRIEF HISTORY OF ICE

Shepherds and Englishmen

The first real evidence of ice climbing comes from the sixteenth century. Alpine shepherds attached spiked horseshoe devices to their feet, and these, along with iron-tipped alpenstocks, allowed them to negotiate the slippery ice on the steep slopes they crossed while controlling their flocks in high Alpine valleys. These same shepherds certainly challenged medieval superstitions that held there were demons on summits and that glaciers were dragons that would steal down at night to drain the udders of sleeping peasants' cows! Chamois hunters and crystal gatherers later pushed higher into the mountains in quest of their prey, furthering knowledge of Alpine terrain.

In the early 1800s, tourists from England began to holiday in the Alpine villages. The tantalizingly inaccessible mountaintops piqued the Victorian sensibilities of these wealthy gentry, and they hired local peasants to guide them amongst the peaks. By mid-century, a symbiotic relationship had been established, whereby the shepherds earned a living as guides and were thus exposed to English culture, while their employers were educated to the mysteries of life in the mountains. Such mutual interest led to improvements in equipment and to the first ascents of classic snow and ice routes. The shepherd's three-pronged "crampon" was replaced by nailed boots; the alpenstock, which had been taller than a man, was shortened; and an adze was added for chopping steps to climb steep slopes of ice.

The latter half of the nineteenth century—the so-called Golden Age of Mountaineering—saw all the summits of the Alps reached. Then climbers tackled new and harder routes. The first ice climbs were almost always led by one of the great step-chopping guides, such as Melchior Anderegg, who spearheaded the first ascent of the Brenva Spur on Mont Blanc in 1865, or Christian Klucker, who climbed the North Face of the Lyskamm—and loved to climb whether he had clients or not.

In the final decades of the century, some Alpine guides traveled with their employers as far away as Canada, New Zealand, Russia, and Argentina, helping to establish their sport in those places. In their own mountains, the Germans, Swiss, Austrians, and French continued to range over ever-steeper and icier ridges and faces. Some of these Europeans were guides, but an increasing number were amateurs who were climbing simply for their own pleasure, following the example of British climbers who were setting new standards on rock.

Scottish Gullies and North Walls

The Scottish Mountaineering Club was formed in 1889. Although the general trend in the Alps was toward rock climbing, by 1920, Scots had extended the art of pure ice and snow climbing in gullies and had introduced the concept of mixed climbing by attempting difficult summer rock climbs under a coating of ice and snow. The outstanding practitioner, Harold Raeburn, led Green Gully on Ben

Climbers experiencing what the Scots call "full conditions"
(Photo: Jeff Lowe)

Nevis in 1906, cutting steps with a long axe and wearing nailed boots as in the Alps. On a 1974 pilgrimage, I made an ascent of the route as one of my first climbs in Scotland. Even with the latest "revolutionary" ice technology adorning my hands and feet, I was impressed by the steep initial pitch and the beauty of the final run-out to the summit plateau. In 1920, Raeburn made the first winter ascent of Observatory Ridge, an iced-up rock route that still enjoys the respect of modern climbers. When the ice is thin, insubstantial, or rotten over rock, technological advances are less important than the skill and spirit of the climber. In Scotland, Raeburn's difficult climbs were unsurpassed until the 1950s.

In 1908 a technological advance was made that wouldn't be wholeheartedly adopted by the recalcitrant Scots for forty years, yet it increased the security and speed of climbing on the ice and snow faces of the Alps. Oscar Eckenstein, an experienced British

The nailed boots, hemp rope, ten-point crampons, and collapsible 90cm straight-pick ice axe that represented state-of-the-art ice-climbing gear during the classic "North Wall Era" of the 1920s and '30s (Photo: René Robert)

The north side of Mount Robson, the crown of the Canadian Rockies, has provided generations of North American climbers with new challenges. In 1938, when Switzerland's much more difficult Eigerwand was climbed, the North Ridge (left skyline) of Mount Robson represented the top of the game on this side of the Atlantic. Robson's broad, snowy North Face (center left), which is comparable to the North Face of the Triolet, was not climbed until 1963. But Mugs Stump and Jim Logan's 1978 climb of the vertical runnels of the Emperor Face (above the climber) was on a par with any ice climb in the Alps. (Photo: Mike Munger)

climber, created a ten-point crampon and invented a "flatfoot" climbing technique that allowed many climbs to be done with few or no cut steps. This Eckenstein technique was quickly adopted by the French, who found it excellent for the névé of the Western Alps.

With the new crampons and an axe one-third shorter than the old shoulder-high style, alpine ice climbing entered what has been called its most productive era. The great guide Hans Lauper capped his brilliant career in 1932 with the first ascent of the Northeast Face of the Eiger—the well-known Lauper Route, seldom climbed and still highly respected. In 1924 special pitons for ice designed by Fritz Riegele were used by Willo Welzenbach on the Northwest Face of the Gross Wiesbachhorn. Between the two World Wars, Welzenbach distinguished himself as the best of a bold new generation of ice enthusiasts. Climbs that he undertook, such as the north faces of the Gross Fiescherhorn, the Grand Charmoz, the Gletscherhorn, and the Lauterbrunnen Breithorn, remained, even into the 1960s, some of the most difficult in the Alps.

Following Welzenbach in the classic "North Wall Era," Jacques Lagarde and Henry de Ségnone maximized the Eckenstein crampon technique on the North Face of the Plan in 1924. Perhaps the finest exponent of this technique, Armand Charlet, climbed the Nant Blanc Face of the Aiguille Verte in 1928 with Camille Dévouassoux. Robert Gréloz and André Roch made the first ascent of the classic North Face of the Triolet in 1931. In the same year, Franz and Toni Schmid, brothers from Munich, climbed the North Face of the Matterhorn, the first of the three most famous north walls in the Alps to be climbed. The next to fall was the Croz Spur, a rock and mixed route on the Grandes Jorasses, in 1935. The remaining and greatest wall, the Eigerwand, was finally climbed in the summer of 1938 by Anderl Heckmair, Ludwig Vörg, Fritz Kasparek, and Heinrich Harrer. On this most controversial and heralded Alpine climb of all time, Heckmair was the natural leader. Although the Eigerwand is not a pure ice route during the summer, Heckmair used twelve-point crampons designed by Laurent Grivel in 1932 to frontpoint up the ice fields in a fraction of the time it would have taken to cut steps. His performance defined the frontiers of the Alpine art until the late 1950s.

Routes climbed on the classic north faces in the Alps and in gullies of snow-ice and buttresses of snow, rock, and verglas in Scotland were not improved upon until after World War II. Existing equipment had already been pushed to near its absolute limits, and most of the obvious and attractive lines had been done. In modern technical terms, the top pure ice grade climbed in the Alps at the time would be about AI3, while in Scotland a mixed standard of M4 may have been achieved.

Though standards were not being set on ice in other ranges of the world during this period, many good climbs were made in the Northern and Southern Alps of New Zealand, in the Caucasus, and in the Canadian Rockies. These areas offer scope for ice as great as that found in Europe, but their contribution to the sport would come later. The next advances would once again spring from the crucibles of the Alps and the Scottish Highlands.

Postwar and into the 1960s

Scottish winter climbing was taken a step beyond Raeburn's most difficult climbs during the 1950s, mainly by Tom Patey, Jimmy Marshall, Hamish MacInnes, and their friends. Using axe and crampons, cunning and craft to their fullest in a uniquely eclectic Scottish blend of step-cutting, frontpointing, flatfooting, and mixed climbing, these pioneers established many of the best climbs of the day. The most impressive were MacInnes's ascent of Raven's Gully in 1953, Bill Brooker's mid-1950s ascent of the Eagle Ridge of Lochnagar, and the ascent by Graeme Nicol, Patey, and MacInnes of Zero Gully in 1957. Their efforts left a future generation of climbers to struggle in their footsteps. Marshall's ascent of

Parallel Gully B in 1959, and his climbs of Gardyloo Buttress and Orion Face Direct the following year (these with the brightest of his apprentices, Robin Smith) were also landmarks from this adventurous era. All of these climbs were rated Scottish grade V. By the system of rating used in this book, the overall standard of the most committing of these routes is grade IV, with a technical difficulty of class 5. Throughout the world, harder ice climbs were not made until the 1970s—and then only with the aid of new technology.

During the first two postwar decades, most Alpine climbers found enough challenge in repeating the great routes of the 1930s. A few harder climbs were made, such as the North Face of Les Droites by Cornau/Devaille in 1955, the Grand Pilier d'Angle of Mont Blanc by Walter Bonatti and Cosimo Zapelli in 1962, and the Shroud on the Grandes Jorasses by Robert Flematti and René Demaison in 1968. All these first ascents were major events, accomplished by some of the best climbers of the day, pulling out all the stops, facing terrifying objective hazards, and launching wholeheartedly into the unknown. When Reinhold Messner made his landmark eight and one-half hour solo of Les Droites in 1969, the era was brought to a resounding close.

Because of the large scale of these Alpine routes, the overall commitment rating had reached grade V, with the hardest of the climbs, Les Droites, having a technical difficulty of AI4 to 5. The introduction of the Salewa tube screw in the mid-1960s made later climbs much safer.

In North America the standard was slightly lower, with a climb like the Black Ice Couloir on the Grand Teton, first climbed by Ray Jacquot and Herb Swedlund in 1961, meriting IV, AI3+; the first solo ascent by Charlie Bell of the Willis Wall on Mount Rainier in the same year, a IV, AI3; and the Snowbird Glacier on Mount Patterson in the Canadian Rockies, climbed in 1967 by Charlie Locke, Ken Baker, Chic Scott, and Don Vockeroth, about the same standard.

An anomaly occurred in 1954 in Alaska, however,

when the experienced team consisting of American Fred Beckey, German Henry Maybohm, and Austrian Heinrich Harrer (of Eigerwand fame) made the alpine-style (that is, without fixed ropes and moving the high camp up with them as they progressed) first

Hamish MacInnes was one of the most active Scottish climbers in the 1950s and '60s. He invented the Terrordactyl, developed mountain rescue to a high art, and also wrote mystery novels. The Scottish populace came to view Hamish as a national treasure.
(Photo: Jeff Lowe)

ascent of 12,339-foot Mount Deborah by the West Face and West Ridge. This climb has seen only a few repeats in the intervening years, and none in less than the three days required for the first ascent. Mount Deborah definitely merits an overall grade V.

Another exceptional North American climb occurred a decade later. Jules Verne once said, "Anything one man can imagine, other men can make real." Such facile pronouncements are familiar, but perhaps only a delusion of the species. However, six men made a climb in 1965 that makes me feel Verne was right.

Mount Logan is located in the St. Elias Range, Yukon Territory, Canada. Its 19,850-foot central peak is the second highest point in North America, only 470 feet lower than the summit of Denali. Logan is a huge mountain with a summit plateau comprising nearly ten square miles and ridges that span twenty-four miles in an east-west direction.

Three south ridges drop 14,000 feet to the Seward Glacier. The Central Ridge consists of six miles of unbelievably contorted cornices, crags, and ice slopes. It is so large that one-fifth of the ridge would still be a major climb. To climb it in semi-alpine style (i.e., fixing ropes between camps, but not down to base) was an impossible dream in 1965. But that didn't stop Al Steck, John Evans, Frank Coale, Jim Wilson, Paul Bacon, and Dick Long from doing it.

After three weeks of intense effort, during which the climbers wondered at the sanity of their actions ("This route is sheer madness!"), they had not yet reached a "bump" on the ridge at 13,000 feet, which they had designated the Snow Dome. With less than half the ridge climbed and much more than half their food consumed, most parties would have elected to retreat while that option was still open. But these men kept at it. Evans later described the ridge in an article in the Sierra Club journal *Ascent*: "A high-wire in the sky, artistically daubed with a stiff meringue of snow; a bottomless fantasy of cornices and flutings."

Finally, on August 6, one month after starting out, they reached the summit. " . . . [W]eaker than we realized, we staggered like drunks. . . . " But they were six very happy and satisfied drunks, for they had gone out on a limb—and isn't that where the fruit is?

Early in the climb, Steck had been ascending a couloir on the side of the ridge when he heard a buzzing sound and instinctively protected his head against what he thought was a falling rock. But the buzzing continued. No rock could fall so slowly. He looked in the direction of the sound only to see a tiny hummingbird hovering and darting above his red pack. The incongruity of this sight stayed in Steck's mind throughout the climb—a source of wonder and comfort that sustained him through the difficulties. The gigantic climb was eventually named after the tiny creature.

The South Ridge of Logan was indeed a breakthrough. To this day, no climb in North America has required a greater level of commitment. But technically the Hummingbird Ridge (VII, AI4?) was of less importance. The only innovation used extensively was a snow shovel instead of an ice axe for carving a path through the cornices.

In the postwar years and through the 1960s, many superior routes were also being climbed in other mountains of the world. Climbs such as Alpamayo in Peru, the Caroline Face on Mount Cook in New Zealand, and the West Face of Mount Ushba in the Caucasus were excellent, although at a lower standard than contemporary climbs being made in the Alps.

During the 1950s and '60s, different nationalities still clung to their own preferences with regard to the techniques used to climb ice. In Scotland step-cutting was the standard; in France the Eckenstein flat-foot method had been so completely adopted that it had also come to be known as "French technique"; while the Austrians and Germans had for quite some time favored frontpointing in almost every instance. During this time, the small number of ice climbers in the rest of the world had to sort out for themselves which of the techniques was best, usually coming to the conclusion that frontpointing with short axes and daggers (handheld ice picks) on hard ice required football-sized calves, that step-cutting for more than a rope-length necessitated the arms of a gorilla, and that French technique was totally unsuited to the human anatomy. A truly international blend of all these techniques would become the future norm.

The New Ice Age: The Great Curve

Of all the early pioneers of Alpine north walls, Anderl Heckmair is probably the most well known because of his brilliant leadership of the first ascent of the Eigerwand. In a virtuoso display of talent, he frontpointed the ice fields with such confidence that years later Heinrich Harrer still wrote with amazement about the performance in his classic book, *The White Spider*. But Heckmair's technique was not the only thing he had going for him. There is an old black-and-white photograph taken during the Eiger climb that shows Heckmair using a short axe with a distinct down-curve to the pick. This simple curve increases the security of an axe placement many times over, thus allowing faster and safer climbing. In the late 1960s this "revolutionary curve" was discovered once again.

In 1966 the American climber and equipment designer Yvon Chouinard climbed one of Europe's great ice walls, the North Face of Les Courtes, with Layton Kor, another American. On this climb they used frontpointing technique, along with an "ice dagger" and an ice axe. The security of this sort of "clawing" was minimal, but Chouinard suggested that in time of trouble, the dagger, which should be attached by a cord to the climber's waist, could quickly be driven in, thus providing a makeshift belay. The future of that particular idea was limited, but Chouinard was inspired by the climb in two important ways that, in retrospect, created the future.

First, the long session of frontpointing on Les Courtes nearly destroyed Chouinard's and Kor's calf muscles. This led Chouinard to adopt and proselytize French technique, which, though harder to master, is more relaxing on climbs that are not overly steep. (He later went on to develop rigid, adjustable crampons that made frontpointing less strenuous.) More importantly, French technique forces the climber to carefully study the ice, thus coming to know it better—the first step on the road to creative ice technique, where the ice becomes a medium for expressing the climber's art and craft rather than an enemy to be "conquered." Although pure French technique is seldom used anymore, it is worth practicing.

Secondly, Chouinard's experience in Europe prompted him to experiment with the pick of the ice axe, curving and drooping it to make it stick better in the ice. He also added a curved pick to his widely used Yosemite hammer. With one of these modified tools in each hand, normal 40° to 60° ice slopes suddenly became much less difficult, and, although it would be a few years before it happened, the way was now open for extended climbs on extremely steep and vertical ice.

Heckmair's Eiger performance had been thirty years ahead of his time. With the popularization of Chouinard's drooped pick and Hamish MacInnes's concurrently developed Terrordactyl (an axe with an extreme downward angled pick that worked exceptionally well for hooking on mixed climbs and soon became the favorite tool in Scotland and the

Yvon Chouinard almost single-handedly brought modern ice climbing to America. Seen here in the Cairngorm Mountains of Scotland in 1974, Chouinard introduced the revolutionary curved pick in the late 1960s. This invention, combined with his teaching and writings on the subject, which always championed finesse and simplicity, made Chouinard one of the most influential ice climbers in history.
(Photo: Jeff Lowe)

Canadian Rockies), ice climbing was changed for all time. Now even the greatest of the existing routes was possible for average climbers.

The North American Contribution

Mountain climbing in all its forms was slower to develop in Canada and the United States than in Great Britain and Europe. By the early 1960s, however, Americans had developed new equipment and techniques for rock climbing that allowed them to make the first ascents of some of the world's greatest rock walls in Yosemite Valley of California. In mid-decade, some Yosemite climbers traveled to the Alps and made the hardest rock climbs of the day, using hardware and techniques they had brought from home. At the same time, these Americans were introduced to ice and snow climbing, an interest they brought with them when they returned home. Unfortunately, except in Alaska, the opportunities for alpine-type climbs on glaciers and ice fields is limited to only a few areas in the high mountains of the United States. In winter, however, frozen waterfalls and ice-filled chimneys are plentiful throughout the northern states, particularly in the northeast and the intermountain region of Colorado, Utah, Wyoming, and Montana.

In the early 1970s, the standards of the hardest Alpine and Scottish climbs were equaled in New Hampshire with such climbs as John Bouchard's first solo winter ascent of the 600-foot Black Dike (III, WI5-) on Cannon Mountain, which Chouinard had described as "a black, filthy, horrendous icicle, 600 feet high, unclimbed," and John Bragg and Rick Wilcox's ascent of Repentance (III, WI5) on Cathedral Ledge, which consists of four pitches of hard ice climbing on a 5.9 rock route. These eastern routes were impressive and provided the impetus for a ten-year growth in the popularity of ice climbing in the region. But it was in Utah and Colorado that the new standards were set for free climbing on ice.

By 1971, my brother Greg Lowe had already used the new ice gear on the first ascent of an obscure but, for the time, phenomenally difficult climb on Mahlen's Peak Waterfall in northern Utah. The crux pitch, under the conditions of the first ascent (WI6), is seventy-five feet of vertical and overhanging ice, which Greg led entirely free with almost no protection. In one bold stroke, ice climbing had been brought up to par with rock standards. In the mid-1960s in Idaho's City of Rocks, Greg had been among the first to lead 5.12 on rock in classic, completely free style. The same strength and abilities had now been applied to ice, opening up a vast and exciting new arena for adventure.

Greg Lowe, shown here making the second ascent (1972) of his standard-setting climb on Mahlen's Peak Waterfall, was one of the first climbers to fully exploit the potential of curved picks and rigid crampons. Greg's line followed the vertical, overhanging left edge of the icefall and would today be rated WI6. Greg is the originator of the modern internal-frame pack, passive and spring-loaded camming nuts, supergaiters, Snarg ice pitons (with the author), Hummingbird tools, and Footfang crampons (with Mike Lowe), and other inventions too numerous to mention. In his spare time he is an award-winning cinematographer. *(Photo: Lance Wilcox)*

Greg introduced Mike Weis and me to the beauty and challenge of climbing frozen waterfalls in the winter of 1972, and we found it much to our liking, complementing, as it did, the other three seasons of rock climbing, mountaineering, and skiing that constituted the focus of our existence. On January 2, 1974, Mike and I completed the first ascent of Colorado's Bridalveil Falls (III, WI6). We found 400 feet of near-vertical, vertical, and overhanging ice spiced with cauliflower and chandelier-like formations. We discovered that the tube screws and ice pitons commercially available at that time would only fracture the extremely cold and brittle ice into large plates and chunks, but Greg had lent us half a dozen homemade chrome-moly tubes with tips beveled to the inside. These could be driven in without destroying the ice, allowing us to climb Bridalveil with some protection. They were later developed into Snarg ice pitons.

While Americans were making their initial explorations of winter icefalls, a group of expatriate Brits led by Bugs McKeith, Rob Wood, and George Homer, along with locals Tim Auger, John Lauchlan, and Laurie Skreslet, were busy searching out the best of the frozen waterfalls in the Canadian Rockies. Their excellent climbs included Bourgeau Left-hand (III, WI5), Takkakkaw Falls (IV, WI4+), the technical test piece Nemesis (III, WI6), the Weeping Wall (III, WI5), Weeping Pillar (IV, WI5+), and Polar Circus (V, WI5). Although this group's first ascents tended to use fixed ropes and aid-climbing techniques (such as aid slings attached to the tools), it wasn't long before all the Canadian routes were free-climbed. These free ascents were, at first, the work of visiting Americans like John Roskelley, Dave Wright, Duncan Ferguson, and Greg Davis, but soon the locals Jack Firth, Albi Sole, James Blench, Ray Jotterand, Skreslet, and Lauchlan resumed the lead role.

In Quebec, Claude Bérubé and Regis Richard climbed the 1,000-foot Le Loutre (IV, WI5) in 1977 completely free, signaling the beginning of a Canadian

Mike Weis eyeing the crux second pitch of Bridalveil Falls during the first ascent in January 1974. Two weeks of 20°F temperatures had produced very brittle ice, adding to the difficulties. *(Photo: Jeff Lowe)*

dominance of waterfall ice, although Mike Weis and I established Curtain Call (III, WI6) in the Columbia Icefields in 1979, and New Englanders Kurt Winkler and Jim Theisen plucked Quebec's ultraclassic La Pomme d'Or (IV, WI5) in 1980. In the late 1970s Lauchlan and Jim Elzinga put up what at the time was probably the hardest high-mountain waterfall climb in the world: the 2,500-foot Slipstream on Snow Dome in the Columbia Icefields, grade IV, AI5+ by the first ascent line through the upper serac. Slipstream was surpassed in 1984 by the ascent of Gimme Shelter on Mount Quadra by Kevin Doyle and Tim Friesen. This very thin climb ascends a near-vertical and vertical 1,000-foot smear formed by

The West Face of Patagonia's Cerro Torre is one of the finest ice climbs in the world.
(Photo: Jon Krakauer)

water seeping from a hànging glacier and is probably grade V, WI6–7. Doyle and Friesen ended their climb under the ice cliff, however, leaving the complete ascent for a later party.

Amalgamation

Although technical standards were being set by American and Canadian climbers during the last years of the 1970s, climbers in the Alps, New Zealand, and elsewhere were only slightly behind on waterfalls and equal on the mountain ice routes being done in North America. The Balfour Face (IV, AI4) of Mount Tasman in New Zealand was done as early as 1971 by Bill Denz and Brian Poole, and the Northeast Couloir of the Dru (V, AI4, A2) was climbed in four days in winter 1972–73 by Walter Cecchinel and Claude Jager. In 1975 Rab Carrington and Al Rouse introduced Scottish-style mixed climbing to the Alps with their winter ascent of the thinly iced slabs of the North Face of Pèlerins (V, WI5, M6?). Jean-Marc Boivin and Patrick Gabarrou climbed the strikingly beautiful Super Couloir on Mont Blanc du Tacul (V, WI4–5, M6) in 1975, and the following year Alex MacIntyre and Nick Colton climbed the difficult direct line (V, WI5, M6) that now bears their names on the right flank of the Walker Spur of the Grandes Jorasses.

Roughly equivalent climbs were made around the world. Mike Weis and I climbed Canada's Grand Central Couloir on Mount Kitchener (V, WI4, M6) in 1974. Rouse and Carrington did the Citadel-Sticil Face combination on Shelter Stone Crag (IV, WI3, M6+, A1), one of the most difficult Scottish routes, in 1975. In Africa in 1975, Mike Covington and Yvon Chouinard made a direct climb of the Diamond Couloir (IV, AI5), and the Breach Wall of Kilimanjaro (V, WI6?) was done by Reinhold Messner and Konrad Renzler in 1978. John Bouchard and Frenchwoman Marie-Odile Meunier made the first ascent of the South Face of Peru's Chacraraju by its most impressive direct line (V, AI6?) in 1977.

In winter of that year, Henry Barber and Rob

The author's 1979 solo first ascent of the South Face of Ama Dablam was a landmark in Himalayan ice climbing. *(Photo: Jeff Lowe)*

Taylor introduced American waterfall techniques to Norway, making the first ascent of the Vettisfossen, 1,000 feet of Bridalveil-type intricate climbing. Norway has some of the longest and prettiest waterfall climbs in the world, and after Barber and Taylor showed the way, such Norwegians as Hans Christian Doseth, Thomas Carlstrom, and Ulf Geir Hansen continued to exploit the potential. Hyndnefossen (III, WI6?), Döntefossen (V, WI6?), Black December (IV, WI6?), and Togfossen (V or VI, WI6?) are all-time classics of the genre.

By the late 1970s and early '80s, waterfall climbing was well established throughout the Alps. Two adventurous Italian ice climbers emerged during this period: Gian Carlo Grassi and Renatto Casarotto, who, together and with others, developed waterfall ice climbing in their home country and traveled widely. Other Italians pioneered the extensive water ice terrain found in the Alpine valleys of Lombardy. In the Cirque de Gavarnie in the French Pyrenees, many exceptional climbs were made, mainly by Dominique Julien, Rainier Munsch, and their friends, with the 1,500-foot Voie de L'Overdose (V, WI5+) being every bit the equal of the big North American waterfalls.

Coming of Age

Within ten years, equipment evolved drastically. Simple curved or angled picks gave way to reverse-curve interchangeable picks, which now sported graphite shafts and specialized adzes. Footfang crampons and Snarg ice pitons made their appearance. Internationally, the number of ice climbers had swelled, and avid aspirants were now cruising climbs within their first few outings that had been the ultimate in the previous decade. In the early 1980s, though, ice climbing took a back seat to sport rock climbing, which seemed more appealing to the young masses.

But the general trend to rock did not halt the expansion of ice-climbing horizons, and the first half of the 1980s saw harder, steeper, pure ice and mixed climbs and the introduction of the highest standards to the world's greatest ranges. The mountains of Alaska, the Andes, and the Himalaya were now fair game for lightning-fast, adventurous climbers. One Alaskan climb that pushed horizons was the ascent by Nick Colton and Tim Leach of the striking couloir on the Northeast Face of the Rooster's Comb (V, AI5, M6) in 1980.

Without a doubt the finest overall ice climb in North America to date is the North Buttress of Mount Hunter (VI, AI6, M6?), the route completed in 1983 by Todd Bibler and Doug Klewin, two climbers from Seattle. Their ascent capped many determined efforts by Klewin, Pat and Dan McNerthney, Rob Newsom, and, especially, Mugs Stump and his New Zealand partner, Paul Aubrey. The latter pair, in fact, are often given credit for the first ascent, even though their route varied significantly from the classic line on the buttress and they retreated from the top of the upper rock band with 300 to 400 feet still to go to the junction with the Northeast Ridge, and a full 2,500 feet remaining to the summit. Without in any way diminishing Stump and Aubrey's "Moonflower Buttress" line, Bibler and Klewin corrected these omissions and deserve full credit for the first ascent of the classic North Buttress route.

The earliest of the "Ice Climbs of the '80s" actually occurred at the end of the previous decade. In 1978 Frenchman Nicholas Jaeger made a series of solo climbs in Peru that were technically as hard as anything in the Alps, at elevations around 19,000 feet. Perhaps his finest routes were the South Face of Taulliraju (V, AI5–6?), a 3,000-foot extreme route done in eight hours, and the South Face of the East Peak of Chacraraju (V, AI5–6?).

The West Face of Cerro Torre in Patagonia was first climbed in expedition style by an Italian team in 1974, but its first alpine-style ascent came in 1977 by Americans Jay Wilson, John Bragg, and Dave Carmen, establishing it as one of the great ascents of the ice world. When it was climbed completely free by fellow Americans Mike Bearzi and Eric Winkelman in 1986, it became, along with the North Buttress of Mount Hunter and the Hungo Face of Kwangde, Nepal, one of the most attractive challenges available.

In 1979, after working on a television film of the second ascent of the Southwest Ridge of Ama Dablam in Nepal, I made the first ascent of the 4,500-foot South Face (VI, AI5, M5+) of this 22,500-foot peak in ten hours. The difficulties were similar to—but longer than—those found on the hard Alpine climbs of the 1960s and early 1970s, such as Les Droites or the Grand Pilier d'Angle. This was the first time such a major new technical route had been soloed in the Himalaya.

These climbs set the stage for the coming years of technically demanding alpine-style ascents of Himalayan ice faces. The best of these include the

1980 ascent of the East Face of Dhaulagiri (VI, AI3, M4?) by Englishman Alex MacIntyre, Frenchman René Ghilini, and Poles Wojciech Kurtyka and Ludwik Wilczyczynsk, with technical difficulties similar to some of the 1930s Alpine routes, but done on a 26,000-foot peak; a fairly technical new route

Randy Racliff climbing "The Shaft" on the North Buttress of Mount Hunter, Alaska (Photo: Bill Belcourt)

on the South Face of Annapurna (VII, AI4, M5?) in 1984 by Spaniards Enric Lucas and Nil Bohigas; a solo winter ascent of the Southeast Spur of 23,500-foot Pumori (VI, AI4, M5), which I made in three days in December 1983; the West Face of 26,000-foot Gasherbrum IV (VII, AI3, M4?), one of the most attractive of all the great Himalayan walls, by Austrian Robert Schauer and Kurtyka in 1985; the North Ridge of Rakaposhi (VII, AI4?), also in 1985,

by Dave Cheesemond, Kevin Doyle, and Barry Blanchard; and the Hungo Face of Kwangde (VII, WI6) in 1982 by David Breashears and me. The 5,000 feet of climbing on this relatively low (20,000-foot) mountain maintains a high standard for the entire climb and is a forerunner of fantastic routes to come. Kusum Kanguru, Kangtega, the North Face of Cholatse, the Northeast Face and West Face of Ama Dablam, and the North Face of Thamserku are all excellent climbs that have been made in recent years. By the time the experienced Slovenian climbers Marco Prezelj and Andrej Stremfelj made the first ascent of 23,000-foot Menlungtse by its South Face in one day in 1992, high-standard, alpine-style ice climbing had already been practiced in the Himalaya for more than a decade.

Off-Season High-Mountain Water Ice

At first, ice climbing was primarily a summer alpine sport, with occasional winter forays into the high places. Then climbers began tackling low-altitude waterfalls, which are frozen only in winter. In the high mountains, however, spring and autumn conditions and temperatures give rise to a hybrid type of climb: frozen drips, flows, runnels, and chimneys of water ice. Thus ice climbing has become a year-round sport for its most ardent devotees. Actually, some of the best climbs of the 1970s, such as the Super Couloir on Mont Blanc du Tacul and Slipstream in Canada, fall into this category.

In the early-to-mid-1980s, certain people began to really seek these off-season opportunities. High on Mont Blanc many great routes were discovered by Patrick Gabarrou, Jean-Marc Boivin, Christophe Profit, and others. Climbs such as Cascade de Notre Dame (V, WI5?) and the Hypercouloir (V, WI5+?)—ribbons of live water ice rising for thousands of feet between granite pillars—are prime examples of the genre. The Alps have seen hundreds more climbs like these since the mid-1980s.

Luckily, off-season ice is available in all the high, snowy mountains of the world, not just the Alps. In

Wyoming, the Teton range offers good off-season ice climbing, particularly on the Northeast Face of the Grand Teton. Here, in 1979, Charlie Fowler and I climbed the Route Canal (IV, WI5+), and Steve Shea soloed Shea's Chute (IV, WI5) in 1980. One of the finest examples of the genre I can think of, mixing high-standard waterfall ice climbing difficulties in a high-mountain environment, is a route called Striving for the Moon (VI, WI5–6) on Mount Temple in the Canadian Rockies. It was first climbed in 1993 by Ward Robinson and Barry Blanchard, two of the world's greatest alpinists.

All Mixed Up

The Scots virtually invented the sport of mixed rock and ice climbing, and they have continued to explore its possibilities. On Ben Nevis, in Glencoe, on Lochnagar, on Shelter Stone Crag, and in the corries of the Northwest Highlands, climbers such as Al Rouse, Rab Carrington, Alan Taylor, Murray Hamilton, Ken Spence, Rab Anderson, Mick Fowler, Rob Milne, and too many others to name have elevated the practice into new levels of technique, strength, and boldness. Hundreds of tricky, all-absorbing climbs have been made. Tilt, Central Grooves, and Inclination on Stob Coire nan Lochan, and Deep Throat, Migrant, and Fallout Corner in the Cairngorms all offer an M6–7 experience intense enough to keep the most jaded climber awake, struggling to fit body and mind to the contours of iced-up rock.

In Colorado, Utah, Wyoming, and Montana, the intricacies of mixed climbing have attracted a hard-core following. Duncan Ferguson has been active in Colorado since the mid-1970s, establishing ephemeral, unprotected thin-ice desperates (up to M6)

Top: **Duncan Ferguson climbing off-season ice on the North Face of Hallets Peak, Rocky Mountain National Park, Colorado** (Photo: Jeff Lowe) Bottom: **The author making the first ascent of the Teriebel Traverse, Vail, Colorado—a modern mixed route, tools on rock, hands on ice (M6–7)** (Photo: Dan Levison)

The elegant pillar of La Dame du Lac in France (*Photo: François-Guy Thivierge*)

in Rocky Mountain National Park on Mount Meeker, Longs Peak, Hallets Peak, and others. Mark Wilford, Charlie Fowler, and I did the classic iced-chimney, Birdbrain Boulevard (IV, M6), in 1985, while Alex Lowe, Greg Davis, and Mike Bearzi pushed the top technical levels up a notch or two on climbs like Hot Doggies (M7, Lowe), Prophet on a Stick (WI7, Lowe), Womb with a View (M7, Davis/Bearzi), and Secret Probation (M7, Davis). The hardest of all the technical problems, Octopussy (M8), though a very short 130 feet, puts mixed rock and ice climbing on the same level of athleticism as modern sport rock climbing. I accomplished this test piece in a magic moment at winter's end 1994, inspired by unusual fitness and the quiet confidence and support of my belayer and wife-to-be, Teri Ebel.

The mixed-climbing renaissance is also in full swing today in the Canadian Rockies. One of the birthplaces of frozen waterfall climbing, the "Alps of Canada" are home to some of the most difficult pure ice climbs in the world. The futuristic Terminator (IV, AI6+) on Mount Rundle was climbed by Californians Jay Smith and Craig Reason in 1985. The double overhanging candlestick of Fearful Symmetry (WI6+), climbed by Bruce Hendricks and Joe Josephson in 1992, is equivalent to France's La Dame du Lac (WI6+)—the prettiest ice pillar I have ever seen, climbed by Thierry Renault in 1992—or the Fang (WI6+) in Colorado, when climbed in the thin conditions of its first ascent made by Alex Lowe in 1981.

But the push onto ever-thinner ice really began in the winter of 1987 when Jeff Marshall and Larry Ostrander climbed the 700-foot Riptide (M7?) on Mount Patterson, described by Marshall as a "five-pitch horror." Then, in 1991, Troy Kirwan and Joe Buzowski climbed Mixed Master (IV, WI4, M6?), a seven-pitch, fully mixed route that finishes with what has been described by Joe Josephson as a "ten-inch-wide vertical ice seam." In 1992, shortly after making the first ascent of Fearful Symmetry,

Hendricks went on to solo the first ascent of Blessed Rage (IV, WI6, M6?), an impressive 650-foot climb above Emerald Lake near Field. Hendricks turned the hat trick when, in 1993, he and Josephson established the aptly named Sea of Vapors (IV, WI7+?) on Mount Rundle, a fleeting and ethereal 500-foot swipe of frozen mist close to the Terminator. The Terminator itself, a four-pitch ice dagger renowned for its purity of line and on prominent display above the town of Banff, seldom touches down. It was climbed in this "unformed" state by Serge Angellucci, Jeff Everett, and Karl Nagy in 1993. Their variation, which is called T2 (IV, WI6+, M7, A2?), takes a mixed start leading to the upper ice fang, and presents one of the most compelling technical challenges to be found anywhere.

In the Alpine countries, mixed climbing has always been a part of the high-mountain game. On some of the ice climbs that have already been mentioned (such as the Super Couloir Direct on Mont Blanc du Tacul and the MacIntyre/Colton on the Grandes Jorasses), mixed ground actually presents the greatest difficulties. In the early 1990s, the American Marc Twight pushed hard on several new routes, such as Beyond Good and Evil (V, M6, A3?), a saber slash on the North Face of Pèlerins, which he climbed in 1992 with Englishman Andy Parkin. But some of these routes have involved considerable aid climbing, in contrast to the free ethos that prevails in Scotland and Colorado. In the Stubai region of Austria, however, Andi Orgler and others have established a number of the highest-caliber mixed rock and water ice routes on some of the lower outcroppings. The major activities of this sort in Austria have taken place since the mid-1980s and include pure ice climbs like Andi's Hängender Garten (III, WI6).

In France and Italy the most difficult new ice routes are mixed. Climbs such as Visa pour l'Amérique (IV, WI6), by François Damilano, Godefroy Perroux, and Philippe Pibarot, were made on very thin, evanescent ice as early as 1987, setting the

stage for more recent climbs of even greater difficulty. The Tête de Gramusat in the Val de Freissinières harbors a number of fine pure ice lines of
world-class quality on its steeply banded, 1,400-foot
cliffs; and the route Blind Faith (V, WI6+, A2), first
climbed by Thierry Renault and me in January of
1992, has an eighteen-foot roof on the fourth pitch,
where Renault used three pitons for aid (it will go
free at M7+ or 8). The overall route is one of the
most exciting I have done. La Lyre (V, WI7+), the
long, 1,800-foot route in the Haute Savoie region,
also climbed in January of 1992 by Renault, Wilfried
Colonna, and Denis Condevaux, has a crux overhanging rock slab sparsely stuccoed with small blobs
and drips of ice. The talented Renault says La Lyre
was one of the most intense climbing experiences of
his long and varied career.

It seems that 1992 was a good year for French
ice in general, and for Renault in particular. In
January he also opened the shorter 300-foot route
L'Aventure C'est L'Aventure in the Haute Maurienne,
after thrilling a watching crowd when a small icicle
he had been hugging with his legs broke at the overhanging crux just as he planted one tool in the ice
above. Struggling through a series of still-difficult,
unprotected moves, Renault gave this climb a rating
of 7+, the highest in France. The only other climb of
this difficulty is Nuit Blanche on l'Argentière Glacier
in the Mont Blanc region, first ascended by English
climber Stevie Haston and Frenchman Patrick
Naudin in January 1994.

The sport of ice climbing has come a long way,
particularly since the introduction of curved picks
(classic and reverse), rigid crampons, and reliable ice
screws. In the high mountains of the Alps, Andes,
Canadian Rockies, Alaska, New Zealand, the
Caucasus, and elsewhere, the ascent of alpine ice
faces, gullies, couloirs, and ice cliffs has become
more than just a pastime for a small group from the
lunatic fringe. And more aggressive adventurers
have sought the wispy dribbles, smears, flows, runnels, and chimneys of seasonal ice that appear each
year. Waterfall specialists, assisted by improved
reverse-curved picks and curved shafts on their ice
axes, Snarg drive-in screw-out tube screws, and,
more recently, extremely sharp ice screws that are
easy to place with one hand, monopoint crampons
for water ice and mixed climbing, improved fabrics
and clothing design, and greater familiarity with the
techniques and demands of the medium, have progressed to the point where it took a single day for
Randy Racliff and Marc Twight to accomplish the
first climb of the dangerous eleven-pitch Reality
Bath (V, WI6?) in the Canadian Rockies in 1988.
And a climb like La Pomme d'Or in Quebec, which
required two days on its first ascent in 1980, was
soloed in 1989 in two hours via a harder direct variation by Guy Laselle.

Today there are probably a hundred climbers of
Guy Laselle's caliber around the world, and many
thousands of men and women who are expert on ice.
It is impossible to keep current with all the new
routes that are being opened and all the new climbers
who are flocking to the sport, but they are everywhere out in the ice world, motivated like no others
to find a way to combat global warming!

There is still plenty of pioneering left to do.
Grab your tools and go find the adventure you want.
The ultimate ice climb remains to be done. It might
be found in May on the East Face of the Moose's
Tooth in Alaska, or in winter on the North Face of
Latok I in Pakistan. Perhaps I will see you there!

The author enjoying the weather on the summit of the Grand Teton, Wyoming, after making the first winter ascent of the Black Ice Couloir/West Face combination, February 1972 (Photo: George Lowe III)

One Man's Frostbite

▼ ▼ ▼ ▼

THE ICE EXPERIENCE

FEAR AND CONFIDENCE

It is July 20, 1967. A hot Teton afternoon. Summits hover in the haze above Cascade Canyon, whose pines and stream-crossed meadows provide the background for a sixteen-year-old's approach to his first ice climb. The boy's boots leave perfect waffle-prints in the dust of the old trail as he takes long strides to keep up with his older partner. They are headed toward a logjam in the creek, across from the rocky bulk of Storm Point.

The boy's mind is filled with stories he has read of ice climbing in the European Alps: spindrift avalanches on the White Spider, Rebuffat's climb of the North Face of the Matterhorn. Scary stories they are, yet beautiful; descriptions of a world he fears but wants to know—cold bivouacs, glistening mornings, snowy days, the crunch of steel points biting into ice. But that dream lives across an ocean in mountains that are fairy-tale castles to the boy. The hills in his mind are romantic, but vague and shapeless when compared to the crags that surround him now. The boy scans the Guide's Wall of Storm Point; he remembers the texture of the rock and the surge of blood and muscles required by the twin cracks of the last pitch.

The young man and the boy come to the ford in the stream. They cross the network of naked timber, rucksacks a challenge to their balance, and on the other side they stoop to drink. The metallic taste of the cold water lingers in their mouths as they start up the hillside to the hanging canyon of Valhalla. Behind them the sun drops below a craggy ridge, and they climb, puffing through the fir trees.

The forest thins, straggles, ends, disgorges the serene man and the sweating boy. The boy's thighs groan with painful relief at the final steps into twilight Valhalla. The man turns and watches the boy drop his rucksack onto the rich turf that covers a portion of the basin. The streamlet that bisects the meadow in a string of half-loops fills the air with gentle sucking and popping noises. The pair make camp against a square boulder. The man brings water in a mess tin; the boy lights the stove.

While the soup is heating and sending beef smells into the air, the man points up at the West Face of the Grand Teton, which looms above them in the dusk. He tells the boy that between the main peak on the left (which is just losing its final

Yes!

To dance beneath

the diamond sky,

with one hand

waving free . . .

—Bob Dylan,
Mr. Tambourine Man

alpine glow) and the lower shoulder silhouetted on the right lies the Black Ice Couloir. The boy tries to see into the gully through the increasing darkness, but his straining eyes discern no secrets.

Curled up on his foam pad against the square rock, and bundled in a down parka, the man snores. The boy shivers under the stars. His legs are cold. He tries to see himself on the ice of the couloir, but he has trouble with the vision. He feels young and afraid at the thought of the steep gray ice he has heard about around fires at Climber's Camp. He recalls tales of rockfall caused by tourists on the Owen route, which crosses a rock-strewn ledge above the couloir. He imagines the strain on calf muscles. They say it is like pitch after pitch of unprotected 5.8 slabs. The boy's fears keep him awake and shaking slightly in waves, synchronized with the rasping breath of the dark figure next to him. He watches Orion creep across the sky and waits, wide-eyed, for morning.

Years pass; seasons bloom and wilt, freeze and thaw. The boy makes many ice climbs and loses his fear, but not his respect. He becomes a young man himself.

The young man is in the Canadian Rockies. He emerges from his tent at the Columbia Icefields Campground just as a faint glow begins to wash the stars from the eastern sky. He stretches in the cold air. A month of climbing has left him feeling strong and supple, mentally relaxed, aggressive in an adventurous way. The clear predawn promises a perfect day for climbing, but one partner has gone home and another won't arrive for two days. He could spend the day photographing the bighorn sheep on the grassy hillside above the campground, or perhaps reading in the sunshine. But there's a nice new route to do over on the West Shoulder of Andromeda. The young man decides he'll take a peek at that instead. The date is July 21, 1973.

Dressed in wool knickers, tattered green cardigan, and brown balaclava, the young man throws his ice axe and a small pack containing a hunk of cheese, his *cagoule*, and crampons onto the front seat of his beat-up old car. Headlights glow like cats' eyes in the fading dark as the vehicle chugs past tents, vans, campers, and a log cook-shelter, bouncing softly down the dirt road to the junction with the highway, then heads west onto the paved road.

During the three-mile drive to the parking lot at the sightseeing concession ("See the wonders of the Athabasca Glacier from the comfort of an enclosed snow machine!") the young man is treated to one of his favorite sights: glaciated mountains awakening to the first light of a new day. On his left are Athabasca and Andromeda; the Snow Dome and Kitchener are to the right; the tongue of the Athabasca Glacier laps down from the ice field between the two sets of peaks.

At the parking lot below and between Athabasca and Andromeda, he grabs the blue pack and ice axe from the seat. The car door slams as he hops out into a slight breeze. It's chilly, and he wastes little time in shouldering the small load and hopping over the guard rail onto the surface of the moraine. The wooden-shafted axe feels familiar and good in his hand as he scrambles up an unstable hill toward the glacial bench that contours beneath the North Ridge of Andromeda, giving access to the face he wants to climb.

The bare ice of the shelf is weathered like an old man's face and littered with small dark stones that have fallen from the rocky buttress of the ridge. Crunching noises punctuate the young man's footsteps as he rounds the corner of the ridge to see the top of the West Shoulder turn pink at the first touch of the sun. A shallow arête of ice interspersed with rocky steps falls 1,800 feet directly from the glowing summit into the small glacier that still separates the young man from the climb. Yes, a good route, he thinks, taking a deep breath. But to get to the base he must first negotiate a jumble of ice blocks the size of houses and then traverse the upper glacier, whose crevasses still remain partially hidden by last winter's snow.

He avoids most of the short icefall with surprising ease by hugging the base of the North Ridge. A latticework of ramps and bridges winds around the edge of one serac and spans a gap between two others. But the upper glacier is more wor-risome. It is a gently rolling quarter-mile of half-covered crevasses—easy terrain, but dangerous. It is with more than respect in his heart that he bends forward at the waist and begins the probing and poking with the shaft of his axe that will con-tinue until he reaches the foot of the climb. The young man presents a humble figure bowing his way across the snow, dwarfed by the rock ridge behind him and the ice wall ahead.

Arriving below his planned route, the young man rests a few minutes. The sweat streaking his face from temples to cheeks evaporates as he sits on his pack and straps crampons to boots. The sun has reached a point two-thirds down from the top of the face, but it is still cool where the young man sits. He takes a moment more to eat a piece of cheese and regain his composure. The obvious problems of the route—wide bergschrund, steep ice, snowed-up rock, summit cornice—seem far preferable to the unseen holes of the glacier.

Crossing the bergschrund is difficult. At its narrowest it still yawns six feet wide, with a bottom too dark to see. He breaks the overhanging lower lip back until a platform can be made to support his weight. He makes a quick calculation: If he lets himself fall forward, will he be able to span the gap with the full length of his body plus outstretched arms? He decides he can. The shock of contacting the upper wall is greater than he expected. Then, maintaining the bridge with one hand, he swings the axe with the other and plants it well in the ice of the face. Feet swing from the lower edge of the split, and the young man is established on the climb.

For fifty feet the ice is tilted up at 70°. He wishes he had brought along an ice hammer to complement the axe, but the steep part is soon behind him. Conditions are excellent: hard snow, ice that takes points like cork. As he climbs farther, he enters the sun. He pauses a moment on the 50° slope to change to dark glasses and store his sweater in the pack. The rim is etched white against a lake-blue sky. He lopes upward, climbing a narrow gully through one rock band, skirting another by

The author on the summit of Mount Athabasca, a neighbor of Mount Andromeda, a few days before his climb of the West Shoulder Direct, August 1973 (Photo: Christie Northrop)

a couloir on the right, regaining the ice arête again 500 feet from the top. He is feeling as light as the ice crystals that sparkle in the air, immune to the old avalanche runnels that swoop down to the glacier.

Crampons grate on limestone as he climbs through an unavoidable cliff a hundred feet below the summit. The top of the rock tapers into snow that gets looser and steeper. Right under the jutting cornice it reaches 80°, and he has to plunge the shaft of the axe and all of one arm into the snow for purchase.

Directly above him the cornice juts out a full fifteen feet. An insecure leftward traverse of forty feet brings the young man to a place where the cornice has fallen and only a seven-foot vertical step bars him from the top. But a full half-hour is consumed while he carves a groove through the snow. At last, however, his careful efforts are rewarded, and he flops safely onto the flat summit.

He stands up and brushes the snow from his clothes, slowly turning full circle. A panorama of his favorite mountains fills his view. The pyramid of Mount Forbes lies to the south. Double-summited Bryce is to the west, sun gleaming on its ice faces. The broad shield of Athabasca can be seen to the east, and the snow domes of Kitchener, the Twins, and Columbia rise out of the ice field to the north.

Looking down through the notch from which he recently emerged, the young man sees the pockmarks of his crossing on the small glacier at the bottom of the face. He sees how the small tributary glacier tumbles down into the mile-wide stream of the Athabasca. He watches as a tiny red bug with thirty people inside winds its way down a bulldozed road from the snowmobile concession on the lateral moraine to the flat surface of the broad ribbon of ice.

The young man gives a single whoop of joy and then begins the descent down the Skyladder route and back to his tracks on the glacier. By noon he is at the campground, reading in the sun. ▼

THE ALPINE BALLROOM

Climbing frozen waterfalls offers the ice climber the same sort of opportunity to sharpen technique as crag climbing offers the rock climber. But to the alpinist, the skills and strength gained on the waterfall are primarily important in their application to major new routes in the high mountains. Training on winter waterfalls actually makes normal alpine ice climbing easier. The proof of this came fast on the heels of early waterfall ice developments. In the summer of 1971, having just made the first ascent of Mahlen's Peak Waterfall the previous winter, my brother Greg soloed the Black Ice Couloir on Wyoming's Grand Teton in two hours. In 1976 John Bouchard used his water ice experience to advantage when he soloed a hard new route on the North Face of the Grand Pilier d'Angle on Mont Blanc, one of the most impressive Alpine ice walls. In 1974 Mike Weis and I were aided by confidence acquired on Bridalveil Falls and other winter ice climbs in the ascent of the Grand Central Couloir on the North Face of Mount Kitchener.

The first ascent of the 3,500-foot North Face of Mount Kitchener was made in August of 1971 by Chris Jones, Gray Thompson, and me. Our line, the Ramp Route, was a very satisfying experience and a difficult climb in its own right. But for me at least, the face held an even greater attraction: the great central couloir that falls from the broad summit of the mountain like the tail of a white comet. I doubt if anywhere else in the Rockies there is a couloir of equal size that is at once so beautiful and steep and singularly imposing. Perhaps I should add dangerous as well, for it is the natural path for rockfall and is often capped by a huge cornice. On my first encounter with the slopes below the couloir in August 1970, with my cousin George Lowe, the weather was warm and the couloir rumbled like Grand Central Station on Christmas Eve.

For several seasons following the ascent of the Ramp Route, yearly attempts were made on the Grand Central Couloir. Brian Greenwood, George Homer, and Bob Beal managed to work a way up the ice and rock buttress to the left of the couloir in 1973. They were actually attempting the couloir, but rockfall forced them to follow a more protected line. In the winter of 1975, at least two determined efforts were made, doubtless in the hopes that the winter cold would reduce rockfall. In the end, the short winter days, brittle ice, and avalanches confined both attempts to the lower half of the face.

Action and

contemplation—

never one without

the other.

—Gaston Rebuffat,
Starlight and Storm

Greg Lowe standing in front of the North Face of Mount Kitchener on the way to an unsuccessful attempt on the Grand Central Couloir, 1973. The next year Mike Weis and the author made their climb.

(Photo: Jeff Lowe)

Such was the state of affairs when Mike Weis and I arrived at the Icefield Campground in mid-August, back for yet another of our annual efforts. On our first try our now-traditional bad luck held, and a snowstorm caught us before we had crossed the bergschrund. Soon the avalanches were roaring, and we were doing the quickstep to get down out of their range.

In the 1970s, Mike was one of my main climbing partners. We had met through a mutual friend in Crested Butte, Colorado, in the autumn of 1970. Although Mike had not been climbing as long as I had at that time, he had shown his adventurous aptitude just a few months after he began by his nearly successful first winter ascent (with John Weiland) of the classic Harding Route on Keeler Needle in the Sierra Nevada. I liked Mike's hard-core, no-nonsense, lumber-camp sensibilities (his father was a logger in Northern California), combined with an innate competence in the outdoors. Soon we were doing new routes together on rock and ice. We made a number of climbs on the sandstone walls of Zion Canyon, Utah, and spent summers on the big faces of the Canadian Rockies. The previous winter we had made the first ascent of Bridalveil Falls in Colorado, which had been a rock and roll sock hop.

Back at the Icefields Campground, waiting for the weather to change, we geared up psychologically for a different sort of rhythm and a more classical, longer-lasting twirl through an immense mountain dance hall. Several days later the weather had improved and looked as if it might hold. We adopted new tactics. We carried minimal food, water, and bivouac gear, starting up at 6:00 P.M. We planned to climb through the night with head lamps and top out the following day. By climbing at night we hoped to be above the zone of bad rockfall by the time the morning sun hit the top of the face.

The real climbing began to the left of the lower of two bergschrunds of the small hanging glacier at the bottom of the wall. The bergschrund itself was impassable without undue exertion. Moving on ice and rotten snow over ice, we climbed unroped, each with his own thoughts, for 400 or 500 feet to about the level of the upper bergschrund. At this point the ice got very hard and Mike cried "Uncle," so we got out the rope. (I was glad for the added security, too.) While the features of the huge amphitheater at the top of the face gradually darkened to a ragged silhouette, we moved simultaneously for six or seven rope-lengths, with two screws between us for safety. At the top of the right-hand *rognon* in the lower ice field we had a bite to eat and drink and prepared our head lamps for the dark hours ahead. I said I thought we would bag the climb this time, but Mike cautiously reminded me that "we've barely gotten started."

From that point on we belayed each pitch. While the leader stomped slowly up with vision limited to the small circle of light projected by his head lamp, the belayer had time for reflection. To spur his thoughts, he could gaze into the infinite darkness of the valley or peer up at the starry sky, head lamp off to save on batteries. We were moving to some sort of ancient cadence, impelled by the natural music of the cosmos to perform a sort of structured waltz in the darkness. For awhile, our sloping dance floor was illuminated by the flashing Aurora Borealis, and a slow-motion riot of color, light, and sensation took place in our heads. Coming at the end of the psychedelic era, this experience drove home an absolute commitment to the superior beauty of untainted reality.

As the gully narrowed and steepened, we encountered the lowest of several polypropylene lines, remnants of an attempt the previous winter. The eastern sky began to lighten. By the time we reached the vertical narrowing of the upper couloir, it was 6:00 A.M.—full light. We were at the top of the fifteenth roped pitch.

The next pitch, my lead, looked as though it had been borrowed from a hard Scottish gully. Initially it was almost a chimney. I could bridge with my left crampon on rock and the other on ice, while using the axe to whatever advantage it could be put. This moderate going came to an end all too soon. The couloir widened, forcing me to climb the thin face of ice and snow itself. With only knifeblades between frozen blocks for protection, the climbing was extremely nerve-wracking. Seldom would the tools penetrate more than half an inch before meeting rock. The crux was climbing out from under an ice mushroom that was crammed into the couloir like a huge marshmallow. It took a couple of hours before I had a hanging belay from a couple of old "Wart Hog" solid ice pitons in the rock at the side of the couloir. We had no jumars or hauling rope, but even with his thirty-pound pack, after a couple of pendulums from underneath the ice mushroom, Mike pulled himself over the bulge by amazing brute strength.

Now the angle eased to a "mere" 65°. The ice was thick and held our points well; we made quicker progress for several pitches. Then we came against the final section of the upper couloir, which had looked well iced from below but turned out to be steep, compact rock thinly veneered with snow. Luck was with us; we found a narrow ice gully leading out to the right onto the rib that borders the couloir. Several hard leads of mixed snow and ice with one or two short but hard rock steps brought us out onto the summit ice cap, just 200 feet short of our goal. In our thirsty and fatigued condition time had moved faster than we had. With the air scratching at our throats, we climbed the last two pitches. The first was ice at a moderate angle. The second—a vertical path on rotten snow through the summit cornice—was as difficult as any, an exhausting capper to twenty-six hours of intense climbing. It was 8:00 P.M. when Mike and I stood side by side in the sun's horizontal rays on Kitchener's summit.

Then we turned, and with the sun a shimmering red disk at our backs, we wobbled through deep snow toward the East Ridge, our descent route. We still had several hours to go before we could rest and get a drink of much-needed water as it trickled from a snowfield in the saddle below the small peak known as K2.

For Mike and me, Bridalveil Falls had been a personal breakthrough, but the Grand Central Couloir opened our minds to unknown reservoirs of endurance, which, from that time on, have been like old friends—always there when they are needed.

Sometimes the best dances are marathons. ▼

GRABBING FRIENDSHIP BY THE ANKLE

Michael Kennedy is a resident of Aspen, Colorado, and the editor of *Climbing* magazine. By reputation he is a good climber, and I have learned that many good climbers are very intense, ready to burst at the seams. This sort of intensity is difficult for me to handle—I have a tendency to shy away—so when Mike and I met over a cup of coffee in 1976 at my brother's house in Eldorado Springs, I prepared myself for a tense, awkward situation. But my fears turned out to be unfounded.

Mike and I talked, among other things, about independent attempts we had each made on the East Face of the Moose's Tooth, a huge Alaskan wall as yet unclimbed. When I asked him the reason for his party's failure, a smile broke through Mike's beard. "At our high point we were hit by an avalanche of ice blocks. One of our anchors was ripped out, and one of our packs was smashed where it sat on a ledge. That was enough for us," he concluded. "Man, we were freaked! We got out of there—fast!"

Embrace Tiger,

return to mountain.

—Tai-chi lesson

I understood exactly. Mike was no arrogant, macho climber, but a man who admits being scared and can smile at his own fear. As we continued to talk, I got a strong feeling that the lanky fellow across the table from me would be a good partner in the high mountains.

In 1977, when I found myself in need of an ice-climbing instructor for the International Alpine School, I thought of Mike. By the end of the course, at our rather boisterous graduation celebration at the Outlaw Bar in Ouray, I knew my first impression of him had been accurate. After accepting my thanks for a job well done, he bought me a Heineken. Over the beer I asked if he would be interested in joining my cousin George and me in Alaska in June to try a couple of new routes on Mounts Hunter and Foraker. "Would I?" Mike responded. "Is the Pope Catholic?"

We rendezvoused at the airport in Anchorage, George arriving from California and Mike and I from Colorado. The other two had never met. It was a blind date, a fact we were all acutely aware of. George and Mike were all good humor and politeness. "Ho, ho," George greeted us at the baggage claim. "Glad to see you guys made it. You must be Mike." They shook hands like two businessmen. I found myself nodding along in an inane, but encouraging, way. Yes (nod), that's

George Lowe III and Mike Kennedy on the Triangle Face of Mount Hunter
(Photo: Jeff Lowe)

Mike, with the beard and the high-pitched laugh, and, yes (nod), that fellow with the young face and hearty manner is my cousin George, the physicist-climber whose top-secret government job matched his (at the time) inscrutable nature. I was the matchmaker, hoping that George's serious mien and Mike's low-key approach would complement each other rather than clash. This can happen so easily on difficult climbs, destroying team harmony and much of the reason for climbing in the first place.

Two days later we were lying in George's tent at the base of the North Face of Mount Hunter, our first objective framed by the arched tent door. The Northwest Spur of Hunter rises more than 7,000 feet from the Southeast Fork to the summit at 14,573 feet. If we were successful on Hunter, we also planned to try a new route on the 10,000-foot-high South Face of 17,400-foot Mount Foraker, across the Kahiltna Glacier from our base camp. But first we had to climb the spur that swept up in front of us. When we landed on the glacier, Mike had exclaimed, "That's a training climb?" Our alpine-style plans did seem a bit flimsy when compared with the obvious strength of the mountain's defenses. It didn't help to know that three good-sized expeditions had already failed on the same route.

But we had made our preparations, caching spare skis at the base of the West

Ridge, our descent route, and loading our packs with enough bivouac gear and food for five days. We planned to climb during the Alaskan night (in June never darker than a Colorado twilight) to avoid the sloppy snow conditions that were certain to exist during the day. The reggae sounds of Jimmy Cliff and Bob Marley and the Wailers helped Mike and me endure the wait.

At 10:30 P.M., as the two of us were engrossed in the rhythm and lyrics of "The harder they come, the harder they fall . . ." George punched the stop button on the tape player. The sun was off the face. Our wait was over. We donned our skis and roped up for the short approach to the base of the spur. The silence was almost as heavy as our packs as we skied up the nearly flat glacier, but none of us really wanted to talk anyway. It was enough just to be starting a big climb, the snow-covered peaks all around us, huge and impressive in the subdued light.

Mike Kennedy and George Lowe III in the bivouac at the top of the Triangle Face
(Photo: Jeff Lowe)

We traded skis for crampons to cross an easy snow bridge over the bergschrund that put us at the base of the route. Mushy snow covered the ice to start, and we climbed simultaneously most of the way up the lower spur. A quick frontpoint led around the end of a rock band that was threatened by a drooping serac, then hard-breathing effort took us up steep, unstable snow. The crest of the spur dropped away on both sides, curving up to taper into an ice bulge that barred the way. But the bluish-white ice looked good. A core of ice extruded as a screw went in. A carabiner clicked. Base camp, 1,500 feet below, already looked small and far away. The winged orange tent seemed like a tiny butterfly lost in a sea of snow and crevasses.

George's crampon points loomed above us as Mike and I belayed him up the steep ice bulge. Mike moved quickly up a corridor of snow between ice towers where the crest became broader. The white profile of the slope above us was sharply etched against a sky of opaque blue as the sun rose from its shallow dip below the horizon. It was 6:00 A.M. We rested and had a bite of cheese and zucchini bread, weighty food perhaps, but more sustaining than "freeze-dried." We had done more than one-third of the climb.

It was nice to sit on the packs, eating and gazing around at the ocean of peaks lapping at the sky. I looked over at Denali, which rose above a row of intervening mountains, and wondered if there were people over there at that very moment staring back, taking a break from the effort of climbing that massive hill. My reverie was soon brought to a halt. "We've made good time up to here," George cautioned, "but the real climbing is just beginning."

I followed the sweep of his hand up the 1,500-foot ice wall to the sharp summit and knew he was right. A pointed ice face we had dubbed the Triangle Face looked straightforward enough, but something we could not see from where we sat had us all a bit worried. From the apex a narrow, corniced ridge led horizontally back from the summit of our spur, connecting it with the main mass of the mountain. From the airplane on the way in, the ridge had resembled a ripsaw blade, its vertical teeth coated with marshmallow syrup. "Let's get started, then," Mike exhorted, reshouldering his pack.

On the face the climbing alternated between good snow and hard ice. The leader trailed both ropes, anchoring each one to two ice screws when it ran out. The others then climbed simultaneously, one belayed by the leader, the other belaying himself with a Gibb's Ascender. The angle varied from about 45° to perhaps 60° as we headed for the right-hand containing ridge, which looked as if it would offer easy going for the last few hundred feet to the top of the face. At belay stances we chortled at our good luck with the weather and joked about making the summit in a few hours.

Our "easy" ridge turned out to be a nightmare. George struggled up through mushrooms and cornices that had the consistency of porridge, but not the cohesion. The snow was rotting in the sun, drooping everywhere, threatening to fall into the space around us, perhaps taking us with it as well. George took hours on his lead, attempting to compact the snow so that it would hold his weight. It was like trying to swim up a 60° knife-edge of sand. Finally he yelled down that he had a belay. "But don't fall. I don't think it'll hold."

Several pitches and much time, sweat, and worry later, the three of us were ensconced on a small ledge we had shoveled out of the snow just under the very top of the face. Almost comically, our rope was draped around the nearest mushroom, like a lasso around a pile of Cream of Wheat. We were not very much cheered by the "security" this provided, but it was all that was available. We had climbed for nineteen hours to get to this place. Mist and light snow moved in. A horizontal ridge that led back from our bivouac site was only 300 feet long, and after that it looked like a stroll to the summit. But those 300 feet were the worst bit of climbing terrain any of us had ever seen. Up close, the drooping ripsaw edge

I had seen earlier from the air took on an even more comically ominous look. Bus-sized mushrooms perched astride the ridge on ridiculously narrow stalks; marshmallow sharks' teeth ripped the air.

We brewed soup on our little ledge and tried to talk ourselves into believing the situation was not quite so glum as it appeared, but I had a terrible feeling in my stomach, as if at any moment the whole mountain would collapse. "It's impossible," I said, and believed it. There was no strong opposition to that viewpoint, but we agreed to rest where we were until early morning hours, to give the evening chill a chance to solidify the snow as much as possible. Then we would give it a go. We tried to sleep.

At one o'clock in the morning I started out on the traverse of the ridge. (Somehow I had grabbed the lead. The suspense of waiting behind seemed less palatable than whatever difficulties the climbing could pose.) I used the shovel in place of my axe because a great deal of snow would have to be removed to get to something more substantial that would support body weight. Losing myself in the task, I shoveled like a wild man trying to tunnel his way back to sanity.

The narrow, incredibly steep ridge was overhung on both sides with cornices, so the trick was to make a trail through them without causing them to fall. Things went well at first, and after a short while the rope back to Mike was stretched taut. Since there was no place for me to establish a belay, he began to follow. I started to enjoy the tunneling and crawling and balancing; thoughts of success crept into my mind as I approached the halfway point along the ridge. I was happy, too, in a way, as I started to carve on a particularly undercut and nasty haystack of snow.

With a sickening "WHOOMP" it suddenly felt as though the earth had begun to rush inward on itself—but the implosion was only in my head. The cornice had collapsed, and me with it. I did not feel too much fear (Will Mike and George hold me, or will they go, too?), but I did flail a lot in a futile attempt to stop tumbling. All in a flash, I felt my left crampon points snag the ice; my ankle made a snapping sound, and I felt tendons rip. Then, just as suddenly, my fall stopped. I was dangling on the rope, sixty feet below the the ridge crest. George called to see if I was all right."Yeah," I replied, "but I think my ankle's broken."

After a prolonged struggle to regain the ridge, during which the only assistance my partners could offer was a tight rope, I crawled back along the path I had so recently chiseled and greeted Mike at the place where he was straddling the ridge *au cheval.* It was the only relatively solid and narrow enough place around—and he had landed there after being jerked off his feet by the force of my fall! The clouds descended around us, and it began to snow again. "Well," shrugged Mike, "I guess we get to go down now, huh?"

The descent of the ice face seemed interminable. First George would rappel down and set up an anchor, then it would be my turn to hop one-legged down to him. Finally Mike would slide down. The storm got heavier, and spindrift began to flow off the face in a continuous sheet. Strangely, our humor was good. We told jokes at the stances. George and Mike accused me of creating an excuse to get back to see a lady I had met in Talkeetna.

On the next-to-last rappel before we reached the flat area below the face, I was alone with George at the anchor. "You know," he remarked, "I'm glad Mike was along on this one. He's solid as hell." When Mike arrived and George slid off again, I had to chuckle to myself as Mike said, "Man, it's great to be with a guy like George in a situation like this. Hey, what're you laughing about? You finally flipped out on us or what?"

We bivouacked at the base of the face, then spent another day getting off the climb, but we finally reached our skis, which stuck out of the snow like outstretched arms. That same day a pilot from Talkeetna just happened to land on the Southeast Fork of the Kahiltna to drop off another party of climbers, so he transported me straight to Providence Hospital in Anchorage, where I found out I had suffered a severe sprain and two bone chips.

Mike and George returned to Hunter and completed the route a few days later. Afterwards they went around to the south side of Foraker and made a ten-day first ascent of the Infinite Spur, which, in the ensuing years, has gained a legendary reputation as one of Alaska's greatest climbs. Their achievements were all the more satisfying because of the new bonds of friendship they had formed. Mike was later to write: "I felt completely comfortable climbing with George. There were no ego games between us, no competition—and the experiences had brought us very close." ▼

MIND MARATHON

Let us live for

the beauty of

our own reality.

—The Chink,
from the novel
*Even Cowgirls
Get the Blues,*
by Tom Robbins

Late one winter, Bill Johnson, a staff writer for *Sports Illustrated*, called me long distance. "Would you be willing to do some ice climbing for an article we have in mind?" he asked. An image of a solitary figure high on a frozen waterfall popped into my head. "Sure," I said, "if I can choose the climb." "No problem there," replied Bill.

So we made arrangements to meet at the end of March in the little ski resort town of Telluride, Colorado. Bridalveil Falls is situated above the Idarado Mine at the head of the mountain valley a couple miles east of town.

The appointed day arrived. Bill, his daughter Tina, and Willis Wood, a photographer on assignment for the story, sat down to breakfast with me at the Iron Ladle. Outside, the town was snowless under a summer-hot sun. Young women, brown as cherrywood and clad in halter tops, walked the Old West streets or lounged on wooden benches.

Bill speared a bite of omelet with his fork, waggling it in front of his neatly trimmed beard as he voiced the question that was on all of our minds: "Hell, Jeff, is the ice going to be safe to climb today?" "I think so," I lied, "but we won't know for sure until we ski in to the base. That is, if there's any snow left to ski on up there." Scratching under his English-style cap, Willis remarked, "Well, we've got good light anyway."

Bridalveil could be seen from the parking lot at the mine, where the three-foot snowpack was shrinking almost visibly. Willis speculated about whether the ice we could see still standing was any good. I held my tongue, certain it was not, though Bridalveil's shaded nook in the cliffs ensured that it would remain in condition longer than any other climb in Colorado. Besides, after all the fuss, I felt obligated to go through the motions.

Bill tossed a bottle of red wine into his pack, along with several oranges and candy bars. "For lunch and a toast to success," he explained. I still had no comment. Removing all unnecessary clothing, we began to ski to the base of the icefall. There would be no climbing today, I told myself silently. The approach up the scenic valley was thus rendered carefree. I had a couple of hours to relax.

But by the time we arrived in the boulder- and snow-filled catch basin beneath the ice, there had been a change in the tone of the afternoon. We discovered that it was cold there in the shade. Even the act of packing a platform to stand on was not sufficient to warm us. Sweaters and parkas appeared from packs and were gratefully donned. Furthermore, there was no sound of running water. Though the ice was thin under some of the bulges, and the dark, underlying rock showed through, it was not melting.

While the others stood around oohing and aahing at the ice, I prepared to climb, commenting, "I'll probably just go up a pitch or so—to that thin spot beneath the overhang—then rappel down." So besides strapping crampons to boots and removing my ice axe and North Wall hammer from the pack, my pre-climb activities included uncoiling a rope to trail behind me—not for safety, as it would simply dangle from my waist, but for use on the rappel. I also included a few ice screws to use in anchoring the rappel. In spite of these precautions, there was even then a little voice in the back of my head whispering, "It will go." But for the moment I succeeded in suppressing that sound.

As I began to climb, my mind was in neutral. No hopes. No expectations. I was just exploring to see what the ice was like. The rope that dangled from my waist was my umbilical to earth. "As soon as the ice gets bad," I thought, "or the climbing too difficult for comfort, all that is necessary is to place an ice screw and rappel." In a way, the security this knowledge provided was comforting—but comfort and concentration don't mix very well. To climb unprotected on Bridalveil, and do it safely, would require total focus. The rope began to tug at the back of my mind, asking for attention I could ill afford to give it.

The first sixty-foot apron inclined at an angle of about 75°. Huge cauliflower-like formations characterized this section of relatively easy climbing. It was a simple matter of maintaining balance over my crampons while sliding up through the slots and bulges, using ice clumps for handholds and occasionally planting the pick of the axe. Working my body into position this way was a pleasure. There was a further delight: here, at least, the ice was good—firm as a solid old oak and only slightly brittle.

Too quickly, the apron lay below and the ice reared up vertically for fifty feet, capped by the first crux of the climb, a three-foot overhang. Was that gentle downward pull on the rope real or imagined? No matter. Mind Control said, "Go up. The ice is good."

In the steep section below the overhang were two pillars, spaced about two feet apart. In the shallow trough between them the ice was thin enough for the green moss growing on the rock beneath to be visible in places. By stemming between the pillars, one foot on either side of the trough, I could maintain balance, weight over my feet to save my arms for when they might really be needed. I placed the picks of my hand tools at the back of the trough primarily as a precaution against falling over backward. The rope trailed down, its final coils still among the feet of my small audience, who, I supposed, were watching intently, though

High on Bridalveil Falls, an unhurried rhythm develops.
(Photo: Willis Wood)

they were of no concern to me. This was a private affair, regardless of how many people observed it.

It took a long time to find a way past the overhang. The problem was bold, but the solution intricate, and I lost myself in an effort to find the combination that would unlock the passage. The underside of the ledge was a cathedral apse. At its apex I had to scrunch up as high as possible and perform an ablution: ice hammer dangling by the wrist-loop on my right hand, left axe placed diagonally around the edge of the roof, I reached into a slippery hole at a point where the ice began to jut out to form the ceiling. I found a small indentation that was just enough, but my fingers were washed in waves of cold that seeped through my wool gloves. They would soon be numb and useless. Mind instructed body: "Stay calm." Vision became acute, and time slowed until there was plenty.

A crampon-shod left boot came floating into view, headed for purchase on a boulder-sized bump at the lip of the overhang. Contact was made and points bit into the ice, small flakes fracturing off and drifting down out of sight. Then the right foot flowed from underneath the edge, coming to rest near its mate. The right hand abandoned its frigid hold on the ice and regrasped the ice hammer. The silver blade arced through the air, then ice shards slowly burst above the overhang as the hammer thunked solidly. I straightened once again into a position of balance, and time resumed its normal pace. Beads of perspiration dripped from my forehead onto my glasses. My mind relaxed, but only slightly.

A few moves higher there was a good ledge for standing. At the moment I stepped onto it, the rope at my waist gave a hard jerk. This time there was no question: it was stuck somewhere below, tangled in icicles. As if stubbornly refusing to allow me to go on, the cord resisted all my attempts to free it from above. It seemed the penance of the overhang would grant me no heaven. Feeling quite defeated, I placed two ice screws as an anchor and rappelled to the source of the problem, which was easily remedied by a simple flick. Once cleared, the rope swooped invitingly earthward, tempting me to follow it.

My body wasn't tired, but my mind wanted to rest. In spite of that desire, the little voice that earlier had whispered of an unlikely possibility now sounded a bit louder, and it had worked its way into the realm of conscious consideration. As I

reclimbed the overhang, well protected by the rope from above, I decided to continue. But some nagging doubts about the remainder of the route still lingered. What about the rotten-looking section at the halfway mark? Was there a way around the huge overhang at 300 feet? More urgent doubts crowded in regarding how long I could maintain such intense concentration without a lapse. I would continue the climb, yes, yet I hadn't the confidence to abandon the rope.

The second hundred feet of climbing contained no unusual problems, and a controlled but enjoyable rhythm began to direct my moves. The ice that had appeared from below to be rotten was not; there was just a subtle change in hue, perhaps due to the millions of tiny air bubbles trapped within it.

"The climb will go," the inner voice shouted. And softer, but with conviction: "Get rid of the rope. It's only distracting you." I was happy with these commands but couldn't bear to watch the rope—and my attachment to it—fall summarily away. I left it tethered to an ice screw and continued.

Unleashed, my body and mind felt much lighter. No thoughts of failure. My entire entity became aligned with gravity, but only as a reference point for balance. Real difficulties seemed to disappear under the energy of a unified approach. Body obeyed mind, seeming to understand its purpose. In turn, mind appreciated the way body supplied stimuli. Smooth, cold, blue monochrome. A brittle clatter. Swing, breathe. Connect, connection. Almost . . . almost . . . almost. . . .

Unexpectedly I felt a change in orientation, as if the ice was falling forward in front of me. I realized after a moment that my vertigo was the result of a reduction in the angle of the ice. Adrenaline spurted through my system when I looked up to see that an easy slope was all that separated me from the top of the climb. But the adrenaline had to be overruled. To rush now would be folly. To climb all that way with concentration and then scramble sloppily up the last bit would negatively color my whole experience. Every step—to the end—must be made as carefully as every other.

The deep, water-worn gorge at the top of Bridalveil Falls was the exit tunnel from the immediate experience of the climb to the conceptualized world I now returned to. Relief came in jerks and spasms. First, a welling of tears; then a restraining. Next, a more enjoyable satisfaction and relaxation of control. Once again the world formed itself for familiar, joyful examination. Crags and sky, wispy cirrus clouds, pine trees and snow, wool, steel, flat, forest.

The whistle down at the mine blew, indicating a change of shift or closing time. The sound echoed through the hills. The sun began to set down-valley above the Lilliputian town of Telluride, and I began the slog through knee-deep snow that would take me around the edge of the cliff and down to the newly remembered people at the base of the falls.

A beer and companionship would suit my fancy just now. ▼

Untethered from the rope, mind and body feel lighter.
(Photo: Willis Wood)

THE HUNGO FACE OF KWANGDE

On top of Cold
Mountain the

Lone round moon

Lights the whole clear
cloudless

Sky

Honor this
priceless natural

Treasure

Concealed in
five shadows

Sunk deep in the flesh

—Han Shan,
Cold Mountain Poems
(translated by
Gary Snyder)

I first saw Kwangde's North Face in November 1981, after the American Medical Research Expedition to Mount Everest. That expedition had been long on learning, short on the art of free-willed movement over technically difficult terrain that excites me. At the end of the expedition, my then-wife, Janie, met me at Lobuje, a yak herders' summer village below Everest base camp, and the two of us spent ten days wandering along the trails and through the villages of the Solo Khumbu. Everywhere we went we met Sherpa friends who welcomed us in and seated us in favored positions by their fires. They fed us potato pancakes with spicy yak butter, which we washed down with enough chang, the local alcoholic beverage, to keep us smiling. All the while the mountains were magnificent: towering amidst swirling afternoon clouds or the watery light of dawn, or silhouetted against a cobalt sky filled with stars. My camera was ecstatic, while my climber's bones ached for that pillar on Pumori, that face on Lhotse, that ridge on Teng Kangpoche.

One afternoon we strolled up a path we hadn't traveled before. Almost suddenly, the foreground ridge across the river dipped and, like a curtain parting, revealed the northern flank of Kwangde rising above the small village of Hungo. Reptilian tongues of ice flicked down over dark boilerplate slabs of granite. From the moraine at the foot of the wall to the jutting summit spire, only three snow ledges broke the extreme angles. Fifteen hundred meters on the map, nearly 5,000 feet. Janie, who doesn't climb but who knows me well, had a great suggestion: "Why don't you come back and climb it, Jeff?"

Almost exactly a year later, David Breashears and I set up base camp in an unused potato field in Hungo. Our sirdar and friend, Nima Tenzing, paid off the yak driver who had transported part of our food and gear, and asked several porters to help us carry our stuff to a camp beneath the face. From there David and I wouldn't require any assistance. Nima and his kitchen boy, Sonam, immediately moved into the home of the family who owned the field where we were camped. David and I pitched our tents, but after the first night we were drawn indoors for our evening meals by typical Sherpa hospitality.

By the light of Nima's kerosene lamp we became acquainted with the members of the family. The head of the clan was a Tibetan whose claim to ninety years seemed to be verified by his wizened face and fragile limbs, although such longevity is exceptional in the region. It was extremely painful for the old man to move from his normal lotus position by the fire, so he seldom did. The night before we went up, he told us we were the first tourists to stay in Hungo. He also said that below the mountain was a cave in which a yeti lived, and that if we managed to succeed in our attempt on the wall, it would prove we were the world's best climbers. Naturally, we were inclined to believe all these things!

Base camp in the village of Hungo, below the North Face of Kwangde *(Photo: Jeff Lowe)*

The ancient Tibetan's wife was perhaps thirty years his junior. She had a nearly toothless, kindly grin that drooped on one side, but showed us that she really didn't mind this invasion of strangers. Two much younger members of the household were, according to Nima, the son and daughter of the old couple. This seemed more than a little unlikely, since the boy could not yet have been twenty, and the girl at least several years younger. He had the look of a fugitive from the 1950s climbing era of English hard-men: dirty face, wool knickers, a sweater hanging in rags from his short, stocky frame, and a happily demented smile. She was small, shy, and mute, and signaled by gentle moans and whimpers that she had arrived at our tent in the morning bringing tea. Spending time with these people allowed us to become more attuned to existence in their land and better prepared to climb their mountain.

I was lucky to have David as a partner. Although his alpine and Himalayan experience was limited at the time, his natural climbing abilities were even then almost legendary. As a seventeen-year-old he had earned the moniker "The Kloeberdanz Kid" for his almost casual second ascent of a free rock climb in Eldorado Canyon, Colorado, that had developed a huge reputation as being impossible to do statically. David found a new combination on the crux roof and blew the preconceptions away. In 1975 he went on to make the first ascents of some unprotected and extremely difficult face climbs; the most famous, Perilous Journey, a 5.11X on Mickey Mouse Wall, high above Eldorado Canyon, did not see a second ascent for a number of years and is widely recognized as one of the high-water marks of free-climbing boldness.

I met David in Eldorado Canyon shortly after these climbs and hired him as an assistant for rock and ice climbing courses offered by my International Alpine School, established in 1976. He took to ice with his typical intensity. I remember once having to ask him not to solo climb in front of the students, as he was thirty

feet up an 80° ice fall, testing the limits of climbing with one tool. I shouldn't have worried. As always, he found a way over the bulge, effecting an extreme mantel, getting the frontpoints of his crampons in level with the pick of his axe and carefully standing up. In David's first year of ice climbing we were doing notable new routes together. David's trademark boldness can be experienced on climbs like The Skylight and Gravity's Rainbow in southwest Colorado.

When David and I went to Kwangde, he was undergoing a personal crisis. His early years had been so completely devoted to climbing that his social, financial, and even emotional life had been relegated to a back seat. At twenty-five he was introverted, and self-doubt was inevitable. He openly wondered where he was going with his life. On an acclimatization jaunt into the Thame Valley, we ran into Reinhold Messner and his team, who were trying to make a winter ascent of the South Face of Cho Oyu (which would ultimately prove unsuccessful). Reinhold's overtly successful persona was hard for David to confront and raised questions about his own current lack of direction. I tried to counsel that although Messner's public and financial success was well-earned, he would never be able to measure up to David's brilliance in certain psychologically/physically/technically extreme climbing situations, and therefore David should feel satisfaction with his own abilities. But such talk is facile and ineffectual unless it comes from within.

David's performance on Kwangde proved inspirational to me. His climbing on 300-foot, virtually unprotected thin-ice leads with a heavy pack forced me to climb well also. As usual, the first day on the route was mentally the toughest. The ice was steeper (90°) in places than we had expected, and intermittent; instead of a continuous flow, we had to deal

Above: **David Breashears greeting the sun on the summit of Kwangde**
Opposite: **David Breashears high on the North Face of Kwangde at the end of the fourth day. Makalu is the pyramidal peak in the background.**
(Photos: Jeff Lowe)

with breaks caused by overlaps in the underlying rock slabs. The ice was feather-thin at each key transition, offering less-than-substantial tool placements and very little protection. Spindrift was a problem. High winter winds scoured the summit ridges for any stray flake or grain of snow, and the immense scale of the upper bowls assured that tiny rivulets of flowing crystals eventually joined into a series of streams that traced the fingers of ice in the lower wall, one of which we were following. Often we would have to wait several minutes in the torrent, heads ducked for breath, until the flow eased and we could continue. Contrasting with the inexorable conditions present on the leads, we found a quality of ice unique in our experience. The very currents of spindrift we cursed were responsible for the formation of a climbing medium like unfired porcelain.

Kwangde's ice presented an opaque, yet deeply revealing mirror to David and me. The second day, out of a BAT tent bivouac, David tied two 300-foot, 9mm ropes together to reach a safe belay. I followed his mega-lead and made an easier one of my own, doglegging on steep snow around the lower rock band to arrive below a vertical 150-foot rock band in the middle of the face. The passage was thinly draped with ice separated from the rock by several inches, like a curtain concealing a false window. We spent a second night below this obvious crux, observing, for the first time, clouds creeping up the finger valleys of the Khumbu, licking the bases of Everest, Cho Oyu, Ama Dablam, Tawoche, Makalu, and the other mineral denizens of the region. A waxing moon illuminated the scene. The wind died, leaving us to contemplate personal visions while we passed rehydrated rations between our individual hanging tents.

In the morning David led a short pitch to position us for the crux. I welcomed the next lead, preferring to embrace the unknown reality directly. At twenty feet I placed a couple of questionable pitons in the rock on the left side of the ice and began to weave my way up, connecting the most trustworthy segments of ice. After an hour, near the top of the pitch, with the last reliable protection a hundred feet below, I achieved an uncommon state of equilibrium. My tools continually sliced through the thin, fragile ice, but each time this happened, I was prepared to shift my weight instantly to the other tool and my feet, and work with the placement until it held, never feeling panic. This sort of freedom from animal fear is rare but at times useful, and I have experienced it a number of times on serious routes. Finally, I reached a solid belay on the snow slope above the rock band.

Later that day David led a long, beautiful pitch up a narrowing and steepening gully to the left of a prominent black prow. Although not as difficult as the crux, the last section was a vertical, ice-filled chimney that gave excellent hard climbing. David's pitch led to a smaller ice field above the black buttress. We bivouacked again at the upper edge of the ice field, where it tapered into vertical rock. Once again during the night a nearly full moon shone on the spectacle of cloud fingers filling the valleys, eventually making islands of all the peaks.

The last day on the face began with normal 50° to 60° alpine ice climbing up and toward the right from our bivouac until the slope steepened deceptively into a 300-foot-high bulge of 70° to 85° thin ice. I had started up the bulge wearing my pack. Partway up I hung it from a short Snarg in order to continue running out the full 300-foot rope to arrive at a little rock outcrop and belay above the last real difficulty of the climb. David and I swung several more mammoth leads up 60° ice to a short rock exit from the face. We had already spent three nights cooking, eating, and sleeping in hammocks suspended from anchors in the rock. After sunset on this fourth day, we emerged from the face onto the cold, windy crest of the

Northwest Ridge, 300 feet below the top. We spent hours in the dark, hacking a coffin-sized cave from the ice of an old cornice.

The next morning we greeted the sun like a long-lost friend and scrambled to the summit over the terra cotta blocks of the ridge. On top we shook hands and sat down, our packs still on our backs, to marvel at our position. A few miles east and 8,000 feet below, across the deep canyon of the Dudh Khosi, the villages of Namche Bazaar and Kumjung clung to the hillside like something out of Tolkien, and we could clearly see the trails leading deeper into the Khumbu toward Ama Dablam and Everest. Further east, on top of a hill beneath the ice-topped fortress of Kangtega, the Thyangboche monastery seemed especially well placed for a spiritual nucleus. I asked David if he thought any of Messner's climbs on 26,000-foot peaks could have brought him any greater satisfaction than this. David's answer was simple, and the truth of it could clearly be seen in his dark eyes, which were now shining in the clear, cold air: "No," he said. "This is the best."

Our stay was short. Mere moments of inaction felt like days to us after our all-consuming climb. Fifteen minutes after summiting, we began the long descent.

Just before dusk the next day we arrived back in Hungo and were greeted by Nima, who came running to hug us. Sonam and the old man's son helped us off with our packs. The quiet daughter beamed and scurried into the stone house, soon returning with sweet tea. Several urchins from the few surrounding houses appeared from nowhere, chattering and laughing excitedly. With her eyes rolling back in her head and her tongue lolling out between a large gap in her teeth, the mother pantomimed her fear that we had died on the mountain. She squeezed my hands long and hard in hers, not releasing me until she saw that I understood how much David and I had worried her. In waning light we were ushered into the home of our friends. The old sage sat by the embers of the fire. He waited impassively for us to report on our adventure. We told him we hadn't seen the yeti. ▼

NO SE GANA, PERO SE GOZA

loosely translated:

You're Not Winning

If You're Not

Having Fun

The climbing magazines would have us believe there is a god called 5.14 to whom we must all pay homage. Regardless of the personal value of our efforts, we are often judged, and we judge ourselves, by the numbers attached to the climbs we do. But in the larger context of life outside the gymnastic prime, the quality and content of the climbing experience become more important than the grade. In particular, being alone on a hard new route in the high mountains can add new excitement to a mundane existence.

For two years I had been chained to my desk, writing business plans for my old climbing-gear company, Latok Mountain Gear, negotiating with bankers, listening to employee problems, with scarcely the time to dream about the mountains, let alone get out in them. I was in terrible shape, my mental and spiritual balance askew. For more than twenty years I had climbed or skied at least a hundred days annually; now it was "once in a blue moon."

So in June of 1985, four of us made a quick trip to Peru on the assumption that three weeks were better than none, for we were all feeling similarly overworked and deprived. Immersion in a less hectic culture slowed our pace, and association with the hill people calmed us down. In spite of recent deadly harassment of locals by members of the Marxist *Sendero Luminoso* (Shining Path), and in spite of tales of trekkers being shot and robbed by *banditos*, we felt the peace of walking in a special place, circumnavigating a compact range of fantastic snowy peaks.

None of the others were climbers, but at our starting point in Chiquian, I had loaded one of our burros down with climbing gear. After seven perfect days, we arrived at a 15,000-foot campsite below the striking South Face of 18,500-foot Trapecio. Though I hardly felt strong, I had regained my equilibrium for the moment and succumbed to the lure of a fine-looking ice route. Seldom had I seen a mountain wall at once so attractive and difficult looking.

Two hours of rhythmic and varied snow and ice so riveted my concentration that I literally bumped into the crux. A wall of reddish rock rose 500 feet in vertical angles and steep corners, its center draped in a veil of green, blue, and white ice. It was this icy lacework that had first attracted me to the line. Now that I was face-to-face with the shimmering headwall, I stomped a small platform in the snow and turned outward to squander a moment taking in the view.

A frosty morning in the Cordillera Huayhuash
(Photo: Jeff Lowe)

Immediately the claustrophobic intensity of climbing was transformed into the unbounded exhilaration of looking out onto an expansive vista. Threads of cirrus clouds torn from snowy summits looked like Tibetan prayer flags in an otherwise electric-blue Andean sky. Following the sweep of fluted ice faces, rock walls, and corniced ridges down from their tops, my eyes encountered a succession of snowfields, cracked glaciers, and dark, jumbled moraines. Three thousand feet below and a mile away was the meadow where my friends were taking a day off. As I gazed out over our campsite—a tiny blue speck—in my imagination I could smell a second pot of coffee brewing, watch Janie feeding breakfast scraps to Armando's burros, and hear the soft splashing of Rosa and Luke washing by the little stream.

I felt totally at one with my surroundings. Though wind-borne ice crystals stung my cheeks and the nearest humans were visible only in my mind, I was not lonely, and the slight discomfort only increased the depth of my contentment. I felt like a space traveler who has been stranded on a planet that is better than paradise, for here it was not only possible to fill the soul with beauty, but also to find a worthy challenge. Shivering slightly, I started up the wall, and for the next twenty minutes, the warming joy of easy movement on 70° ice was mine.

At first the ice rose up a deep corner in frothy white bulges. An unhurried rhythm, balanced over my feet, felt less like fighting gravity and more like walking in place. The ice moved down in front of me, an illusion that was strengthened by thin streams of spindrift falling all around. I would take five or six crunching steps, splaying one foot sideways and frontpointing with the other, then switch the position of my feet, taking an extra breath at each transition. In this way, each calf muscle was alternately tensed and stretched, eliminating fatigue. Holding the head of my axe in one hand and the bottom of the shaft in the other, I lightly shoved the pick into the ice in front of my face at every other step. Soon, however, the ice thinned to less than two inches, and the angle increased to vertical. I placed and tied off two Snargs, hung my pack, and set up a self-belay. The easy going had come to an end.

Above, both walls of the corner steepened to overhanging. At the same time the ice became very thin, like a crust of frozen foam that had spilled over the side of the mountain, opaque enough to hide any cracks in the rock but offering almost no resistance to downward-slicing metal points. I paid out forty feet of slack to allow me to reach easier-angled terrain. It was clear from the large loop of extra rope left dangling from my waist that I could not count on the flimsy purchase of the tied-off ice pitons to hold a fall. This forced me to mentally shift gears from high-speed cruise to four-wheel low. I switched into that place in my consciousness that is acutely aware of the seriousness of the situation. The entire universe reduced itself to an area perhaps ten feet square. Anything beyond that perimeter was out of reach and therefore extraneous to existence.

My first attempt to move up the corner was rushed and awkward. Gently I stepped back down to the highest resting place, feeling balance return to the center of my gut like a baseball to a catcher's mitt. A few deep breaths forced the tension from my body, and I resurveyed the situation. The problem was that the right wall leaned severely leftward, forcing me to stem onto the smooth, undercut left wall where there was no ice. Another attempt at my original solution would obviously yield the same results as before, and at first there seemed to be no alternative. Yet I knew there must be another way, and as I continued to breathe and relax, an image began to form in my mind. I saw myself from a detached perspective, twenty feet in space behind me. Although my tactile senses remained centered in the icy corner, this overview allowed me to visualize a single move executed on the right wall, followed by stabilizing movements back into the corner.

Reaching to the right, I swung my axe at an icy hollow where I knew it would stick securely. As I twisted my body to face the right wall directly, I shivered with a current of déjà vu: the moves felt as comfortable as a well-rehearsed series of dance steps. Thunk, thunk. Step, step. Stem left back into the corner, a couple of moves laybacking off the picks, and I found myself on good, thick, 80° ice.

I untied the knot in the rope at my waist, freeing the entire length, and climbed to its end up the steep, massive flow. The wind picked up and spindrift instantly filled the hole I chopped for a screw. As I rappelled the line to retrieve my pack, I could look off to either side of the icefall and see clouds from the north pouring over the edges of the face and churning in the turbulence. The swirling snow softened the sharp dark angles of the containing buttresses, but behind me to the southwest the rock peaks of the Puscanturpa group still rose clearly out of the glaciers. This storm was merely a localized disturbance, but one that would make the climbing to come even more of a challenge. After shouldering my pack and removing the anchors with disconcerting ease, I jumared back up the rope to survey the situation above.

From my top anchors the icefall steepened for a final rope-length into a dead vertical filigree of insubstantial gray ice fifteen feet wide. Although the climbing appeared difficult and dangerous, I thought I could see several places where the ice was thick enough to allow the placement of secure screws. Without much more thought I started up, the full rope hanging down between the belay and myself.

I climbed along the right edge of the ice, hooking rock holds with my right axe and crampon points and getting some wobbly placements in the ice with my left. After fifty feet, the rock holds petered out, and the ice curtain became even less substantial. The only protection I could manage was a poor knifeblade in a shallow crack, and I had trouble ascertaining the security of this arrangement through the constant rush of spindrift draining from the upper bowl down the central line of the face—my route. Part of me was revolted by the idea of launching onto the ice in such horrific conditions with such a questionable backup, but another part, the adventurous part, was exhilarated.

My first attempt to get out onto the ice resulted in a sheet ten feet square falling out from underneath my crampons, leaving me dangling from my tools, stuck in the aerated ice above the fracture line. Painful, nearly overwhelming spurts of adrenaline shot through my limbs, but years of climbing had taught me how to absorb it almost as quickly as it had shocked me. In a few seconds panic subsided. Very gingerly I found crampon holds in the bare rock and pulled gently over the fractured edge of ice. I was totally committed now. Backing off was unthinkable.

Above, the ice was a gossamer shroud of crusty, poorly bonded snow crystals over rock. The darker, solid-looking sections had appeared far more substantial from below than they were in reality. I half-chuckled, half-moaned. I had wanted a difficult climb, but this was diabolical.

Sweat and spindrift soon formed a bubbly crust on my glasses. There was nearly a hundred feet of this vertical maelstrom to endure. At first I was on the verge of despair as, with each new axe placement, the blade would slice downward several inches before catching; but slowly a feeling of control returned as I

**Trapecio's South Face,
through the clouds**
(Photo: Jeff Lowe)

discovered that each placement was consistent, however insecure. I gradually lost the fear that there might be one hold that simply could not be made to stick. Soon my arms were starting to burn with fatigue. I forced myself to conserve energy by using the lightest grip on my tools that I dared and by hanging straight-armed as much as possible. I settled into a complicated rhythm that felt right: three deep breaths hanging straight-armed with the feet high; one breath straightening up, replacing one tool higher, then immediately hanging straight-armed from the new placement; two more breaths removing the lower tool, placing it higher, and hanging straight-armed from both; then a rest breath before carefully walking my feet up into position to repeat the sequence.

My concentration on correctly performing the cadence of movements allowed me to ignore the hot coals in my forearms and to forget the potential horrendous fall. At one point I even felt a shiver of thanks for this challenge that was more than I had bargained for. Seldom had the edge felt so close, yet still been within my abilities. Even so, the dangerous urge to lunge past the final few feet of the icefall onto the summit snow slope was almost overwhelming. I resisted the temptation and pulled over the top on the shafts of my tools.

The relief was intense. My entire body slumped down of its own accord and, as I sank into the soft snow, my mind also seemed to slump in its cranium. The summit was still 500 feet higher, but I had no stomach for the slog. My whole being was revolted by the idea of being exposed to any more hazard. I didn't care that I was depriving myself of the first ascent of the entire face. I had gotten all I needed from the climb.

After three long, spectacular rappels, a careful face-in gallop down snow to the top of the lower ice pitches, more demanding down-climbing, and one final rappel, I reached the foot of the wall. Dragging my rope, I plunged down the lower snow slope to the edge of the moraine at the base of the face. It was four o'clock.

At the base of the face there was scarcely a breath of wind. I dropped my pack on a low boulder sticking out of the snow and paused a moment to enjoy the lightness in my shoulders. After coiling the rope with a series of expansive movements like a man pumping an accordion, I sat down and pulled out an orange. Biting into the skin, I was startled by the pungent explosion that filled my mouth and nose. The only smell in this mineral world of rock and ice had been my own sweat. The pleasure of returning to valley life washed over me in a wave of joy.

A sound close behind shook me from my reverie. Turning, I saw it was Armando, clattering up the steep moraine in sandals. Grinning widely, he puffed up and clasped my shoulders with both hands. "Jeffe," he greeted me. "Muy bueno, Jeffe! Trapecio es muy difícil en la cara sud."

"Gracias, amigo. Si, la cara sud es un escalade grande."

Leaving the snow and raising dust clouds as we glissaded down the steep moraine, we returned to camp. Janie met us in the meadow, giving me the king of hugs and the queen of kisses. I was happy and content and would have liked to live forever. ▼

CASCADE CLIMBING IN FRANCE

For almost two decades the commonly held conceit among North American ice climbers has been that they set the standard for the esoteric activity of climbing frozen waterfalls. Even European climbers seemed to agree, many of the best of them making a pilgrimage to Canada to do such classics as La Pomme d'Or in Quebec or Weeping Pillar, Polar Circus, and the like in the Rockies. But a trip to France in 1992 convinced me that the Continent is once again spearheading a revolution in yet another form of ascent. Just as with alpinism and sport climbing, intense pressure from a large climbing population, coupled with truly extensive waterfall ice in many of the Alpine valleys, has revealed a treasure trove of outrageous routes.

Recently, the main employer in the small industrial village of L'Argentière La Besée closed its doors, leaving the town in financial difficulties. Consequently, the town fathers have welcomed the recent influx of ice climbers. In January 1992 they hosted their second International de la Cascade de Glace, an annual meeting of ice climbers, media representatives, and spectators.

Arriving from Colorado late on a Friday night after a long journey by plane, train, and automobile, I caught the tail end of the first evening's talks and movies at the Maison de Ville. When the lights came on and the crowded hall began to empty, I ran into Thierry Renault, one of France's best all-around climbers. He invited me to join him on an area classic, Cascade des Viollins (III, WI6 in the new guidebook) the next day.

In his mid-thirties, Thierry had the unquenchable desire for difficulty that usually characterizes a younger man. For several years he had been searching for the most radical ice climb he could find. In excellent English he conveyed his passion for this aspect of climbing in terms I could fully understand. His enthusiasm nearly reached the intensity of a feverish disease. Unfortunately for me, it seemed to be communicable, and in the next few weeks I found myself with a full-blown case of water ice fever, something I thought I had become immune to years ago.

Even jet-lagged and fatigued, I was able to appreciate the boldness of Georges Chantriaux's 1982 solo first ascent of Cascade des Viollins. The initial 250 feet of 80° to 85° ice lead to a 130-foot, free-standing "cigar," which Thierry led. At the top of the Chantriaux route, Thierry and I made the first ascent of a

In this book

I have given special

prominence to the laws

that govern gravity.

—Stephen Hawking,
A Brief History of Time

two-pitch variation up an easy ice face and two tiers of thin, vertical pillars. The last pitch was mine. It began with thirty feet of delicate, pigeon-toe frontpointing up a free-hanging fang and finished with forty feet of unprotected stemming between a vertical rock wall and a curtain of poorly bonded icicles.

Saturday evening the participants (who had come from all over Europe, as well as the handful of us from farther away), along with an estimated audience of two thousand, were treated to a spectacle on the hillside at the edge of L'Argentière la Besée. Here water had been diverted to ice-coat a couple of crags, creating the stage for a morality play, complete with lights and sound effects that would have done justice to a Broadway production. The drama ended with the hero battling the devil as he and the heroine escaped up a fifty-foot, 75° slab of ice against a backdrop of fireworks. *C'est fantastique!*

On Sunday I was dragged out of bed at dawn by François Damilano, Thierry's main competition for the title of France's leading ice specialist. For ten years François had been responsible for some of the finest and hardest new ice climbs in France, as well as in the Canadian Rockies and other areas. Whereas Thierry's technique was almost flamboyant in its artful balance and precision, François climbed in a very straightforward and efficient manner, with no extra flourishes. François had plans that would up the ante over Thierry's variation of the previous day. Together with Jean-Marc Porte, the editor of *Montagnes* magazine and a very personable fellow but not a very experienced ice climber, we headed for the Val de Freissinières and an unclimbed line of tenuous smears, chimneys, and pillars on the 1,200- to 1,500-foot-high Tête de Gramusat.

François Damilano, belayed by the author, begins his ill-fated dance with the big icicle.
(Photo: Jean-Marc Porte)

Thierry Renault on aid under the big roof *(Photo: Jeff Lowe)*

François led the route's short but difficult fifth pitch in great style, climbing up under a six-foot-wide roof on a tongue of ice, then turning out to face the valley and stepping into space onto a stalactite hanging from the lip. Finally he spiraled out to the front face and ascended to a ledge above the roof. Going second, Jean-Marc, along as reporter and photographer, swung repeatedly out into space. Dangling, exhausted, he pleaded softly, "What am I *doing* here?"

When my turn came, I found the pitch to be excellent and a true grade 6. Stepping out onto the stalactite 600 feet above the beginning of the route, my heart was in my mouth, even with the toprope!

It was now my lead, and we faced the obvious crux of the route, a seventy-five-foot, rotten, free-hanging icicle that failed by five feet to connect with our ledge. I took a long look at the creaking monster and told the others that it was time to turn tail and run. I was really surprised when François disagreed, saying he would like to give it a try. Reluctantly I put him on belay, double-checking that we had bombproof anchors well out of the fall line. Jean-Marc said nothing, but readied his camera.

Ten minutes later, with François one-third of the way up, having placed one screw, the icicle snapped at the roof line, and down went François, lashed like Ahab to Moby Dick! The calamitous roar lasted several minutes as the entire lower line of our climb was scoured by a hundred tons of ice that triggered an avalanche down the steep, 1,000-foot approach slopes. I saw a crowd of people on the valley road scamper away from the avalanche's path and feared the worst for François, but only a moment passed before his shout came up: "I'm OK!" Soon he was back on the ledge. François and I giggled like schoolgirls at our good fortune to be alive, agreeing now that it was time to go down. Jean-Marc stared at us as if we were both from Mars.

Thierry wanted another shot at me. He had picked out another new line on the Tête de Gramusat, left of Gramusat Direct (VI, WI6, done in 1991 by François and the Scotsman Robin Clothier). The next day I caught my first glimpse of the future of frozen waterfall climbing as Thierry and I spent ten hours on our new plum, Blind Faith (VII, WI7-, A2). Of its eleven pitches, two in particular stand out. The fourth pitch (WI6+, A2) tackles a fifteen-foot rock roof to a hanging tongue of ice. Thierry used two pitons for aid here, which allowed him to spear the tongue of ice with one tool and swing over. Following the roof with our pack was quite exciting, as I had to unclip from Thierry's last aid piton before I could make the final long stretch to plant my axe in the icicle. If I had fallen then, I would have been left hanging in space 500 feet above the approach slopes with no way to get back onto the ice. Luckily, I was able to make the move up and around the corner of the roof onto vertical ice. I was surprised, however, to see that the pitch continued to be severe. The rope snaked up through another thinly iced overhanging corner, which, going second, I found to be as difficult as the lower roof had been. Joining Thierry at his belay above the band of overhangs, I congratulated him on an excellent lead. He asked me how difficult I thought the climbing was, and I said probably WI6+, A2; but if the roof was done completely free, it would probably be M7 or 8.

The way was now easier as we surfed waves of ice to the right and up for several hundred feet. The seventh pitch (WI6+), again led by Thierry, ascended a free-standing pillar, which gently overhung for sixty poorly protected feet, surmounted a big "umbrella," and continued up another steep, free-standing pillar for ninety feet more. Following Thierry's lead with our light pack was almost too much for me, and I arrived at the belay with barely enough strength to open a carabiner. My taste for waterfall ice had been reborn!

It was getting dark fast. Thierry and I climbed the final four or five pitches of WI3 and 4 with no intermediate protection between belays. Even so, it was 7:00 P.M. and dark when we climbed into the trees at the top. We pulled out our head lamps for the traverse through snow to the top of the descent route, which required seven rappels down a buttress on the side of the cliff. We arrived back in town at 10:00 P.M., tired from a long day, but happy.

Val Cenis is a quaint alpine town in the Haute Maurienne. The Maurienne and

Haute Maurienne are not notable for especially great peaks, but the terrain is excellent for ski touring, and the valleys have a large number of frozen waterfalls. François, who is the primary liaison with the French press for the sport of cascade climbing, chose Val Cenis as the site for this phase of the meeting because climbers of all abilities could enjoy themselves here. Perhaps most importantly, the press could be brought to a spectacular vantage point on the edge of a deep gorge overlooking the area's jewel, the 400-foot, grade III, WI5 Glacenost.

During the weekend this climb was done by at least a dozen roped teams. There was an orgy of picture taking; for much of the day, the climb enjoyed full sun under blue skies. I waited until the sun and most climbers were off the ice on Saturday afternoon before taking my own solo spin. I found perfect ice and a grand ambience.

Saturday evening's fine banquet was preceded by a tribute to the late Italian ice climber, Gian Carlo Grassi. Beautiful slides and music communicated Grassi's great spirit and passion for this singular sport. Grassi was one of the leading exponents of the European school of extreme ice climbing in the 1980s. He discovered and climbed many of the best off-season water-ice routes in the high mountains and pushed the limits of safety while making the first ascents of many alpine ice falls. He was also one of the first Europeans to travel to Canada to make ascents of the classics, such as La Pomme d'Or, Polar Circus, and the Weeping Wall. His death the previous year had been a blow to the world ice-climbing community.

On Sunday, Thierry demonstrated state-of-the-art mixed climbing to the spectators as he opened a new route to the right of Glacenost. After ascending a poorly protected overhanging rock wall with occasional patches of ice, he locked his legs behind an icicle only eight inches in diameter. Stretching up to the thin ice above, Thierry planted his pick, and at the same moment, the icicle he was straddling broke. His feet swung free, and the peanut gallery wet its collective pants. Of course Thierry didn't fall, commenting later that the route was hard, but only M7+!

The artificially supported tower of ice created for the Competition d'Escalade at Courchevel in February was staggering in its beauty—a crystal version of a desert sandstone spire. I immediately longed to climb it. Standing over 100 feet high and weighing an estimated 450 tons, luminous blue in the shade and dazzling white in the sun, the tower was truly a work of art.

Ropes outlined the route boundaries on each side. Protection was fixed for clipping on the lead. As in golf, the lowest score would win. Points were counted for every placement (or attempted placement) of a tool; a slip of a foot cost five penalty points. Overall style was judged on a scale of 0 to 20, with 0 being perfect. Twenty minutes were allowed for climbing a route, and three points were subtracted from the competitor's overall score for each minute less than the full twenty taken to reach the top. Saturday's qualifying rounds were held on three separate routes, the top three finishers from each route advancing to Sunday's finals. The

Frenchman Roland Georges on an overhanging arête in the finals of the competition at Courchevel *(Photo: Jeff Lowe)*

Sunday finals also included points from a speed climb. All pretty complicated!

Watching some of the other competitors on the opposite side of the tower from my qualifying route, I wondered if I could move as smoothly and precisely through the bulges and roofs. It was a month before the Albertville Winter Olympic Games, and CBS was in the area to do background pieces to run during its coverage of the Games; so when my turn came, François, looking like a big bug, jumared alongside me with a CBS camera strapped to his helmet. Clipping the pro and passing overhanging sections without hanging around to place ice screws was a joy. I had to laugh to myself: "Just like sport climbing!" In the middle of the course the judges told me to go back down a few moves and use my tools after I had started climbing with my hands. Ohhh, I didn't know about that rule! After ten and a half minutes of really enjoyable ice climbing, I was up, slightly surprised to find out later that I had the lowest score in the qualifying round.

But my self-satisfaction was short-lived. Going first in the Sunday finals, I was attempting to clear the initial roof, but my attention was focused on the upper sections of the fantastic route. I made the classic beginner's mistake of placing my tools too close together. Down I came, along with a chunk of the overhang! The crowd groaned, and, with a sheepish grin, I walked out of the competition area. Humility is good for the soul!

The following climber, a local lad by the name of Bruno Soursac, looked surprisingly good, negotiating the twisting, overhanging path in under eleven and a half minutes. Romain Loval made a mistake similar to mine, but half a foot lower. (Oh, good, I'm not the only stupid one!) The following two competitors each ran out of time before reaching the top. Going fifth, Richard Ouairy showed the form that allowed him to solo Canada's Weeping Wall, Polar Circus, and Ice Nine all in one day in 1991. Then the colorful Italian, Enzo Marlier, defied all probability by struggling to the top after repeated near-falls and missed clips, a reflection of his 3:00 A.M. antics on the dance floor earlier that day. Next to last, Thierry appeared more nervous than if he was facing a class-8 death-lead, but he still completed a masterful ascent, a couple minutes slower than Bruno's, but with greater control. Doni Maillot went last with a solid, but not sparkling, climb.

Suddenly I was awakened from my role of spectator to go first in the top-roped speed competition. This was a new and somewhat ridiculous experience for me. I have spent all my life learning precision and control, and here I was slamming, jerking, and flailing my way up the ice. To my surprise, I had the second fastest time after the first round—one minute, twenty-three seconds to Bruno's one minute, seventeen seconds. After several more head-to-head heats, I ended up third behind Bruno and Doni. Speed counted in difficulty results in some way that I couldn't understand, and falls by both Richard and Thierry moved each down a notch in the final difficulty standing. The overall results put Bruno in first, Thierry in second, and Doni in third. (François later told me that in future competitions, difficulty and speed would be completely separated.)

All in all, the ambience and organization of the Courchevel event were superb, complete with Gallic energy, Van Morrison on the loudspeakers, and an incredible fireworks display on Saturday night that transformed the tower into an erupting ice volcano! ▼

OCTOPUSSY

Over the years, the frozen waterfalls on the limestone cliff bands east of Vail, Colorado, have provided ice climbers with a playground/laboratory on which to improve old skills and, occasionally, to develop new ones. The Rigid Designator area is particularly good in this regard. Easily approached and in a location normally free of avalanches, the Designator stands like a Doric column, the crystal centerpiece of a 100-foot-high arc of inky rock. When it was first climbed in 1974 by Bob Culp, it was, at WI5, one of Colorado's hardest ice climbs, surpassed in difficulty only by Telluride's Bridalveil Falls (WI6), which Mike Weis and I climbed the same winter.

Just to the right of the Rigid Designator is the Fang (WI6+), a free-hanging, 130-foot pencil of ice even more difficult than Bridalveil in the thin conditions of its first ascent, which was made by Alex Lowe in 1981. It is hard to find more challenging climbing on pure ice than the Fang in skinny conditions. But recently ice climbers have started to do more and more difficult mixed routes—climbs that marry the physicality of gymnastic sport-climbing moves to ice-climbing gear, the uncertain medium of ice-plastered (and sometimes unplastered) rock, and winter conditions.

As far back as 1980 I suggested the introduction of the 7th classification, M (for "mixed") 7, for Alex Lowe's lead of a climb called Hot Doggies in Rocky Mountain National Park. (At the time Eric Winkelman and I were suitably impressed trying to follow the climb on a toprope. I fell off the five-foot horizontal overhang at the crux, dangling in space awhile before I could get back onto the bulge of ice. Alex fished me up like a big tuna!) By 1991, there were a handful of M7 climbs in Colorado, including Secret Probation, located 300 or 400 feet left of the Rigid Designator on the same band of rock. Greg Davis made the first free ascent of this short but ruggedly athletic route up a rock overhang into a very thinly iced rock corner.

I spent the winter of 1993–94 in Colorado, concentrating my efforts in the Vail area. In January I made the first ascent of the Teriebel Traverse, which traverses thirty-five feet left across rotten rock from partway up the left side of the Rigid Designator to ascend a short ice pillar with a complex move out onto a fragile, free-hanging curtain of ice that cascades over the lip of the roof above. Toward the end

Above, left to right: **Clipping the protection for the first unsuccessful attempt on Octopussy . . . Beginning the roof . . . Preparing for the first Tarzan swing . . .**

Previous page: **What next?**

(Photos: Brad Johnson)

of the winter I did the first ascent of the Seventh Tentacle, pushing the possibilities of dry tooling, leading up a smear of ice that licks down to within twenty rocky feet of the ground behind the Fang. This eighty-foot climb turned out to be the first pitch of my most interesting effort of the season, Octopussy.

In April I went up to Vail, determined to end a good winter ice season on a strong note. After climbing the Seventh Tentacle, my belayer and fiancée, Teri Ebel, jumared up, and I set out on a thirty-foot leftward rock traverse until I was directly behind Octopussy's frozen tentacles, which were dangling from the edge of the ten-foot horizontal roof I had been passing beneath. With great effort, by stretching almost horizontally, I managed to place two good pitons in the roof. Clipping into them proved to be incredibly strenuous, but this was only the beginning of the wildest set of mixed climbing moves I have ever done.

Hanging from a tiny hook placement in the limestone roof, I cut both feet free and simultaneously turned my body in midair, swinging like Tarzan to stick my other pick into the nearest tentacle—which I managed after two tries. This left me dangling between my outstretched arms, wondering what to do next. Another ape swing was all I could come up with, but I missed the first stick and had to exert great effort on several subsequent attempts before I finally got it. Absolutely pumped, I pulled into a front lever with my frontpoints barely contacting a more substantial icicle five feet away and started walking my feet horizontally upward, making a few more vertical progressions with my tools before my feet slipped. Unable to kip back up into position, with no strength or feeling left in my forearms, I shrugged my picks from their meager lodgements and dropped free into a swinging fall.

After a two-day rest we returned to Vail, entirely unconvinced I would be able to get any farther on the climb, but with a new idea. On my first attempt, I discovered a tiny, shallow vertical slot for my pick in a corner just under the higher of the two pitons in the roof. I turned upside down and threaded my left leg over my right elbow, wedging the toe of my boot under the rock roof, performing a figure 4 in ice climbing gear. I was then able to lever myself up into a high, stable position and take a good swing at the ice at the lip of the roof with my left tool. Unfortunately, just as I swung, the right tool placement popped and I plummeted into space. Shit . . . and EUREKA! This was going to work! On my next attempt I got a solid ice placement with my left tool, but once I unhooked myself from the figure 4, I was left dangling from one rapidly weakening arm, trying to do a one-arm pull-up to make a diagonal placement up and left into the ice above the lip of the overhang. I couldn't do it, and I fell off again!

The third time, however, was magic. This time I did a second figure 4 immediately following the first one, which allowed me to get a good stick higher up with my right tool. I knew that if I untangled from the figure 4 and dropped my feet, I would still be hanging well below the lip of the roof, faced with another series of impossible (for me) one-arm pull-ups and swings before I could get my crampon points into the ice. But as I gazed up into the maw of Octopussy, I was inspired by a new possibility.

I disentangled from the second figure 4, then immediately inverted again and stuck my feet directly up into a space between the tentacles of ice and the gently overhanging rock wall above the roof. I could get heel-toe jams this way, which allowed me to take most of the weight off my arms. Since I was facing upside-down and backward from the wall, I was able to do a series of inverted sit-ups, alternating pick placements until I was five feet above the lip of the roof. At this point, I dropped my feet from the slot and kicked into an upright position. Ten more feet of grade 5+ ice brought me to a good screw placement and the end of the difficulties. I yelled to Teri that I had made it, and she gave a whoop of joy that I am sure was heard down in Vail. I had wrestled with the eight tentacles of difficulty and, just like James Bond, had come out on top of Octopussy—at class 8, technically the hardest mixed climb I had ever done! ▼

Base camp on the Kahiltna
Glacier, Mount Hunter,
Alaska (Photo: Jeff Lowe)

Accoutrement
▼ ▼ ▼ ▼

THE NECESSARY CLOTHING AND GEAR

THE NECESSARY CLOTHING AND GEAR

While ice climbing is not about the gear used in its practice, there is, indeed, much to admire and learn from in the materials, design, construction, and function of modern ice tools and clothing. Understanding the technology is the first step to being able to make enlightened choices that will enhance your ice climbing experience. Climbers who refuse to educate themselves as to the strengths, weaknesses, and functional characteristics of the equipment, and who treat it shoddily, seem to have more than their share of epics and accidents. But there is no need to buy every new toy that comes along, either.

Clothing

Dressing for warmth and comfort in an activity such as ice climbing, which can take place under conditions ranging from those found at the dry, frigid poles in winter to a near-freezing rain on Ben Nevis in a thaw, is an art in itself. Although new fabrics and insulations have greatly increased comfort and survival probability, there are as yet no true "miracle" solutions to the age-old problems of wet and cold, and to the threats of hypothermia and frostbite.

Until the advent of synthetic fibers, wool was the most efficient material for everything from socks to sweaters to trousers, mittens, hats, and underwear. Unlike other natural fibers, such as cotton, wool does not lose all its insulating characteristics when wet. For all basic garments wool is still an acceptable material, and it is often possible to find good secondhand or surplus wool garments at a modest price.

However, ever since Chris Bonington kitted out his 1970 expedition to the South Face of Annapurna with synthetic underwear and fiber pile jackets, the superior characteristics of these manmade substitutes have been recognized. Synthetics are much lighter than wool; they wick moisture away from the body, provide better insulation, and dry very quickly. When effectively layered, synthetic garments can comfortably see you through widely varying temperatures and activity levels.

Feet

A thin synthetic wicking sock transports moisture away from the skin and should be layered under a heavier synthetic or wool insulation sock. Terry-knit provides more cushioning, making blisters less likely. (To inhibit sweat, an antiperspirant may be used on the feet.) Add high gaiters with overboots or supergaiters for colder conditions.

Boots specifically designed for ice climbing are quite specialized. They may be made of plastic or leather, and they may be one piece or of double construction with a removable inner boot. (*Plastic* is used here as a catch-all term for the wide variety of polymeric compounds that boots are made of.)

Plastic boots—currently the most popular due to their low maintenance and waterproof characteristics—are commonly of double construction. As yet, no manufacturer has offered a plastic boot with sufficient ankle flexibility to suit my taste, nor are most of the standard inner boots very well made or very warm. Expensive special closed-cell foam inners are available for some models; these are indeed warm, but the foam breaks down quickly. Many plastic boots also suffer from an ill-fitting shape that sacrifices control and an overall rigidity that makes graceful movement on ice about as easy as dancing in ski boots. On the other hand, many leather boots are nearly as stiff in the ankles, and no leather boot maintains its water repellency without frequent treatment.

A good single leather boot allows better feel on pure rock sections of mixed routes. Combined with an overboot that can be removed anytime crampons are not being worn, or with a supergaiter (an overboot that leaves the boot sole exposed), a single boot is warm enough for most people under normal ice-climbing conditions.

Plastic boots really come into their own in conditions of extreme cold or high altitude—or both. In these situations the need for an absolutely waterproof and reliably insulated covering is greater than the need for ankle flexibility and sensitivity. The best plastic boots available perform nearly as well as leather boots on technical ground and are often lighter.

The choice between plastic and leather, then, depends completely on whether or not you can afford two pairs of boots—a pair for summer alpine climbing (leather), which can be used in many winter conditions with the addition of a supergaiter, and a pair of plastic boots for expeditions and the coldest winter conditions. If you can have only one pair and you are going to climb mostly summer alpine routes, a pair of leather boots will probably suffice. If you are climbing mainly in the winter, then plastic boots are probably the right choice.

I look for these features in an ice boot: a very stiff but not rigid sole; a good quarter-inch lip at the heel and toe to accept crampon bindings; a rigid, roomy toe that will stand up to step-kicking in hard snow; a flexible ankle that allows full range of motion with little resistance or irritation at the boot top; light weight; and a fit that holds the heel firmly in place. A good fit, with no pressure points and plenty of room in the toe area, is crucial to maintaining good circulation and is the key to warm feet in single or double boots.

Whether leather or plastic, ice-climbing boots are designed to prevent moisture from getting inside, so they also effectively prevent the escape of perspiration. Thus your socks may eventually become moist and lose some of their insulating value. Putting a plastic bag or waterproof nylon sock between a thin liner sock and a thick insulative sock will keep the outer sock dry. Surprisingly enough, your foot does not end up drenched in sweat, since the body regulates perspiration according to the humidity of its immediate environment. This so-called Vapor Barrier Liner (VBL) theory contends that a waterproof layer worn over socks (or long underwear or inside a sleeping bag) limits the cooling effect created when perspiration evaporates into the atmosphere. In practice, I find vapor barrier liners to be uncomfortable, but others have used them successfully.

Lower Body

Synthetic underwear transports perspiration away from the skin surface to help keep you dry. Over this first layer I wear a medium-weight, single-sided fleece, farmer John–style stretch suit, but pants or *salopettes* of the same kind of fabric are equally appropriate. Stretch fleece allows excellent mobility, sheds snow quite well, and offers considerable warmth, while permitting moisture to freely escape.

Choosing underwear with a windproof crotch panel extends the viability of your inner layers, making it less necessary to add a windproof outer layer. For very cold conditions or for standing around while on belay, fleece or down trousers with full side zips provide an easily donned (or doffed) final insulating layer. A "rainbow" zip in all layers that extends from the side of one thigh up and around to the small of the back and down to the opposite thigh makes answering nature's call much easier, even in a harness. Windproof/waterproof *salopettes*, or pants, or a one-piece suit with full side zips should be the final layer

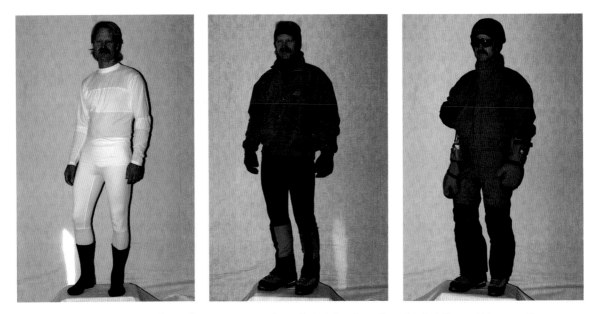

Left: **Synthetic moisture-transporting long underwear constitutes the ice climber's base layer.** Center: **Synthetic fleece mid-layers can be worn as outerwear in good weather with the gap between the boot-top and lower pant leg protected by high gaiters.** Right: **In full storm conditions the integrity of the insulating layers is maintained by coated or waterproof, breathable jackets, bibs, and mitts. A helmet and dark glasses protect the head and eyes.** (Photos: Greg Lowe)

of protection against the elements. You might find insulated down or synthetic-fill overpants necessary for alpine winters or Himalayan climbs.

Upper Body

I prefer to wear a full, long-sleeved underwear suit under the farmer John–style fleece suit, which automatically gives me the same initial layer over my entire body. Other garments can be added or subtracted as required for warmth: a light windshirt and/or fleece jacket with a high zip collar; a windproof/waterproof jacket or one-piece suit; a down or synthetic-fill parka for extreme cold.

Hands

A good combination for hands is a thin, stretch-synthetic liner glove inside a fleece glove or mitt, covered by a windproof/waterproof shell. Neoprene "wet suit" gloves work well in extremely wet conditions, while ski gloves provide decent protection and good dexterity in dry conditions. Wool gloves, when slightly damp, offer an amazing grip on ice in cold temperatures. Down or synthetic insulated mitts are best for the coldest climbs.

Head and Face

As much as 40 percent of the body's heat loss occurs through the head. Your shell parka should have a secure neck-closure/hood combination with a visor to protect the eyes from wind, snow, or rain. The hood should allow a complete seal around the face, without restricting your vision in any direction. On sunny days, a visor, cotton golfer's cap, or baseball cap provides shade, while a synthetic fleece balaclava is the traditional and best head insulation. If it is cold enough for a down or fiberfill parka, it is cold enough for a hood of the same insulation. Waterproof/windproof hats lined with fleece or insulated with fiberfill, complete with ear flaps, cheek protectors, and visor, are perhaps the most versatile of all head coverings.

An insulated face mask of windproof material prevents frostbite in high winds and is very light.

Dark Glasses and Goggles

On glaciers and snowfields it is necessary to wear dark glasses to avoid snow blindness and other eye damage caused by ultraviolet and infrared rays. Even on a cloudy day, infrared rays can blind you—almost without discomfort, until it is too late. To be adequate for high mountain use, glasses must filter 100 percent of ultraviolet and infrared rays. The best usually come with leather side guards and, sometimes, nose guards. If you wear prescription sunglasses, make your optician fully aware of the need for total ultraviolet and infrared blockage.

In very stormy weather and high winds, goggles are sometimes necessary to maintain any vision at all. However, fogging often renders goggles useless, especially for those who wear prescription glasses. Various methods of ventilation have been devised to help alleviate this problem, the most successful to date being goggles equipped with a small, battery-operated fan—admittedly quite a technological solution! Alternatively, lenses may be treated with antifog cream. Goggles or protective glasses are also recommended to shield the eyes from flying chips of ice.

Hardware

Ice climbing is a tool-intensive activity, and every individual ice climber seems to have a cherished opinion about which axe is the best, which crampon

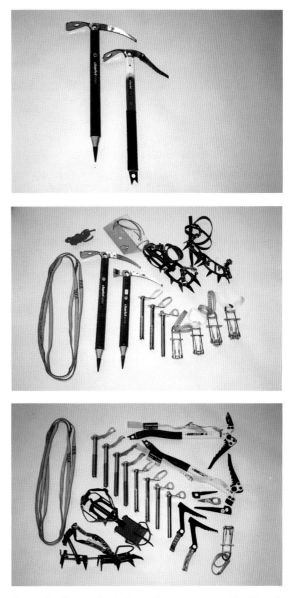

Top: **The major difference between an axe with a classically curved pick (on the left) and one with a reverse curve (on the right) is that pulling out on the shaft tends to lock the classic curve into the ice, but it dislodges the reverse curve. Also, on lower-angle slopes (up to about 60°) the classic curve is easier to plant in the ice without bending over so far that you feel you are crawling.** Middle: **A standard array of alpine ice-climbing gear includes: flexible twelve-point crampons; a 60 to 70cm ice axe with classically curved pick; a 40 to 50cm North Wall hammer; several tubular ice screws; a handful of** slings and rock protection devices; a deadman or snow picket(s); and mechanical ascender or prusik for crevasse travel. *Bottom:* **A standard selection of gear for waterfall ice climbing includes: monopoint parallel-sided crampons; a matching set of reverse-curve tools with 45 to 55cm shafts, one with a cutting adze and one with a pounding anvil; half a dozen or more tubular ice screws; several Snarg-type pitons; a hook piton or two; and slings and rock gear as appropriate to the chosen route.** *(Photos: Greg Lowe)*

the most versatile. Ice gear is expensive, and designs are ever-changing. It is best to try out several different models of axes and crampons to see which ones suit you. A lot of good used gear is available; it could be just what you need—and might fit your budget, too.

Axes and Hammers

Ice axes come in countless variations on two basic styles: one-piece heads or modular tools. One-piece heads cannot vibrate loose, but pick loosening shouldn't be a serious problem on well-designed modular tools. Tools with interchangeable parts allow you to replace worn or damaged components, as well as to switch out the picks and/or adzes to better suit your purpose on a specific climb.

The market bristles with pick designs, some useful, others less so. The pick of a traditional ice axe juts out 90° from the shaft. Many of the techniques described in this book are not possible using such an axe. A classical curve matched to the shaft length and arc of a natural swing is best for all-around alpine ice applications. Properly designed reverse, or banana, curves also permit a natural swing, and perform well with shorter shafts and on steeper ice. They are the common choice for water ice. Even more steeply angled picks hook well on rotten or chandeliered ice, but require an unnatural downward flick of the wrist at the end of the swing. Some people prefer a lower-angle reverse curve pick for steep alpine *gulotte* (gully or chimney) climbing. Tube picks tend to fracture very brittle ice less than other styles because forces are directed into the tube rather than out into the ice. Combined with a tubular adze, tube picks cut the fastest and cleanest bollards.

Other factors affect the function of a pick: whether or not the top and/or bottom is beveled; the shape and depth of the teeth; the overall cross-sectional shape and dimensions, that is, how tall the pick is, and how thick; whether or not it exhibits positive or negative clearance; and the hooking angle of the point and first tooth. Beveling on both top and bottom makes the pick much easier to extract from the ice without compromising the security of the placement. Teeth along the entire underside of the pick help the tool stick in the ice, but if they are too deep (more than about 0.2 inches), the pick will be hard to remove. A thin cross section displaces less ice and therefore causes less fracturing, but if it is too tall and very thin, sideways vibrations will result and the pick will slice through soft or rotten ice. Positive clearance gives smoother performance in self-arrest, while negative clearance is required in thin ice and will hold well with shallower penetration in thick ice. A very aggressive hooking angle at the first tooth is absolutely essential on thin ice and mixed climbing to avoid the "skating" tendency of inadequate hook angles.

Adzes are mainly used for chopping. Most good axes have an adze almost perpendicular to the shaft. The adze should have sharp corners for cutting. Exotic, wavy edges add nothing to function. Secondary uses of the adze are torqueing in mixed climbing situations and in climbing slopes of snow-ice or rotten ice that a pick would slice through. Specialized adzes that have a steeper droop or hooking angle work better for these purposes and are shaped more like a pointed spade than a flat-edged shovel. Such an adze may also have notched sides that grab the edges of cracks for torqueing.

Shaft length and configuration depend largely on personal climbing style, strength, size, and type of climbing normally done. The strongest and best shafts are aluminum-alloy, fiberglass, or carbon-fiber-wrapped, thin-wall alloy. Metal shafts should be covered with smooth, soft rubber for insulation and a good grip; carbon fiber and fiberglass shafts are warm enough as they are, yet they, too, are easier to hang onto if they are equipped with a rubber grip. Cross-country ski waxes can be used on bare shafts to increase gripability.

For alpine use, the best ice axe has a straight shaft between 60 and 70cm in length, depending on your personal style, preference, and body size. If you plan to do only extreme alpine climbs, you can get by with a shorter axe, but tools less than 60cm long are difficult to use for self-arrest. The spike and ferrule at the bottom of the shaft should be smooth and gradually tapered for good penetration in snow. A second tool for alpine ice can be either a short-shafted alpine hammer or a North Wall hammer with curved pick, pounding anvil, and 45 to 55cm shaft.

For waterfall and extreme alpine routes, I like to carry a matched set of tools with reverse-curved picks and curved shafts. Curved shafts aid in reaching over bulges or around pillars, and they reduce the wrist bend that occurs while hanging from the tool, thus diminishing fatigue. Spikes on these technical tools should be stubbier than those on traditional ice axes, allowing a full grip at the very bottom of the shaft about an inch above the point of the spike. This assures that the spike stays out of the way when you swing the tool on steep ice or in tight places.

Although theoretically useful, a leash from the tool to the harness will often entangle the climber. I have seen minutes wasted and strength squandered while climbers attempted to sort themselves out. A good wrist loop, on the other hand, is crucial for steep ice climbing. On short stretches of very steep ice, a quick wrist loop can be fashioned for an alpine axe or hammer by wrapping a prusik loop around the handle or a short runner of the correct length through the carabiner hole in the tool's head. For waterfall ice and extreme alpine ice, tools should have permanently attached wrist loops. Most tools designed for this type of climbing are factory-equipped with functional, adjustable wrist loops. There are also a number of commercially available wrist loops, some of which offer better support than the factory-equipped variety. If the wrist loop is too narrow, it will tend to cut off the circulation to your hand; if it is too wide, it hinders flex in the wrist. I have found the best width to be about one inch. The length of the wrist loop must be properly adjusted so that you are supported with your hand in the proper position at the very bottom of the shaft.

Carry your tools in holsters on your harness or on a separate belt. Most leather or nylon webbing holsters and harness gear loops used as holsters make withdrawing or inserting the tools an awkward task. Carpenters' holsters with wire loops are easiest to work with, although they sometimes hang up in chimneys and other tight situations.

Crampons

Crampons come in these basic configurations (with endless variations): rigid with twelve points (two projecting forward and ten downward under the boot); hinged in the middle, with either ten or twelve points; and ultralight, with eight or fewer points. Footfangs fall outside the standard categories, being rigid crampons with twenty points and parallel side rails. Crampons with a single frontpoint, the monopoint, were introduced in the late 1980s.

The geometry of the points is crucial and determines how well the crampons work. The length of the points, the relationship of the frontpoints to the secondary points, the spacing of the points under the foot, whether or not the points follow the outline of the boot sole or are in two parallel rows, these and other variables affect performance. Not all crampons work equally well in all ice and snow conditions. Many hardcore climbers own two pairs, one for waterfall ice climbing and one for alpine use. I prefer vertically oriented monopoint crampons for water ice climbing and dual horizontal frontpoints for alpine ice. If you do not want to own two pairs of crampons, a single pair of adjustable rigid or hinged twelve-point crampons will serve you well on summer alpine climbs, winter icefalls, rime-coated rock, or frozen névé.

The best crampons are adjustable to fit a wide range of boots. Fit is critical to the performance of crampons. Each model has its own fitting parameters, so it is not possible to do more here than generalize regarding a few considerations. Longer points obviously work better in snow ice and névé. Adjust frontpoints long for these conditions, extending about 1.2 inches in front of the boot toe. For hard alpine gully ice and black ice, 0.75 inch of frontpoint is all you will need. Paradoxically, frontpoints for waterfall ice climbing should be adjusted long, about the same as for snow climbing.

Crampons with straps must fit tightly so that they will stay on the boot when you pick them up without the straps holding them on. Crampons with a toe-bale/heel-clamp binding should be adjusted tight enough so that it takes significant force to lever the heel clamp up.

Straps used to be the only method of attaching crampons to boots. Nowadays, the best straps are made of neoprene-covered nylon that remains flexible in wet, freezing conditions. Whatever the strap component, the straps should use a pin-style or double-locking-ring buckle, rather than a friction-type buckle. Beware of straps attached by a single rivet; rivets are prone to failure.

Most of the best models of crampons offer a ski-type, toe-bale/heel-clamp binding to secure the crampon to the boot. These bindings have numerous advantages over straps: they are quicker and easier to put on and remove; they provide a more positive grip on the boot; they apply no pressure over the toe or foot that would restrict circulation; and they are less prone to breakage. I highly recommend this kind of binding. To ensure secure attachment, your boot must have a welt of 0.25 inch at the toe and heel for

Crampons with dual horizontal frontpoints are best for alpine ice. They should fit tightly on the boots. (Photo: Ian Tomlinson)

the binding to grab. Do not attempt to use this type of binding on a boot with less purchase than this.

Care of Gear

Sharp tools penetrate the ice easily, fracture it less, and enhance your security, so attend regularly to the sharpness of your crampons and picks. Except for the special functional modifications recommended in this book, file all points in the same configuration as they came from the factory, whether they be crampon points or picks. To avoid overheating the steel and damaging the temper, never use a power grinder to sharpen your points. I always carry a small mill file along with me, stashed in an accessible place.

Dry and lightly oil metal parts after use to inhibit rust. Before each climb, inspect all crampon straps, wrist loops, hammers, and axes for fraying, hairline fractures, and fatigue cracks. Also check screws and bolts for tightness. Liquid compounds such as Locktite provide extra insurance that bolts will stay tight.

Protection Hardware

The reliability of protection on snow and ice is as variable as the medium itself, although the latest protection devices for ice often can provide security as great as that afforded by a well-placed half-inch bolt in solid rock. Along with improvements in experience, technique, and strength, the new ultrasharp ice screws and Snarg-type pitons have allowed climbers to achieve higher levels of difficulty.

Tubular Ice Screws

Depending on the quality of the ice, a well-placed tubular screw will hold from two thousand to five thousand pounds, providing excellent protection. In rotten ice, screws hold very little. Obviously, longer screws with larger diameters and deeper threads will hold better in snow-ice and rotten ice. In solid water ice, long screws are unnecessary. In practice, 90 percent of the time you can get by with screws eight to

On scree approaches and low-angle snow and ice, telescopic ski poles are more functional than an ice axe for assisting balance. They are light-weight and can easily be stowed on the pack when not in use. *(Photo: Ian Tomlinson)*

ten inches long. For very thin ice, thread a few of your screws through the tight openings sewn into the ends of quickdraw-type runners. As soon as the screw touches rock, it is a simple matter to wind this runner down the threads to create an excellent tie-off at the ice surface. This precludes the need to carry shorter screws and allows the use of screws in series, as recommended for thin ice in the technique section of this book.

One problem with tubular screws is that the core of ice tends to freeze to the inside wall of the screw. An ice-filled tube cannot be placed again until the ice has been removed, which can be extremely difficult unless the screw design addresses this problem. Several effective solutions have been discovered. A differential inside diameter forces the ice through a slightly smaller opening at the tip, so it can be shaken out the back. Several of the very finely machined stainless steel or chrome-moly screws now

on the market have such aggressive cutting teeth that the ice core is pulverized as it is forced into the tube; these screws can usually be cleared by tapping them against the head of a tool.

Ice Pitons

The new generation of sharply machined ice screws are so easily placed that they have largely obviated the need for ice pitons. However, pound-in protection is still occasionally useful. Ice pitons come in two main styles. Hook-type pitons have a design similar to the pick of an ice tool. Although their solid cross section tends to fracture brittle ice quite badly, they can often be fitted rapidy into a pick hole in a weakness between icicles, or slammed home for quick, temporary protection. While these protection devices often can be removed by pulling up and out on the carabiner, sometimes they must be chopped out by the second.

For hard-ice conditions, the pound-in, screw-out tube piton (commonly known as a Snarg) offers superior holding power compared with the hook styles of ice protection. A full-length slot from the rear of the tube to within about half an inch of the tip allows mechanical clearing of the ice core with the pick of a hand tool.

Deadmen, Snow Stakes, and Pickets

In relatively soft snow, the best protection can be arranged with the use of *deadmen*, cabled aluminum plates ranging in size from about six by eight to ten by twelve inches. (The smaller sizes are called *deadboys*.) Deadmen are pounded in the snow at an angle of about 45°; if properly placed, they tend, under load, to "sail" or "fluke" deeper into the snow, providing variable security. On harder snow—in particular the walls of bergschrunds, cornices, and the like—tubular, V-shaped, or T-cross section snow stakes can provide useful protection. These are pounded directly into the snow at an angle to resist the expected force of a load. Snow stakes range from about eighteen to thirty-six inches long, for use in different snow conditions. A variation is the tubular snow picket, which usually has holes drilled throughout its length to increase holding power. These can be one to three inches in diameter and about the same length as snow stakes. A great benefit of this tubular design is that they can be used to make V-thread anchors (as described in the chapter Protection and Belays).

Energy-Absorbing Devices

The reliability of a questionable ice or snow anchor can be enhanced through the use of an energy-absorbing webbing device deployed between the piton and the rope. Such devices, either friction-plate-and-web arrangements or, more simply, Air Voyagers or Screamers (webbing strips that rely on the ripping of a series of bar tacks to absorb the force) limit the force that can be applied to the anchor to around seven hundred pounds.

Ropes

"Dry," or water-repellent, ropes are a major boon to the ice climber as they tend to freeze up much less than untreated ropes. It is important to check the manufacturer's information regarding the dry treatment. If every strand of the rope is treated individually before the rope is constructed, the water-repellent characteristics will last the life of the rope. Most treatments wear off with use, however, so the advantage may eventually be lost. Water-repellent treatments have the added advantages of reducing the friction of the rope through carabiners and against rock, and enhancing the abrasion resistance of the sheath. For easy snow and glacier tours, an 8mm or 8.5mm dynamic rope is probably adequate, while on long, hard routes I carry a doubled 8.5mm or 9mm rope, which gives insurance against cutting and may be used single strand for long, rapid leads on easier terrain. Of course, you can use 10mm or 11mm single ropes as well.

Accessories

In addition to clothing and hardware, a number of other items are, at various times, essential for ice climbing.

A harness for alpine ice climbing should be either lightly padded or not padded at all and have adjustable leg loops. A chest harness should be added for extensive glacier travel. *(Photo: Ian Tomlinson)*

- A head lamp is often useful on short winter days or for predawn alpine starts. Lithium-powered lights shine many times longer than those powered by regular batteries, but they are expensive and require special bulbs. Alkaline batteries are next best, and cheaper. Batteries stored near the body will last much longer than those exposed directly to the cold in a pack.
- A harness with adjustable leg loops will accommodate a variety of clothing. For glacier travel a chest harness, used in conjunction with a sit harness, is a good idea to reduce the chance of a broken back caused by a heavy pack.
- A closed-cell-foam-insulated water bottle, or a thermos, will keep liquids from becoming undrinkable solids.
- A map and compass—and at least rudimentary knowledge of how to use them—will help you navigate in a whiteout.
- An altimeter can tell you how high you have climbed, or warn of a change in weather.
- A thermometer can tell you just how cold you really are, while an inclinometer lets you know just how steep the ice really isn't!
- A small repair kit, with a file, spare picks, wrenches for tools and crampons, and so forth, is a smart idea.
- A first-aid kit is always advisable.
- A helmet with a UIAA certification label may forestall the use of the first-aid kit.
- A mechanical belay/rappel device is essential.
- A mechanical ascender that positively grips icy ropes is a useful option to replace the prusik knot in glacier travel.
- A lightweight shovel is essential for freeing victims from avalanches or digging a snow cave.
- Snowshoes or skis ease approaches and/or descents in deep snow.
- A pack is necessary to carry clothing, equipment, food, and drink. You probably already own a small pack for rock climbing, which will do fine as you start out; but if you choose to buy a pack for ice

A good ice-climbing pack has the following features: medium to large capacity (3,300 cubic inches for a day to 6,000 cubic inches for Himalayan alpine-style climbs); an easily accessible place to carry two ice axes, crampons, rope, skis, and shovel; an adjustable but lightweight frame and harness system; some expansion capability for oversized loads; durable but lightweight coated fabric; double-stitched, taped seams; # 8 or larger zippers. (Photo: Greg Lowe)

climbing, it should have these features: padded adjustable shoulder straps and waist belt; load-stabilizing straps at waist belt and top of shoulder straps; compression straps on sides of pack bag; convenient attachment points for axes, crampons, skis, and so forth; and a removable foam pad or internal frame.

After all this talk of exotic equipment and clothing, I want to reemphasize that owning the latest and greatest ice-climbing paraphernalia is not the goal. To get started, you can use army surplus woolies or old ski clothes, purchase well-cared-for used axes and crampons, and take off for the snowy hills.

The author on the North Face of Mount Fay, Canadian Rockies *(Photo: Ian Tomlinson)*

The Cold
Dance Review

▼ ▼ ▼ ▼ ▼

THE BASICS OF CLIMBING ICE

Winter conditions can completely alter the nature of a climb. During the first winter ascent of Wyoming's Black Ice Couloir in January 1971, the author's party encountered a savagely beautiful landscape.
(Photo: Greg Lowe)

THE BASICS OF CLIMBING ICE

It is possible for the novice ice climber to advance rapidly through the ranks of difficulty and accomplish some very impressive climbs within the first season. But technical ability on hard ice is only a secondary measure of a good ice climber. Far more important is the depth of a climber's experience with, and knowledge of, a host of related concerns. The climber must understand the phenomena of avalanches and mountain weather; have a knowledge of snow conditions and the ability to navigate successfully and travel safely on snow and glaciers; and know how to avoid the hazards of falling rock and ice, collapsing cornices, and altitude illness. If an accident occurs, a good climber is fully prepared to effect a self-rescue and administer appropriate first aid. The best ice climbers are equally at home traveling on foot, skis, or snowshoes. They have developed an unconscious rapport with the mountains and are constantly filtering information from the environment through a screen of intuition and hard-won knowledge. Almost without thinking, this provides the appropriate response to any set of circumstances. Go slow, be cautious, and build experience gradually.

In addition, a number of considerations may help the aspiring ice climber progress to higher levels of safety, performance, and enjoyment. Once the basic skills have been acquired, specialized physical and mental training and new perspectives on the choice and use of equipment will shorten the apprenticeship and allow the climber to begin to lead desired routes sooner.

Important Basics

Weather

The wonder of a single snowflake outweighs the wisdom of a million meteorologists.

—Francis Bacon

Winter is not a season, it's an occupation.

—Sinclair Lewis

A little-praised side benefit of learning to ice climb is that the climber begins to recognize the beauty of savage weather. Such weather is responsible for the arc of a cornice, the spreading wings of icicles on a frozen waterfall, the sharp-edged clarity of the atmosphere when a cold front pushes out the storm, and the quickening of the blood and brain on frosty predawn starts. Sleet, snow, sun, wind, wet, thaw, gust, gale, blow, freeze, whiteout, haze, mist, fog, clouds: the ice climber is treated to a kaleidoscopic experience of high and wild places. Gradually learning to cope with ever more harsh conditions is as rewarding as learning to climb steeper and harder ice. Successfully interpreting the meaning of high cirrus clouds turning red in the sunset, or a sudden rise in temperature accompanied by a cessation of wind and lowering clouds not only allows retreat to be made in time to avoid an epic, but offers the satisfaction of being intimate with one of the most fascinating aspects of nature. The ice climber learns to face the storm with a grin, and the sun with dark glasses and adequate sunscreen to protect nose and lips!

Navigation

Normally the mountaineer can find his or her way using the many landmarks that are part of the alpine scene. During storms and whiteout conditions, however, landmarks disappear, and map and compass skills become essential. The ability to take a bearing from the map and follow it through the mountains; the art of locating your position on the map by triangulating two bearings taken on prominent landmarks; and the skillful avoidance of hazardous terrain and dead ends through knowledgeable scrutiny of the contour lines on the map are all critical skills.

But total reliance on map and compass is not necessary or even desirable. If there is no map or the compass has been lost, then a finely honed sixth sense, like the one that allows the Polynesians to navigate unaided from island to island across large expanses of open water, comes into its own. We are all born with this instinctive sense of where we are and how to get from here to there, but learning to use it is a long process. This sense is buried by the technology we use in everyday travel, but it can be rediscovered with practice.

Skiing and Snowshoeing

Deep, soft snow can render foot travel impossible, so some winter ice climbs can be approached only by ski or snowshoe. The advantages of snowshoes are that anyone who can walk can learn to use them immediately; they are more compact than skis when they must be carried; and they usually cost less than skis. Some snowshoes are only about twice the size of a boot sole and, while not very useful in fresh powder, they may be carried in the pack on technical ground, ready to be pulled out for use on easier sections of snow.

Skis, on the other hand, allow faster uphill travel—and going downhill, there is no comparison. Not everyone has an easy time mastering the skills of skiing, but persistence, along with some instruction from a friend or professional, will soon pay dividends that are more than simply utilitarian. The skier

playing with gravity learns to identify a sort of internal gyroscope that performs a more subtle, but equally important, role in ice climbing. It is neither necessary nor appropriate to deal here with all the varieties of ski equipment. Suffice it to say that for approaching ice climbs, the ski/boot/binding combination must allow the heel to move freely up and down so that a motion similar to walking is achieved.

Bivouacs

An old adage says if you carry bivouac gear, you will use it. The extra weight of the gear will cause you to go so slowly that you will certainly be caught out at day's end. If an unplanned bivouac is a possibility, a point can be made for limiting equipment to the absolute minimum required for survival. A water bottle and bivouac sac, along with climbing clothing and a pack to sit on, should suffice.

A slight extra degree of comfort might be allowed for planned nights out. A three-quarter length pad of 13mm closed-cell foam, cooking pot and stove, food, and ultralight sleeping bag will improve things.

When the snow is deep enough, a snow cave is always a better shelter than a tent or bivouac sac, but to make one you will need to carry a shovel.

Special Training

It has often been said that climbing itself is the best training for climbing. But this is not always true. Sometimes the very practice of climbing gets in the way of advancement. For instance, I have stressed that one of the goals of an ice climber should be to achieve nearly effortless upward movement. Ironically, however, if you come too close to realizing this goal, your future progress may stagnate due to lack of strength. On the other hand, if you rely on muscle alone, you may be able to get up most hard, strenuous routes, but be unprepared for delicate climbs.

Coordination between eye and hand or foot and tool is enhanced by the practice of other sports and

Skis offer the quickest access to, as well as the most enjoyable descents from, some ice climbs.
(Photo: Greg Lowe)

activities that use tools. Soccer, cricket, baseball, and tennis, for example, all depend upon the dynamic manipulation of an object or tool through space and time using either hands or feet. Skiing is the best parallel sport for normal alpine ice climbing, as it involves both hands and feet in precise, simultaneous, balanced movements, coordinated through sight and sensation. Rough carpentry definitely helps in learning to swing tools accurately and with subtle power, while cabinet making and fine woodworking are excellent introductions to the subtle qualities of well-designed tools and their interface with the medium being worked.

Modern and classical dance, the martial arts, and certain Eastern practices—especially tai-chi, which is directly concerned with centering and movement—can bring you in closer touch with your body and improve its quality of motion. Meditation or self-hypnosis may aid concentration and prepare the mind to face new problems, while stretching or hatha yoga will make you more supple and teach you better breathing. All of the foregoing are somewhat helpful in increasing functional strength, but gymnastics and weight training are best for developing climbing muscles, and running, biking, or other aerobic exercise builds endurance.

Although few climbers will practice all that I preach here, the point is that anyone's climbing can benefit both from a holistic approach to physical and mental balance, as well as from a specific program of strength, endurance, and agility training. Furthermore, this training can be varied and enjoyable. Imbued with the right spirit, there are numerous opportunities to "train" for ice climbing, even if you live three thousand miles from the nearest frozen water!

Nutrition

I am not an expert nutritionist, but it does seem important to make a couple of observations regarding diet for the ice climber. Although carbohydrates provide the best source of energy for most sports, the special demands of ice climbing (cold conditions and long-term output of effort) would seem to indicate a need for greater proportions of protein and fat. Caffeine is a vaso-constrictor, which cuts off blood to extremities. Therefore, tea and coffee cannot be recommended since they increase the likelihood of injury due to cold. (But I drink a lot of both!)

Bouldering on Ice

You can practice ice bouldering while unroped at the base of a frozen waterfall or on glacial seracs in those areas where a fall poses no threat of serious injury. As with bouldering on rock, ice bouldering enables you to really push your technical ability without the distractions of exposure and high risk. You can work out new, very specialized techniques. You can develop strengths to deal with specific problems. And on ice in particular, you can discover, realize, and expand upon the limitations, potential, and strength of each tool—and the ice itself—in a fairly safe manner.

Although ice bouldering is relatively less dangerous than lead climbing on ice, remember that in even a very short fall, crampon points can snag in the ice or on your own pant leg, snapping an ankle or tearing a calf muscle. A toprope reduces the chance of such occurrences. But the constant use of a toprope may also lessen the degree of concentration applied to each move, and you will consequently learn more slowly. Ice bouldering definitely has a place in a climber's development.

Learning from Others

Friendly competition among a small group of climbers will sometimes yield surprising results, as each individual's imagination, creativity, strength, and motivation are gently pushed, prodded, and inspired by others. However, any kind of scorekeeping attitude among the group is usually counterproductive for all, except the top dog who makes the hardest moves of the day and is in a position to reap temporary ego benefits at the others' expense.

It is better when everyone is let in on the secret of just how a move was done—what it felt like to accomplish it—not in the sense of good/bad or easy/hard, but more along these lines: "As I was lay-backing around the lip, I found that my left crampon held better when I placed it out onto the thin ice and just sort of shifted my weight onto it without kicking it in. I just sort of pushed and stood up. It felt like the points melted their way in."

Plateaus

Sooner or later your progress as an ice climber will seem to halt, no matter how much you try to improve. The first thing to remember is that this is natural, and that one of the causes for the plateau may be that you are trying too hard. These cycles in performance may be due to a stagnation in your acceptance of the experience; your senses may have become dulled by what you think you already know. This is the time to back off, get loose, and remember that it is all a game and should be fun.

Planning

Commonly, planning involves drawing up lists of equipment, food, and so forth in the hopes that some important item or detail will not be over-looked. This is great as far as it goes, but such paper-work should be supplemented (and can eventually be almost entirely replaced) by what I call "long-range imaging," or taking the skills of visualization you have learned to use in dealing with technical problems and applying them to an entire climb, trip, or even three-month expedition. It is simple, really. You just do the climb, imagine the trip, or run the expedition in your head a few times, letting all the possible scenarios run their course. Actually it is only controlled daydreaming, but it is a powerful and effective tool.

Packing Light and Right

Excess weight in your pack or on your body can kill your aspirations. You will never move fast if you go by the book (even this book!) and always carry the famous "ten essentials," which, in any case, seem to vary from one authority to the next. For a given climb there may, in fact, be only three essentials: ice axe, crampons, and skill. Head lamps, water bottles, helmets, harnesses, extra clothes, first-aid kits, avalanche beacons, stoves, sleeping bags, tents, spare matches, toilet paper, great literature, jumars, ladders, and the kitchen sink all have their place in the scheme of things; but if you put them all in your pack each time you go, you won't be going far, believe me. I have tried it more than once. Be bold. Leave something behind and see if you miss it.

Moving Fast and Conserving Energy

You do not necessarily move fast in the mountains by running. A thoughtful choice of route and careful timing, along with a light pack and good pacing, can have many possible benefits. This common-sense approach might save half an hour because you do not have to backtrack through the icefall to find a way out of the cul-de-sac you have blindly wandered into; it might cut the time of ascending a slope in the late morning slush by three-quarters simply because you were there two hours earlier; it might save energy, effort, and time because you are not carrying your home on your back; and it might eliminate the need for long rests to "catch your breath," which you never would have lost if you had adopted the right pace from the beginning.

When it comes to equipment, another thing to consider is that light is not always right. For example, I have found it less tiring to use a pair of "old-fash-ioned" heavy leather boots for mountain routes simply because the flexible leather ankle is not con-stantly trying to throw me off balance when I step up onto a boulder, or forcing me to frontpoint on long slopes of moderate ice as do modern plastic boots. Remember, total effort expended is equal to the weight of equipment multiplied by the efficiency of that equipment as exploited by the skill of the climber.

Many ice climbs are positioned directly in avalanche paths. The large bowl above Colorado's Blue Ribbon Gully can funnel enough spindrift alone to cause problems for a climbing team. *(Photo: Jeff Lowe)*

Staying Warm

Staying warm while ice climbing is often quite easy. The climbing itself is strenuous enough so you will probably err on the side of being overdressed while you are moving. In very cold weather it is especially important not to overheat and drench your clothes in sweat, which will cause an instant chill when you stop to belay or rest. Learn to anticipate the exact clothing you will need to wear and adjust things accordingly before committing to a pitch. If the climbing is so difficult that you are leading without a pack, a light parka in a stuff sack can be clipped to your harness, ready to be put on at the end of the lead, before you start to cool down.

When you feel your hands or feet getting too cold, stop immediately and warm them up. Vigorous swinging in a wide arc is the quickest way to force warm blood to the extremities. Keep a constant bit of awareness focused on the temperature of all extremities, including the exposed and delicate nose, cheeks, ears, and chin. These are often frostbitten without the victim even being aware of a problem.

Protect your core temperature with an adequate intake of the right foods and liquids, and try not to exhaust yourself. Take pride in never succumbing to cold injuries, a more subtle accomplishment than climbing itself, but equally satisfying and more difficult in the long run.

Avalanches

Avalanches of various kinds pose perhaps the biggest threat you will face as an ice climber. On the approach to a climb, a new snow or slab avalanche may be a possibility. Slopes above may release and funnel onto you while you are on an ice face or in a gully or couloir. Under thaw conditions, an entire winter's snowpack may slide on a gentle slope of water-lubricated granite slabs. Knowledge of the basic phenomena associated with avalanches can help you avoid exposure in the first place and lessen your chances of being caught in an avalanche if you must travel or climb in dangerous conditions. The information presented here is enough to give you a basic understanding of the factors involved in avalanche prediction and avoidance, but it is not enough to make you an expert.

Always err of the side of caution. Even the most acknowledged authorities take this approach when in the field. There are simply too many variables to gamble your life on. However, with time and sensitive awareness, you will eventually develop a feel for conditions that will serve you well.

Snow avalanches are of two main types: *loose*

snow avalanches, which start at a point and gather mass in fan-shape as they fall; and *cohesive slab avalanches,* which start sliding over a large area all at once, creating a well-defined fracture line. Either type of avalanche requires a trigger, which may be the weight of a climber, a falling rock or cornice, the collapse of a weak layer in the snowpack, a sudden change in barometric pressure or temperature, wind, the tug of gravity, new snowfall, a combination of the above, or something else!

Of the two types, slab avalanches are frequently the most damaging and deadly, and are often triggered by the victim's weight on a stressed slab that is weakly bonded to the ground or other layers within the snowpack. An avalanche of either type need travel only a short distance to gain deadly force and mass. People have been buried at the bottom of a thirty-foot slope.

Care must be exercised in negotiating corniced ridges. The potential fracture line is often lower than it might appear, requiring a traverse well below the ridge crest. *(Photo: Jeff Lowe)*

Steepness is one of the factors that influences whether the introduction of a trigger will release the slope. Slopes of 30° to 45° have a low enough angle to allow snow to accumulate significant depths with poor bonds. Avalanches most often occur on these slopes, but in unstable conditions they may occur at angles greater or less than this.

Slope configuration is another determinant. Slab avalanches usually occur on convex slopes, breaking at the crest, but they may also break on a concave slope if other factors overcome the natural compression.

Snow on north-facing slopes (south-facing slopes in the Southern Hemisphere) receives little or no sun and often is slower to stabilize than snow on other aspects. South-facing slopes exposed directly to the sun are especially dangerous in the spring and summer. Slopes of other aspects to the sun are variously affected. Slight changes in aspect can have dramatic effects on slope stability.

Snow tends to be removed from windward slopes and deposited as slabs on leeward slopes, which are often unstable. If surface features such as rocks, trees, or brush are present and sticking up through the snowpack in significant quantity, they help to anchor the snow. Once these features are buried, avalanche hazard increases.

If the rate of new snowfall during a storm is more than one inch per hour, avalanches are quite likely to occur. If wind is present, the danger increases rapidly. New snow is not necessarily deposited evenly on every slope, so be alert for variations in depth. When six inches or more of new snow builds up on a slope without sloughing, avalanche conditions are dangerous. In the absence of new snowfall, wind alone is a major contributor to instability. Sustained winds will transport loose snow into gullies and slopes on the leeward sides, forming slabs.

Snow crystals are not all the same. Star-shaped, angular crystals interlock better than needles or pellets, creating a more cohesive snowpack. After falling, however, snow crystals begin to change as wind rolls them along the surface, as well as under the force of gravity, the pressure of new snow on top, or the effect of atmospheric conditions.

Storms that start with low temperatures and dry snow, followed by rising temperatures, are likely to cause avalanches. The dry snow early on forms a poor bond to the old snow or ice surface. However, if a storm starts warm and gets colder, the new snow bonds well to old snow or freezes to ice, and is thus more stable. Continued cold temperatures hinder slope stabilization, while warm weather aids settling and stability.

In prolonged cold, clear winter weather, Temperature Gradient (TG) snow, commonly called *depth hoar*, forms from the ground up whenever the snowpack is thin (two to four feet). The ground is warmer than the upper snowpack, and moisture is leached from the bottom up through sublimation, creating large, weak, angular grains. Under the weight of new snow or in the presence of another trigger, a layer of depth hoar can collapse, causing an avalanche. In the Rocky Mountains this condition is all too prevalent.

Wet snow avalanches occur most often during the first prolonged spring thaw, but in the high mountains, wet snow avalanche hazard may exist throughout the summer, although it generally subsides later in the season.

The art of avalanche avoidance requires a combination of observation in the field and an understanding of the factors that predispose a slope to avalanche. As you travel through the mountains, watch for old avalanche paths, in particular those that show signs of having slid earlier in the winter or season, as these slopes will be most likely to slide again. Fresh avalanches indicate conditions are hazardous, at least on slopes of the same aspect, elevation, and snowpack history. If the snow settles with a "whoomp" around you, and especially if the snow cracks and the fractures travel for some distance, do not cross the slope. Avalanche danger is

high! In warm weather, snowballs or "cartwheels" that roll down the slope also indicate danger.

If a slope is suspect, or if you simply have no idea of the stability of a slope, a snow pit dug through the snowpack to the ground will provide much valuable information. To be meaningful, the snow pit must be dug on the actual slope under question or on a slope of similar aspect and other characteristics. After digging the pit, lightly brush the strata to expose the cross section of the snowpack clearly. Ice crusts, weak bonds between snow layers, and particularly depth hoar will show up. Take a handful of snow from each of the layers and try to from a snowball. If it holds together well, then that layer is probably stable. If the entire snowpack exhibits this cohesive tendency, then in the absence of poor bonds between layers or an underlaying surface of ice or depth hoar, it is probably quite stable.

The safest routes follow ridge crests on the windward side below the potential fracture line of a cornice. On dangerous open slopes or wide couloirs, climb up or down the edges in a straight line; switchbacks in the middle of the slope are likely to cause an unstable slope to slide. Traverse dangerous slopes or couloirs at the top, above the release zone, if possible. If you can't cross above the release zone, it is worth making an even longer detour below the slope to cross on a flat well away from the bottom of the slope, if possible.

If you must cross a suspect slope, only one person should cross at a time, the others waiting their turn in a safe location, keeping a careful eye out for the exposed individual. Roped belays are only useful on small slopes. The force of a major avalanche makes it impossible to hold a victim. Do not assume that a slope is stable simply because one person crossed it safely; each person must be watched carefully while crossing. Pick your line to take advantage of rock outcrops, ridges, or other havens.

While traveling in dangerous areas, unhook the waistbelt of your pack, remove your ice-axe or ski-pole straps, unhook the safety straps to your ski bindings, and ensure that you can quickly drop your pack if necessary. Beware of gear slings and runners over pack straps that make it impossible to rid yourself of this very effective "snow anchor." Wear your gloves and hat, and secure all openings in your clothing to avoid frostbite and hypothermia if you are caught and trapped in an avalanche.

If you are caught in an avalanche, get rid of all equipment and your pack, and try to stay near the surface of the tumbling snow by "swimming." Direct your efforts to making your way to the side of the avalanche. As the snow slows down, keep your hands in front of your face, trying to create an air pocket when the snow stops. You will survive longer when you are buried if you do not panic, giving your partner(s) time to find you.

The members of the party who are not involved in the avalanche should mentally mark the spot where the victim was first caught, and also the place last seen. A fan-shaped area bisected by an imaginary line drawn between the first and last places seen is the most likely area for the victim to be found. Articles of clothing or equipment may indicate the location of the victim and should be quickly checked by probing with a special probe, ski pole, or ice axe in the immediate vicinity. If this fails to locate the victim, probe and scuff the snow in the fan-shaped area, especially in the places you somehow feel might be most likely to yield results. If the hasty search does not locate him or her, do a grid search, probing the area first at three-foot intervals, and finally every foot. Go for help only if all this fails. *You* are the victim's most likely savior. Chances of survival diminish rapidly after the first half hour, but people have been known to survive for twenty-four hours.

After successfully locating and freeing the victim, treat for suffocation, shock, any traumatic injuries, and, finally, for hypothermia and frostbite, if appropriate. Do not remain any longer than necessary in an area exposed to further avalanche danger.

First Aid

Even the most careful and experienced climbers will, at some point, need to provide emergency medical assistance to themselves or to someone else. The alpinist who does not take the time to become proficient in advanced first aid is neglecting to accept a moral duty. A thorough understanding of basic bodily processes and anatomy also serves the climber well when it is time to choose clothing and food to take into the mountains. Most clubs and organizations offer first aid courses and medical seminars specially tailored to the needs of climbers. You should attend these.

Intuitive Avoidance of Danger

Mountain hazards can be avoided by two methods. The first is the scientific, or textbook, approach that monitors conditions through the use of thermometers, hydrometers, barometers, wind meters, inclinometers, snow pits, shear tests, and other carefully plotted observations. This approach is very appropriate and should be carefully studied and adapted.

But the scientific approach to avoiding hazards should be viewed as an adjunct to, rather than a replacement for, an intuitive rapport with the mountain environment. No matter what your instruments and rational observations say, if you have a deep-seated feeling that conditions just are not right, then do not go on. At times you will find you have misinterpreted your feelings and turned back for the wrong reasons, but eventually you will learn to separate those unfounded feelings of dread from the genuine subconscious, computerlike accumulation and evaluation of data bombarding your senses from all angles and perspectives.

Taking Responsiblity

Falling rock, collapsing cornices and seracs, storms, loose rock, hidden crevasses, weak snowbridges, and avalanches are often termed "objective" hazards, since there is apparently little the climber can do to

Catherine Destivelle climbing the final snow arête to the summit of Switzerland's Eiger after making the first female solo of the North Face in the winter of 1992 *(Photo: Jeff Lowe)*

alter them. But such hazards, as well as cold and altitude, are often used to excuse accident or tragedy. However, haven't we chosen to expose ourselves to these possibilities in our decision to spend time in the mountains? Should we not accept the responsibility for our decisions and their resulting consequences? If we do admit that a skull broken by a falling rock or a life smothered by an avalanche is our fault, then aren't we more likely to be extra cautious, scrupulously avoiding times of excessive danger, doing our utmost to learn all we can about the rhythm of the mountains and inserting ourselves into that rhythm only at appropriate times and places? Shouldn't we have the patience to wait if necessary and never to go in those places that are always unsafe?

We should cross the zones of rockfall only when the rocks are frozen solidly in place, avoiding the morning thaw and evening freeze. We should allow enough time for new snow to settle and stabilize before we commit ourselves to the avalanche slope. We should rope up when snow hides the crevasses, unrope to move faster when that is appropriate, be prepared for freezing temperatures and storm, allow time to acclimatize adequately, test our holds before weighting them, all the while listening to and trusting both our intuition and intellect, never gambling recklessly.

Absorbing the Mountain Essence

Ambition feeds on itself; it can never be satisfied; you can only let go of it.

—Doug Scott

Success in ice climbing depends as much on attitude as on the mastery of individual skills. Whether you can gain the maximum enjoyment of the sport by advancing as rapidly as possible depends to a large extent on how you view yourself. Leave preconceptions behind; open up all your senses and feelings; try to do something new without passing judgment on your own or others' efforts to learn.

Moving on Snowy Terrain

Snow Climbing

Snow climbing may not be as exciting to do or watch as hard ice climbing, since it lacks the "fly on a pane of glass" quality, but snow often requires a more refined understanding and technique. On a double-corniced Alaskan ridge or a steep face of Andean cheese ice, insecurity reaches a zenith never matched in other types of ascent.

Timing and Route Finding

More than any other consideration, when and under what conditions you do a snow climb determine how difficult and/or insecure the ascent will be. For instance, a prolonged warm spell followed by a hard frost will turn a hillside of bottomless mush into a delightful slope of crisp névé, which in the morning may be too hard to climb without crampons, but which will yield perfect steps at 10:00 A.M., after an hour's exposure to the sun. In another hour the snow may rapidly regress to its former sloppy midday state, requiring three or four times the effort and time. Learn to predict when such "windows of opportunity" exist in the mountains and develop this skill at prediction through thoughtful observation. Capitalizing on your mistakes imparts the deepest knowledge.

Just as important as *when* you climb is *where* you climb. On any given day conditions will vary greatly from one aspect of a mountain to another. You may travel on good windpack on the lower East Ridge, flounder through three feet of dangerous sugar snow as you traverse out beneath the North Face, which may offer a path up the edges of spindrift-gouged avalanche runnels, and finally reach the consolidated snow on the southern slopes—perhaps softened just enough to allow a wonderful sliding descent back to camp at 1:00 P.M.

Each facet of the mountain also contains a multitude of subtle conditions, less dramatically variable than those found on opposite sides of the hill, but just as important to the climber. You will learn to

Left: **Piolet manche,
that is both hands
on the head of the
axe, shaft plunged
into the snow**

Above and opposite page: **To self-arrest,
drag your pick . . .**

(Photos: Mark Wilford)

identify the slight difference in opacity of the thicker wind crust that just bears your weight, or the firm avalanche debris beneath a mantle of new snow.

Step-Kicking

In both hard and soft snow it is often necessary to kick steps. In hard snow a small platform to stand on is "sawed" into the slope with a forward thrust of the edge of the boot. In soft snow, kicking directly into the snow—sometimes with a tamping motion or two (or six or eight in very soft snow)—will yield a big step that shouldn't give way under body weight.

Self-Belay with Ice Axe

Unroped snow climbing is often safe, with the expectation that the support of the ice axe shaft, shoved as deeply as possible into the snow as a self-belay before each step, will be adequate to catch a slip before it turns into a fall.

Some people are adamant that the pick should point away from the body, thus making injury in a slip less likely and giving a more comfortable grip with the wide adze in the palm of the hand. Others insist the correct way is exactly the opposite, with the adze pointing forward. Their reasoning is that a self-arrest can be applied more quickly if the self-belay should fail. I do not feel strongly either way, but tend most often to point the pick forward because I find the adze provides a more comfortable support.

Self-Arrest

Using the ice axe self-belay and kicking good steps, you will rarely find yourself in an uncontrolled fall on snow. But such falls do happen, so the technique of self-arresting with the pick of the ice axe was developed to stop them.

For practice, you must find a slope with snow firm enough to slide on, and a good run-out. Obviously a slope above a drop-off or one that ends in a field of boulders is not the right place to learn. Do not wear crampons, as you could snag one and break your ankle. If, in a real fall, you are wearing crampons, bend your legs at the knees and keep your feet away from the snow. Although a fall can leave

. . . swing your lower body below you, away from the pick . . .

. . . roll onto the shaft, controlling the pick at just above shoulder level . . .

. . . hunch your weight over the shaft and dig in your toes. (Photos: Mark Wilford)

you in any position, even upside-down and backwards (about which more later), begin by trying to stop yourself from a position where your feet are pointing downhill and you are lying on your back. With one hand grasp the axe very near the spike, the shaft diagonally across your chest, the fingers of your other hand curled over the head of the axe, and your thumb wrapped around between the adze and the shaft. If your left hand is near the spike and your right hand is holding the head, let yourself slide a little and roll to your right, toward the pick of the axe. As you roll over onto the pick, gradually insert it into the snow to stop your slide. If the pick of the axe is in your left hand, roll to the left. If you roll toward the spike, it may catch in the snow as you roll, which will almost certainly wrench the axe from your hands. To keep the spike from catching as you apply braking force, pull up on it as you hunch your weight onto the pick. You can also dig the toes of your boots in for extra stopping power.

Once you have the skill to stop yourself at greater speeds from this basic position, try ever more exotic falls, always remembering the basic principles of rolling toward the pick and controlling the spike. The illustrations show the sequence for stopping an upside-down and backward fall. First, try to sit up a bit and drag the pick into the snow at about waist level. This provides a kind of pivot around which your feet can swing. At the same time, begin to roll toward the pick with your upper body. This eventually puts you in a position to effect a classic arrest.

Belays and Protection on Snow

Snow belays and protection are less reliable and require more skill than those on rock or hard ice. Luckily, however, the forces to be controlled are usually not as large, and with experience, roped climbing on snow can be safe enough. We have already discussed the first two lines of defense in snow climbing: self-belay and self-arrest. Ninety percent of the time these techniques will be effective even for a roped party. But if an axe is lost in a fall through a cornice or into a crevasse, an adequate belay must be arranged.

While the party is moving simultaneously over moderate terrain, the members, keeping the rope tight between them, should be prepared to stop another's fall with a self-arrest. When a fall occurs, the belayer instantly drops into arrest position. With practice, falls can be kept short this way, but it is

A sitting belay utilizes the snow between the belayer's legs as a sort of bollard and is backed up by a tie-in to the axe, a deadman, a snow stake, or a snow picket. *(Photo: Mark Wilford)*

best not to expect the technique to hold anything very severe.

The boot-axe belay is more reliable, though still only effective against relatively low forces. After a platform has been stamped in the snow, the rope is passed over the boot and around the shaft of the firmly planted axe. The belayer's weight is kept on both the boot and the head of the axe through a nearly straight arm, while a dynamic braking force is applied by pulling the rope back around the ankle with the other hand.

Still more secure is the sitting hip belay, backed up by the axe inserted horizontally into the snow, perpendicular to the force of a fall. Pass a runner around the middle of the shaft, cut an exit groove for the runner in the snow and have the belayer clip into the runner. If a U-shaped channel for the belayer to sit in is stamped into the snow, this belay can be quite strong.

Snow stakes or deadmen are used both to anchor belays and to provide protection on the lead. In certain hard snow conditions, snow stakes pounded vertically into the snow are quite strong. More often, however, a well-placed deadman is best. Pound the deadman into the slope at a 45° angle and make certain to cut a groove for the cable so that when it is loaded there is no upward force on the deadman.

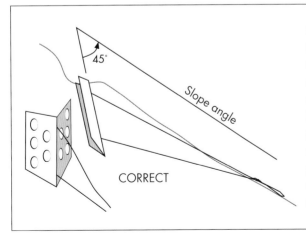

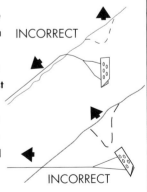

Pound in a deadman at an angle of 45° to the expected direction of pull and cut a slot for the cable at a 90° angle to the face of the deadman. This T-slot must be as deep as the deadman, gradually coming to the surface of the snow so there is no component of upward force exerted on the deadman through the cable.

In the boot-axe belay, shove the shaft of your axe as deeply into the snow as possible, stamp the boot of the uphill foot firmly in front of the axe to give it support, pass the rope over the toe of the boot, around the shaft of the axe, and back in front of the ankle to the braking hand, and lean your weight through your the uphill hand onto the head of the axe to give further support. To stop a fall, pull the rope back toward the rear of your boot, which increases friction. (Photo: Mark Wilford)

Use of Crampons in Snow Climbing

In soft snow crampons may be more of a hindrance than an aid in climbing. The snow will often form a clump between the points, making a heavy, rounded mass that is slippery and awkward to walk on. When you must wear crampons in soft snow, a shuffling gait will keep clumping to a minimum. In the worst conditions, however, you will find it necessary to knock the clumps off with the spike of your axe, sometimes on each step. A plastic or rubber plate that attaches to the bottom of the crampon between the points to reduce snowballing is available for some models. You can also fashion your own anti-balling plate from a sheet of plastic wired to the crampon frame.

When the snow is firm or overlays ice or rock, crampons become more necessary. In frozen névé you will find your points sinking all the way in under body weight, but your feet will stay on the surface. This condition is an ice climber's dream, and very steep slopes can be ascended with ease and security. On the other hand, sloppy wet snow over ice or powder snow over rock can make even gentle terrain quite hair-raising. In these conditions it is often best to frontpoint even on moderate angles, kicking hard to get through the slush, compact the snow into a platform, or attain some support from the underlying rock or ice.

Descending Snow

If there is no safe run-out, the slope is overly steep, or the snow is very hard, it is best to back down the hill, facing in and kicking your toes directly in. Keep your boot soles horizontal. Shove the shaft of your axe deeply into the snow, as low down as is comfortable before each step, thus providing a self-belay if your feet should slip. When the slope is long enough, the snow is good, and you feel confident that you can effect a self-arrest, it is faster to turn and face the valley, using the *plunge step* to go down. Lean far forward and transfer your weight completely with each step, digging your heels in deeply. Descent at a slight diagonal allows the spike and shaft of the axe to be planted low before each step for balance and as a safeguard against a slip; but when that isn't necessary, just walk down the slope with the axe in one or both hands, ready to arrest a fall. On spring and summer snow with a surface of sun-softened corn, you can skate down moderate- and lower-angled slopes in great diagonal strides, eating up distance in very little time. This is actually a modified *glissade*, which is the art of skiing down a slope on your boot soles.

Sitting glissade

Crouching glissade

Standing glissade, turning left

Glissading

In reality, the most basic glissade is not made on your feet at all, but rather inelegantly on your rump in the same manner as a child slides down a snowbank. This sitting glissade is used on snow that is too soft to allow sliding on your boot soles. A sitting glissade should not be used on harder snow, however, because there is less control compared with a crouching or standing glissade, although the lower position allows for a faster self-arrest.

Much drier and more enjoyable, though still somewhat awkward, is the crouching glissade. Hold the axe across your body in the self-arrest grip and apply weight to the spike to control your speed. You will find that turns are difficult, but note that it is easier to turn to the side on which you are dragging the spike. Obviously, then, if you want to turn right, but the spike is in your left hand, you will need to switch hands first. You must practice doing this quickly so unwanted speed does not build up during the switch. To stop, turn to the side with the spike

and apply greater force while simultaneously edging your boots and weighting them equally.

The most controlled glissade of all, and the one with the most potential for fun, is the standing glissade. If you are an expert skier you will take to this technique like a duck to water, but even if you are a newcomer you will be able to link turns and have a good time the first day out. Although the standing glissade is closely related to skiing, it is much easier and more natural since there are no long boards strapped to your feet. As in skiing, however, you will have to bend your knees quite deeply to develop control in turns and to be able to "swallow" bumps and other irregularities in the snow without upsetting your balance. With your back nearly vertical and your knees relaxed and bent, just point your knees in the direction you want to go, edging your boots into the snow at the same time. Keep your upper body quiet—the action should occur from the hips down. Hold the axe in either hand with the pick pointing forward to lessen the chance of

Standing glissade, turning right

(Photos: Mark Wilford)

Standing glissade, stopping. Plunge your axe into the snow for additional stopping power if necessary.

The first cut of a step should be the one closest to your body. With each cut thereafter, slice away successive layers of ice rather than attempting to break a chunk from the main mass.

stabbing yourself in a fall. The usual mistake is leaning back, which will cause your feet to scoot out from under you, depositing you on your backside in a flurry of arms and legs. If you feel your weight more on the balls of your feet than on the heels, you are properly balanced. During standing glissades you will want to feel your weight equally on both feet at all times. This will help to counter the tendency to lean into the slopes while turning, which also causes your feet to skate out from under you.

To come to a stop from a standing glissade, exaggerate the bend in your knees, at the same time reaching forward with the spike of your axe (reach downhill more than across the slope); turn your knees and edge your boots to the side holding the axe (but keep your upper body oriented more directly down the slope). Once you have slowed down enough, plunge your axe into the snow with a nearly straight arm and give an extra emphasis to your edge set. On many slopes it is not necessary to ram the axe in to stop, because proper edging with bent knees will eventually bring you to a halt.

Step-Cutting

Since the advent of curved picks and rigid crampons, few climbers have bothered to become expert at chopping steps, which is a time-consuming process. However, the technique is useful for those climbs when just an occasional step will obviate the need to carry crampons on mountain rock routes, or when a crampon is broken or dropped. Furthermore, in cutting belay and bivouac stances, a great deal of energy can be saved by using proper technique.

Above: **The North Face of Athabasca in the Columbia Icefields, a perfect schoolroom for learning alpine ice techniques.** *(Photo: Jeff Lowe)*
Below: **Teri Ebel gearing up at the Icefields Campground** *(Photo: Ian Tomlinson)*

Mentally outline the step before you make the first swing with the adze. Make a chop at the closest point to your body on the outlined step, and make successive cuts moving farther away. You will find that the ice behind the first chop is easier to remove. In hard snow the adze may enter the snow at an acute angle. A flick of the wrist at the end of the swing will pop out a large chunk. On hard ice, the adze should strike more obliquely in an effort to shave the ice away. If one pass leaves a step that is too small, make successive passes starting just below the first. On steep ice, once the basic step has been fashioned, the overhanging lip above the step can be quickly removed with a couple of blows of the pick.

A basic step is one that accepts the entire boot sole and slopes slightly into the mountain. A series of these would ascend in a diagonal line up the slope, though this may be modified in any number of ways to suit various situations.

Alpine Ice Techniques

Photos on pp. 121–155 are by Ian Tomlinson

Alpine ice climbing techniques cover all aspects of glacier travel, as well as climbing on seracs, ice cliffs, permanent ice faces, couloirs, arêtes, and ridges. The photos accompanying this section were taken in October in the Canadian Rockies in cold autumn conditions. It was my wife Teri's first experience with glaciers and alpine ice conditions. The techniques illustrated represent AI1 to 4 climbing, the normal range of alpine ice difficulties, although there are some exceptional alpine climbs that are harder. The techniques required to deal with those special alpine climbs are explained in the following chapter on waterfall ice techniques.

Glacier Travel and Crevasse Rescue

While it is true that some climbers manage to get away for years with unroped travel on snow-covered glaciers, far too many less fortunate others have been fatally surprised when an apparently safe expanse of snow collapsed and dropped them into the depths of an icy slot. Experience will help you to detect the subtle shadings and depressions that may indicate a hidden crevasse, but no one I know has climbed for long in an alpine environment and not fallen into a hole or two. Where the ice is bare, of course, the crevasses may be seen, and unroped travel is often justifiable; otherwise, use the rope.

For the rope to be a true safeguard, it must be properly employed. This means you must be prepared to stop a fall and to extricate yourself or another from a crevasse. The basic two-person party should tie into the ends of the rope normally, then each climber should take up one-third of the rope in coils and clip into the shortened rope with a figure 8 and locking carabiner. The extra coils may be carried over the shoulder. This extra rope is thus available once a fall has been held and anchored, to be thrown down into the crevasse to the fallen climber. A prusik and 12-foot loop of 7mm cord is tied just in front of the figure-8 knot or ascending device if one is available. If the fall has been successfully held, the axe shaft may be rammed through this loop into the snow and backed up as needed, and the load of the fallen climber can then be taken by the prusik or ascender, freeing the belayer to extract himself or herself from the rope and further assist the victim.

Roped "in thirds" for glacier travel, each climber carries one-third of the rope coiled over his or her shoulder, ready for use in crevasse rescue; the other one-third connects the two climbers.

If you are the one who has fallen, first remove your pack and hang it from the rope, then stand in your foot sling and right yourself. Once the extra ropes from the person on the surface have been lowered to you and have been padded with a pack or ice axe to keep them from burying themselves in the edge of the crevasse, you can then alternately slide up and stand in the foot sling, belayed by the other rope, until you have worked your way out of the crevasse. If the victim is injured or unconscious, mechanical pulley systems can be arranged, but these seldom allow one unaided person to hoist another.

Careful route finding will make a fall into a

No matter how careful you are, eventually you will fall into a thinly bridged crevasse, such as this one. . . . Here I'm dropping the free end of the rope down to Teri. . . . Teri tied in to the free end of the rope and I put her on belay. Then she stood in her prusik, unclipped from her locking carabiner, and hung her pack from her old tie-in point.

crevasse less likely. Traveling against the general grain will lessen the chances of all members falling into the same crevasse, and a tight rope as you walk will keep falls short. Remember that there are generally fewer crevasses where the ice is under compression, such as in dips and the inside of bends in the glacier. Where the ice flows over a hump or on the outside of corners, you will find more crevasses.

If you must cross a suspect snowbridge, it is best for one person to set a boot-axe or other appropriate belay in advance while the leader gingerly probes with an axe to ascertain the strength of the snow before lightly walking or crawling (to distribute the weight better) over the bridge. The other members should be belayed across as well. Snowshoes and skis

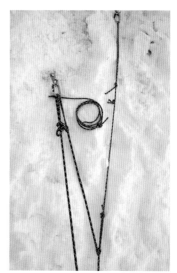

The anchor set-up. The rope to Teri is held by a prusik knot, backed up by a tie-off to the second anchor. I am using the rope directly from the second anchor as my belay at the edge of the crevasse.

Above: **Traveling parallel to the crevasse pattern puts climbers at risk of falling in simultaneously . . . while walking crosswise to the crevasse pattern reduces that risk. Once across the crevasse field, I belayed Teri through using a standard belay anchored to my ice axe.**
Below: **Higher on the glacier we found some crevasses still spanned by snowbridges made of the previous winter's snow. A belay and careful probing were called for. . . . Eventually we came to a crevasse with no easy way around. With an attentive belay from Teri, who was situated well back, I calculated the distance, took the appropriate number of coils in my hand, got a start, and made a leap for the other side, dropping the rope coils in mid-air, and preparing to make a self-arrest upon landing. Teri opted for a long detour.**

On our second day we took a beautiful walk to an ice slope on the northeast side of Athabasca to practice low-angle techniques.

effectively spread body weight over a large area and often make such crossings safer.

The huge masses of ice in seracs and icefalls are unpredictable, since their movement is affected more by the glacier's continuous downward motion than by superficial freeze and thaw. Therefore, whenever possible, avoid routes that require travel through icefalls or exposure to seracs. In those rare instances when, for whatever reason, you choose to accept these risks, remember that speed is the most important safety factor.

Climbing Low-Angle Ice

Depending on the quality of the ice, a natural progression for climbing low-angle ice (up to about 45°) is as follows.

On flat ground walk normally (*pied marche*), but with a stance that is slightly wider than usual to avoid having your crampons snagging the other foot or trouser leg. Hold your axe (*piolet*) in one hand by the head like a cane with the pick pointing forward. On slight inclines, splay your feet like a duck, *en canard*, and follow a straight line. As the slope steepens, make a diagonal ascent and bend your ankles to allow all except the front crampon points to penetrate. Up to 35° or so it is most convenient to keep the axe in the uphill hand as a walking stick, *piolet canne*, but above that angle, with a reasonably long axe, it is best to hold the axe diagonally across your body, *piolet ramasse*, with the inside hand near the spike and the other hand on the head with the pick pointing forward. Whichever way you hold the axe, keep your feet flat, *pied à plat*, to the slope with toes horizontal or pointing downhill slightly as it gets steeper. As you take each step, alternately crossing the feet over each other, you will be moving from a position of balance to one that is out of balance. Move your axe *before* making each step, not during the step.

When it is time to change direction, make a step with the toes pointing slightly uphill, as if you were stepping into the out-of-balance position. But now, instead of crossing the trailing foot over the lead foot, simply splay the hind foot in the new direction. Now switch hands on the axe and you are ready to head off in the new direction. If, because of very hard ice or a steeper angle, you find it awkward to make the full direction change by splaying your feet, you will find it more comfortable to make an inter-mediate frontpoint move with both crampons, between the two splayed-foot moves. Always while climbing ice, move only one point of contact at a time, and in a precise sequence. Avoid the tendency to rush in the beginning, and make certain each move is correctly executed and feels secure.

Descending Low-Angle Ice

Using an axe with a classically curved or slightly drooped pick, it is possible to descend securely either diagonally or facing directly out on slopes of up to 45°, once again depending on the type and quality of the ice. On névé and snow-ice you can descend diagonally *pied à plat* using the axe in the *piolet appui* manner—like a railing, with the head pointing diagonally down in your inside hand, pick punched, but not swung, into the snow. On harder

Roped together on a short rope we made our way in diagonal switchbacks up the beginning ice and snow slopes. Originally we used pied à plat with our ice axes held piolet canne in our uphill hands with picks pointing forward (top). . . . To change directions from right to left, we would stop on a right foot, splay our left foot in the new direction, and shift the axe from the left to the right (uphill) hand, allowing us to head up and left. With each step we plunged the spike of our axe into the snow or ice for additional bal-ance and as a self-belay. A turn to the right was accomplished in reverse order (bottom). Here I have already made my turn and Teri is ready to turn off her left foot.

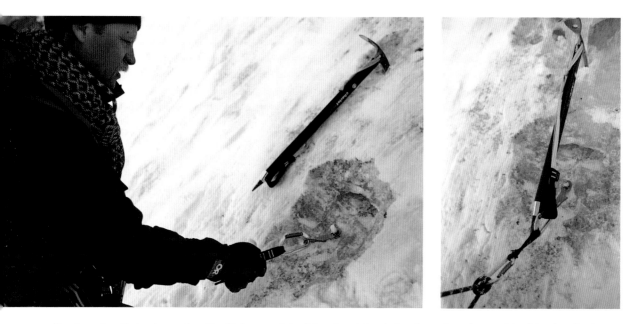

At a place where the ice steepened considerably I set up a belay. I first cleared three inches of granular and unconsolidated ice, then placed a screw roughly 15° beyond perpendicular into the ice, until the eye was flush with the surface. . . . I planted my axe deeply and clipped into it as a backup, thus fashioning a perfectly adequate belay for the low-angle ice we would be climbing.

ice, squat down and plant the pick in an upside-down *piolet ancre* as low as possible, which is called *piolet rampe*. As you step down, a slight outward force on the shaft will lock the pick into the ice and allow you to make aggressive and positive steps down. Sliding your hand down the shaft lets you make two or three steps without replanting the tool. The axe can be quickly removed by popping the shaft back against the ice, grasping the head, and pulling out along the smooth top surface of the pick. This technique is not secure with reverse-curve picks, as pulling out on the shaft dislodges the pick. Coming straight down the fall line in this manner, with toes splayed, en canard, and the feet about shoulder width, is the most secure means of descent.

On very low-angle terrain, simply face the valley and hold the axe piolet canne. Positive weight transfer with each step in all these techniques is an essential element of security. The type and quality of the ice and the skill of the climber will determine at which angles and under what conditions these classical "French" techniques may be employed.

Climbing Moderate to Steep Ice

On most types of ice above 45°, flexing your ankles enough to get all the points in is quite difficult. Here it is more natural to frontpoint. Depending on the type of ice and your own preference and skill, for angles of up to about 60° or so, one of two basic techniques is useful. Either use pure frontpointing combined with one or two tools held in the palm(s), *piolet panne* (adze in palm of hand, pick in the ice), or alternate frontpointing with one foot and using the other foot sideways, *pied troisième*, in conjunction with the axe placed every second step as an anchor, *piolet ancre*. Generally, the first technique is faster, while the second is more secure and reduces strain on the calves. In practice on a long climb, you may find yourself switching between these methods.

Above 60° on most ice you will find pied troisième

Next we worked on various low-angle ice techniques. Upper left: Here I'm using the axe piolet panne in my left hand. My right hand is for balance, and my feet are pied troisiéme. The angle of the ice is about 40°, or class 2. Upper middle: In this detail of pied troisiéme, one foot is frontpointing and the other is splayed across the ice, ankle flexed to allow all the points to penetrate. Upper right: Using the second tool piolet panne gives another point of purchase. Frontpointing with double piolet panne allows very fast climbing on ice of 40° to 50°, but the harder the ice, the less secure it is, and the greater the confidence required. Lower left: More secure and less strenuous is pied troisiéme combined with piolet ancre. Lower right: In the middle of the slope I set up a second belay, cutting a bollard, anchoring to it with the climbing rope, and backing it up with my ice axe.

Above: **Teri followed, practicing the techniques.**

Below: **I also had her practice traversing using pied troisième with double piolet panne . . . and crossing her feet one in front of the other rather than shuffling sideways.**

Opposite page: **When it was time to go down, the bollard became our rappel anchor.**

Far right: **Lower down I kept Teri on a tight rope as she learned to walk down the low-angle slopes. At first her steps were somewhat hesitant. She sat back and wanted to turn her body across the slope . . . but after some coaching she learned to face directly down the fall line and transfer her weight completely with each step, using the axe in the piolet canne position.**

combined with the axe held in self-arrest position in front of the body (which allows you to punch the pick into soft ice with each couple of steps) to be a very useful technique. If the ice is slightly harder, frontpointing with both feet and using a tool in each hand like a dagger, *piolet poignard*, will increase your security. Or you can use the pied troisième/piolet ancre technique. As the ice steepens and becomes harder, you will eventually need to use a technique called *piolet traction*. This involves frontpointing with both feet and using a tool in each hand that is planted piolet ancre with each step or every other step, for balance, and used as a handhold on which to pull up. Piolet traction is often abused by beginners and even experienced climbers. On ice under angles of 50° it forces you to "crawl" inelegantly and waste energy by virtue of being out of balance. It is better to use this method only when it is truly required by the angle or condition of the ice.

When frontpointing, your heels should never be higher than your toes. Standing straight up in balance over the frontpoints with calves relaxed and heels low is actually more secure than if you are tensely poised on tip-toe. Similarly, on any but the steepest ice (or on rotten ice where the surface needs clearing), repeated fierce kicking of the frontpoints does little to promote security, while a gentle but carefully aimed and weighted kick preserves the integrity of the ice and conserves energy.

Text continues on page 138

Top: **Impressed by the beauty and wonder of the day's experiences, Teri paused to reflect during the walk back to camp.** Bottom left: **Our third day dawned clear, and as we headed for the Skyladder Route on Andromeda, the upper part of the mountain's east face was lit warmly by the rising sun. The icefall on the approach to the Skyladder was broken at this time of year, and there was no way to avoid climbing through it to reach the foot of the face.** Bottom right: **We discovered a fairly safe route through the seracs, chimneying through one slot and traversing around a long tower into a broken corridor. Above is the summit of the West Shoulder of Andromeda.**

Left: **The rope weaving in and out of the ice blocks and towers offered sufficient security against a fall, so to save time I placed no ice screws until the rope came tight. Locating a relatively stable section of ice, I set up a belay from screws and brought Teri over.** Top right: **A single ice axe in the anchor position (piolet ancre) offered sufficient security for climbing out the other end of the crevasse and allowed quicker progress than would have been possible using both hand tools planted in the ice with each step.** Bottom right: **Teri did an excellent job balancing and stemming on the ice blocks in the bottom of the crevasse, using her hands whenever possible, and she soon joined me. By the time we had traversed the icefall and glacier above, the storm predicted by the previous evening's high cirrus clouds had moved in, and we abandoned the climb.**

Top: **After a rest day in Lake Louise, we set out for the Neil Colgan Hut above Moraine Lake. We planned to spend a few days there, climbing on the North Face of Mount Fay. Our approach would take us up the broad couloir in the left quarter of the photo. Known for heavy rockfall in warm weather, the 3-4 Couloir is a class 2 snow climb in the early season.** Bottom: **We figured the autumn cold would limit the rockfall, and the hard late-season ice would give us a chance to practice 40° to 50° techniques.**

As the gully steepened 1,500 feet from the top, snow gradually gave way to ice. To begin with this allowed us to practice our French technique.

In piolet ramasse, the axe is held diagonally across the body, and the spike is used for balance. Ankles are flexed—pied à plat—to get crampon points in the ice and a diagonal ascent is made.

A right turn is made off the left foot, right foot splayed in the new direction. Hands change position on the axe . . .

. . . and you set off in the new direction . . .

. . . crossing one foot over the other.

Teri found the ice too hard for a comfortable piolet ramasse, and she adopted a very natural rhythm of pied troisième/piolet canne.

Six or seven rope-lengths from the top, we were surprised by several volleys of rock, one of which struck our photographer, Ian, a bruising blow to his shoulder. I sought a sheltered belay in a crevasse at the side of the couloir, feeling somewhat foolish for miscalculating the hazard. Teri joined me at the belay (top). After assessing the configuration of the terrain above, it seemed safe enough to continue, so long as we stuck to the far right side—climbing the moat between ice and rock at times. Leading on frontpoint and piolet ancre above the crevasse belay (bottom left), I ran out full rope-lengths to belays in safe locations on the rock to the top of the couloir. A few more rocks did fall in the upper reaches but generally down the left and center portions of the funnel. Teri remained calm and plugged away at the rock-hard ice, preferring to use full piolet traction technique (bottom right). The 50° black ice would be rated AI2 or 3.

We found our way in the dark across the glacier at the top of the climb, arriving at the Colgan Hut tired but happy that my poor choice of route hadn't had more serious consequences than Ian's injured shoulder. A foot of snow fell during the night, and the storm continued all the next day and most of the following one, confining us to the hut, where we kept ourselves entertained by eating, reading the log book, and sampling Ian's fine scotch.

The patience to maintain morale while waiting out storms is an important asset in alpine climbing. The storm finally cleared on the afternoon of our second day in the hut, revealing an impressive view of Mount Hungabee. We went outside to greet the sun and to stretch our legs in the late-afternoon light, limbering up for an early start in the morning.

As usual when a cold front pushes out a storm, the next morning was cold, clear, and beautiful. In almost-winter conditions we headed for a series of bulges on the eastern icefall of Mount Fay's North Face (top left), where we could practice techniques for 50° to 105° ice. We found a good bulge up to 70° on the second pitch. I placed a screw (bottom left) and climbed this AI3 section using both my axe and North Wall hammer (right) . . .

. . . and alternating my feet in pied troisième (above left).

Climbing well, Teri followed with full piolet traction, using her shorter, lighter tools, which she was finding very functional for her, as they allowed for accurate swings (bottom and top right).

By going the steepest way we found class 4 terrain on 85° ice on the fourth rope-length. I placed another screw to protect the moves at the top of the bulge . . . which was steep enough to force me to use piolet traction, hanging straight-armed and walking my feet high between tool placements. . . . The angle soon relented to about 60°, and I ran the full rope out to a belay. On alpine ice routes, speed is an important safety factor, and it is good to get used to climbing with a minimum of protection, treating your tool placements as portable belays.

Coming second, Teri used good technique, keeping her body away from the ice . . . until it became steep enough to require a hips-in/back-arched body position for good axe swings.

Traversing and Descending Steep Ice

If you must traverse on steep ice, you will get the most out of each tool placement if you place your tool diagonally as close to your body as possible, just above shoulder height. Then lean as far as possible in the direction of the traverse and place the other tool diagonally at a comfortable arm's reach. You can either take small sideways steps, or, if you are feeling confident, you may cross one foot in front of the other.

Descending steep ice is best done in a similar manner. Place one tool off to the side and as low down and close to your body as you find comfortable. A slight lieback off this tool will allow you to take several steps down, at which time you are ready to place the other tool low down and diagonally off the other side, ready to repeat the procedure. A more secure descent on thin or rotten ice is made by simply backing

With time running out (Teri and I had a plane to catch), I rushed at the steepest line through the upper ice cliff, immediately encountering vertical AI5 conditions . . . which soon became overhanging AI6 and would have been even more difficult if I hadn't run out of steam below the last 25-foot 15° overhang. In the end I was forced to hang on screws to rest.

There was no time left for Teri to try the pitch, and as I explained to her, alpine ice is seldom harder than class 4 anyway. She had had a classic, realistic introduction to the techniques, hazards, and beauty of alpine ice, and she loved it!

straight down with small steps and short placements of the tools at about head level or just above. Placing the tools off to the side allows a better swing and firmer placements, while going straight down gives greater control and allows both tools to remain planted while you step down.

The Coldest Dance: Waterfall Ice

To the extent that a person loses his ability to concentrate, he himself becomes powerless to accomplish, to enjoy, and above all, to love.

—Timothy Gallwey, *Inner Skiing*

We have bicameral minds. Our left brains function analytically; our right brains are more creative. Western culture favors logic and reason over emotion and feeling. This tendency has divorced us somewhat from our senses. In ice climbing it is best when we reinhabit our bodies. The center or balance point from which all movement and all awareness originates is located in the lower abdomen. Anyone who has turned a somersault knows this center, and so, for that matter, does anyone who has "rolled out of bed." Functioning from the center allows us to remain calm in the midst of external confusion. Through sensitized hands, feet, eyes, ears, and noses, real information can go straight to this source of power, where a balanced response is automatic, bypassing the mental screen of ideas, values, beliefs, and conditioning that can put a 90° bend in reality.

The exercises below are designed to help you find your center and get clearer input from your senses. This will allow you to get more out of ice climbing. The mechanics are important, too, however, and here you will find each technique broken down into its component parts. Movements are isolated in the photos as if they were complete in themselves. As you read the captions and study the photos, it is up to you to visualize the flow. Imagine yourself in the pictures; but go further and make a movie out of the stills. Run through the sequences until they are

smooth mentally, and when you actually try them on ice, they will be much more comfortable.

When you do go to the ice, go with an experienced friend or an instructor. After you have donned crampons, insist on taking a little time before you start to climb, and do these things:

1. Open up and start feeling, seeing, hearing, and smelling. Replace expectations with an awareness of the cold seeping up through your boots into the balls of your feet; wriggle your toes to warm them. In a similar fashion, check out the rest of your senses and extremities.

2. Determine the true angle of the ice you have come to practice on. Take two ski poles or ice axes of equal length. Hold one vertically with the point on the slope and make a right angle pointing toward the slope by holding the other pole or axe horizontally at the top. If the horizontal pole or axe fully outstretched just touches the slope, then the angle is 45°. If the appendage doesn't reach, then the angle is less than 45°. If the horizontal member forms a T with the vertical brace when the point touches the slope, then the angle is greater than 45°. Study the detailed structure of the ice.

3. Isolate as many muscle groups as you can and alternately tense and relax each one, starting with your head and working down. Concentrate especially on the calf muscles.

4. Breathe slowly and deeply until your breathing is smooth and relaxed.

5. Still breathing evenly, do some stretching exercises.

6. Recall the last time you felt real confidence. Hold that feeling.

7. With both knees slightly bent and feet at shoulder width, take a step forward, but just before transferring your weight, step back. Do this with both feet and feel your center of gravity.

Now you are ready to climb.

The photographs in this chapter were taken during an extended lesson on Colorado waterfall ice,

Bird Lew and I spent several days in Boulder Canyon covering WI1 to 4 ice techniques, which have already been covered in the alpine ice techniques section of this book. We then traveled to Ouray, Colorado, to work on more advanced techniques.

with Bird Lew as my student. Bird has a long history of rock climbing, including traditional self-protected routes, as well as modern sport-climbing competitions. She had previously done a small amount of high-mountain snow climbing with crampons, but had never experienced technical ice. Although we spent a week on the basics of ice climbing up to WI4, the techniques required for waterfalls are essentially identical to the alpine ice techniques previously discussed. In any case, most waterfall ice climbs have a difficulty of WI3 or more. Here we will join the

lesson at the beginning of week two in Ouray, Colorado. The following waterfall ice and mixed climbing techniques are also applicable to extreme high-mountain ice climbs.

Climbing Extreme Ice

As you approach the vertical, there will come a time when you will no longer be able to stand in balance over your frontpoints. Although it is possible by brute strength to hold yourself vertically up against the ice, a far more efficient method is something I have termed the *monkey hang*.

Beginning at the bottom of a near-vertical, vertical, or gently overhanging section of ice, the correct sequence is as follows:

1. Plant both hand tools comfortably high and far enough apart so that there is no danger of fracturing out the ice between them. Now, hanging straight-armed from the tools and letting the wrist loops do their intended job of holding the heel of the hand so as to allow a light grip on the shafts, walk your feet up the ice until you are in a mild crouch. Since your buttocks are away from the ice in this position, your weight will be pushing your frontpoints into the ice rather than applying a shear force.

2. Now look ahead and choose the exact spot where you will make your next placement. Still hanging straight-armed, loosen the appropriate tool in preparation for easy removal and replacement.

3. With your loosened tool merely hooked in its hole, keep your eyes glued to the exact spot you have chosen for replanting it and, in one smooth sequence, stand up, remove the tool, and positively replant it in the chosen spot.

4. At the instant of penetration, ascertain that the placement is solid and trustworthy and instantly weight the tool with a straight arm. This leaves you in position to replant the other tool and repeat the sequence, or to remove an ice screw or piton from your rack and place protection for continuing the lead. This one-handed method of

Text continues on page 156

Left: **To improve footwork and increase awareness of the configuration and quality of the ice, we spent some time climbing without hand tools on a steep toproped pitch. I have always found this an enjoyable and eye-opening exercise, where all free rock-climbing techniques come into play. . . . Bird's natural finesse was evident, and I think she preferred to climb without the awkward tools in her hands.**

Below: **We broke our first climb, Tubular Bells, in the Uncompahgre Gorge into two short, distinctive pitches.**

The first pitch consisted of a mixture of natural handholds and hooking on cauliflowers, as well as a few chimney moves protected naturally and well with a runner draped around an ice mushroom.

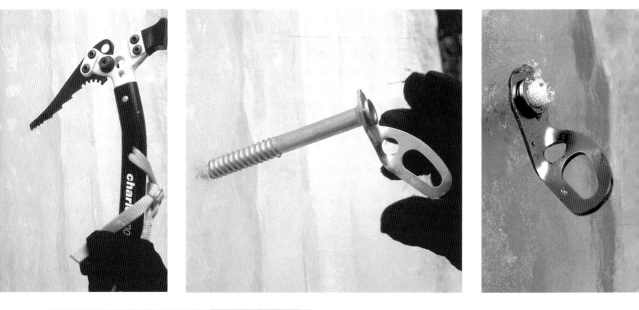

Above: **On a good ledge between two pillars I set up a belay. With the pick of my ice tool I made a good starting hole for an ice screw. . . . Then I placed a screw about 5° or 10° beyond perpendicular to the surface of the ice . . . and continued turning it in until the eye was flush to the surface.**

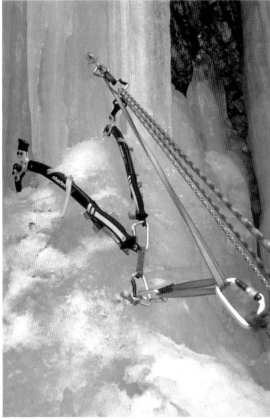

Left: **I placed a second screw two feet above the first and clipped a double-length runner into both. I tied myself into a carabiner which I had clipped into a twist in the runner in such a way as to equalize the force on the screws. I backed up the belay with my tools and clipped the rope to Bird through the upper anchor. If we had been swinging leads this would have been Bird's first point of protection as she passed me and began her pitch.**

When Bird followed she used more natural handholds than I had—a style she was rapidly developing. On a toprope this seemed a good way for her to conserve energy, but on the lead pushing the use of natural holds too far can sometimes be more precarious than using the tools. This pitch was an excellent introduction to WI5- climbing.

Above: **On the next lead I took the steepest line on the pillar, using a modified monkey-hang technique on the WI5+ crux. . . . I waited until I could stand on a basketball-sized lump of ice to place a runner around a small natural column and back that up with a drive-in tube piton. Thus, well-protected, I walked my feet high in an L-position, which allowed me to clear the bulge at the top of the pillar in a secure and controlled manner.** Below: **Bird found the climbing very strenuous, with few opportunities for natural handholds. In particular chopping the piton most of the way out used a good portion of her reserves. From this point on she would call tube pitons "the dreaded drive-ins!" Even so, she shook out and successfully climbed to the top.**

Our next climb was a new route we called Birdcage, in honor of my student. We avoided a possible easier start and began by doing a strenuous diagonal traverse at the lip of an overhang fifteen feet above the ground. I was forced to frontpoint on icicles below the rock roof and make a series of diagonal cross-over pick placements (left) . . . until I could finally stand up and get a good stick in thicker ice on the vertical slab above (WI6-) (lower right). . . . A stretch of easier climbing ended another short pitch on a two-foot-wide belay ledge. I placed rock anchors here (upper right).

Above: **Bird followed the first pitch extremely well, and it became obvious to me once again just how valuable a solid background in free climbing can be to a beginning ice climber. Although it would be imprudent of Bird to begin leading ice very soon, she was able to progress rapidly through the levels of difficulty and enjoy each new technical challenge, finding satisfaction even on a toprope.**
Right: **The second pitch began with one foot and one hand on rock and the other foot and hand on ice.**

I found knifeblade protection in the rock for the difficult pick-torqueing, liebacking, and stemming moves (M6) to get established on the hanging ice. While hanging straight-armed from a good placement of my left tool, I placed a bomb-proof screw in solid ice at the base of the upper pillar.

A couple of diagonal pick placements (lower left) . . . and step-through lieback crampon moves (upper left) . . .

. . . allowed me to pull left around the corner onto the front of the pillar, where there was a ledge to put one foot flat and take a break. The final vertical pillar was still steep (WI5) but offered perfect terrain for classic monkey-hang technique.

Bird found the mixed moves—frontpoints on rock and picks torqueing in cracks—to be clumsy and strange, but she puzzled them out in a show of the phlegmatic fortitude that is one of her greatest strengths as a climber. She had to battle with another "dreaded drive-in" I had placed in the upper pillar, but once she had removed it she climbed in textbook straight-arm, butt-out, feet-high, precision-placement style. When she reached me, she was grinning and openly enthusiastic about her introduction to the joy of complex movement involved in high-level ice climbing.

The next day we delved deep into the Gothic terrain of a 150-foot mineralized golden labyrinth of chandelier-hung mushrooms draped from a huge rock cave and supported by a pillar of poorly welded pencil icicles which required smooth climbing to avoid slicing through with the picks. Crampon holds could be fashioned by kicking the entire toe into the friable surface, making an untrustworthy step. Protection on this 50-foot WI5+ section came only from the mind.

A second, more substantial, pillar led up into the overhangs. Although a fracture line bisected the base, I arranged good protection from screws to begin. The climbing was steep but psychologically less demanding. After twenty or thirty feet I was able to scum a shoulder back against one of the huge icicles (lower left), which allowed me to rest and place another screw in preparation for the crux section through the upper roofs. A couple of traverse moves directly to the right (upper left) put me in line with a groove through the overhangs. Finally, WI6 climbing led up into tight pick and crampon placements in a bomb-bay chimney (right).

Right: **On the initial fragile pillar, Bird was surprised by how nebulous pick and crampon placements can be in a mass that looks solid from a distance. Even handholds she tried would crumble unexpectedly in her grip. Her customary light step was inadequate in these conditions. From my position I could faintly hear Bird's self-encouragement as she dealt with the strange medium. She coached herself through the difficulties, remaining calm and focused as she took in new sensations and learned.**

Above: **Above the chimney thirty feet of hooking led up lower-angle cauliflowered ice to the top of the formation.**

In ethereal, fragile, chandeliered, overhanging terrain like this, an open-minded exploratory attitude is required. Careful, calculated, deliberate climbing, questioning every section of ice and anticipating the effect of climbing on it, whether it will collapse or support your ascent, is the only approach that offers the hope of consistent success and a long life. Bird was forced to focus extra attention on getting adequate pick placements in the confined space of the narrow, overhanging slot. She gave a yell of relief when she finally cleared the overhangs and was able to climb with her hands on the last cauliflowered section.

Our last morning in Ouray we climbed a hollow tube in 0°F conditions. . . . Although the walls of this particular tube were thick and solid, the fragile, eggshell-like nature of the formation was brought home to me halfway up when I planted a tool and the entire feature vibrated with a loud "CRACK." Gingerly I climbed to the top, avoiding placing any more protection so as not to add further stress. Just below the junction of the apex of the tube and the main ice formation I found the one-inch-wide fracture line. With a toprope and without screws in the upper tube, it was safe for Bird to follow the pitch and see for herself one of the potential hazards of waterfall ice climbing. *(Photos: Ian Tomlinson)*

placing protection is the simplest and purest on steep ice, but a deep and narrow starting hole for the screw or piton must be chipped. The technique conserves energy and allows long, clean, vertical ascents.

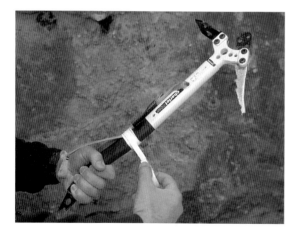

Taping the wrist loop to the shaft of your axe at a place close to the bottom grip reduces the strength necessary to hold on in vertical and overhanging situations. *(Photo: Brad Johnson)*

Clearing a Bulge

Often the most difficult moves on a pitch are at the top or where you must clear a bulge. The normal tendency is to reach far over and plant the tools as far back from the lip as possible. However, this makes it impossible to see your feet as you come over the bulge. What's more, you won't be able to keep your heels low enough as your tendons simply won't stretch that far, and you will find your frontpoints shearing out. It is better to plant your tools just over the bulge and climb and mantel on them until your feet are above the lip. Then replant your tools higher.

Grabbing and Hooking Natural Holds

On steep waterfall climbs you will often find features that provide good natural holds for hands, feet, and tools. Whenever a climb is chandeliered or cauliflowered, it is often better to look for handholds or to simply hook the features with your tools rather than to try to plant your picks solidly. You will find that wet wool gloves or mittens stick well to cold ice, sort of like ice climbers' chalk. With experimentation you will discover that it is more secure to lieback up a small pillar, hooking your picks behind the ice, rather than to risk shattering the fragile column.

Class 6 Ice Techniques

The monkey hang is a good pure technique for climbing well-formed vertical ice. However, you will often encounter grooves, pillars, overhangs, and other formations that make the climbing more difficult. On ice between 90° and 95° you can use a modified monkey hang that includes what I call a *cross-body lock*. This is a kind of turn-out maneuver where, instead of facing the ice directly as you pull up to replant your tool, you rotate sideways. If you are hanging from your right arm, for example, turn your left hip and shoulder into the ice, standing on the outside edge of your left crampon and inside edge of your right crampon. This locks your gently crooked right arm across your chest and allows a

Pigeon-toe frontpointing, keeping the feet perpendicular to the surface of the ice, is easier to accomplish with monopoints. The tripod effect created between the monopoint and the second set of forward-angled points can be more stable than a more standard dual-frontpoint configuration. *(Photo: Ian Tomlinson)*

high reach without the effort of hanging from a radically flexed bicep.

Always look for stemming possibilities that enable you to get the weight off your arms. Many times you can find a small bump of ice to rest on. Even on the steepest pillars you can do a *frog rest*, with your frontpoints together on the foothold and your knees splayed on either side of the pillar so that you are essentially sitting on your heels.

Waterfalls with multiple pillars, roofs, and other features often allow unusual rests. Never pass up an opportunity to take a break by assuming a *chimney position* in a groove or *scumming* a hip or shoulder behind an icicle. *Knee locks* can be achieved between a rock wall and a free-hanging curtain. Icicles can be straddled or encircled with arms or legs, and, if you have equipped your crampons with spurs, you can actually push yourself up the column. When a pillar has a very small diameter (two feet or less), it is necessary to crampon in a pigeon-toed fashion, ensuring that your frontpoints penetrate the ice perpendicular—horizontally and vertically—to the surface. For very technical waterfall ice climbs, spurs on the heel clamps of your crampons will allow you to perform very effective *heel hooks* on pillars, between icicles, and on roofs. Heel hooks are most often used to maintain balance in awkward situations, but occasionally can be useful in making upward progress.

Advantages of Monopoint Crampons

For several years I have chosen to use only monopoint crampons, which offer a number of advantages for waterfall ice climbing. With monopoints it is not crucial to keep your foot absolutely quiet after placing the frontpoint—your heel can swivel and turn as needed to execute backsteps or drop-knee moves, high steps on narrow pillars with your foot directly in front of your waist, or rock-ons over roofs and around corners. You can slot the frontpoint between icicles or take advantage of a single air bubble in the ice. On thin ice you can frontpoint in the same hooking nicks you have carved for your picks, thus avoiding the possibility of breaking the ice. On dry rock, monopoints allow precise use of incredibly small holds, and your foot can swivel without the danger of one frontpoint levering the other frontpoint off the rock, as is the case with dual frontpoints. Monopoints slot readily into knifeblade and bugaboo cracks, and they torque well in baby-angle-size cracks. And surprisingly, if the geometry of the monopoint and secondary frontpoints is correct, monopoints are more stable on pure ice. This is because of the tripod effect created when you drop your heel and the first set of forward-angled points contacts the ice in addition to the monopoint.

Thin Ice Technique

Many climbs of class 6 and above are actually on very thin ice or mixed rock and ice. Thin ice can be durable and well adhered to the rock (such as verglas),

or rotten and loosely anchored, or a solid sheet separated by some air space from the rock, or—worst of all—thin, rotten, and separated from the rock. Occasionally you may also encounter a thin-walled hollow tube of ice with water running inside. Thin ice must be treated gently.

If the ice is well bonded to the rock, gently chip small holds for your tools rather than trying to plant them with a forceful swing. Sometimes you will find a tiny air pocket that, with a light tap, will accept the pick and make a good placement. If the ice is less than vertical and you have modified the hooking angle of your pick sufficiently, you can simply scrape the pick down the ice until it begins to grab, then weight it some more to secure it. In all these cases, you must not apply any outward force on the shaft of your tools, but rather push directly down on your wrist loops, even as you move up. Crampons should

I made the first ascent of a thin-ice route called Silver-tongued Devil in Vail. The lower portion consisted of steep, poorly bonded, and poorly protected climbing, requiring delicate pick and crampon placements, always pulling down on the shafts of the tools, never applying an outward force even as I moved up past them. . . . The ice ended in a moss garden under a rock roof near the top. Slinging a rickety pillar with a double-length runner gave some protection as I made awkward moves up onto the moss, which provided shallow—but reasonably good—sticks for my tools. . . . The moves up under the roof were exceptionally awkward, especially since the pick placements in the moss had to be treated exactly the same as thin-ice placements, i.e., no outward pull on the shafts. *(Photos: Brad Johnson)*

Above: **Extremely thin ice on a vertical wall with small pillars is often best hooked in pockets at the side of the pillars and in locations where the ice is well bonded to the rock. Gently chipping a hold is all the ice will allow.**

Right: **Unable to arrange acceptable protection in the moss (I could only get a hook-type piton partway in before it bottomed on rock), I down-climbed and placed a screw in the top of the pillar, increasing the slim possibility that it might hold a fall by clipping a load-limiting Screamer sling to it. With this protection I was able to climb back up and drive a knifeblade piton in the corner underneath the roof. With these three pieces I felt safe in making the difficult and awkward (M6+ or 7-) dry-tooling moves up and left to the top of the climb. Placing my own protection in the difficult situations on Silver-tongued Devil added a dimension of psychological and physical challenge that is lacking in the other bolt-protected climbs in Vail.**

(Photos: Brad Johnson)

be placed in a similar gentle chipping manner, making several very light taps to chip small holds for your picks. Monopoints can be placed directly in the pick placements as you pass them.

On rotten, thin ice, your points will tend to slice through, so look for areas of greater density within the sheet of ice. Moving the pick just a few inches to one side or another will frequently yield a better hold. Occasionally you will have to continue pulling on your tool as it slices through the ice, hoping it will eventually grab something substantial enough to rely on. On such ice, it is often useful to attempt to climb on the underlying rock with your crampons; in other words, kick your points through the ice and scrape them down until you feel them hook on a rock hold, attempting to spread the weight between the ice and the purchase on the rock. Move smoothly in these conditions so as not to overstress any of your points of contact.

On thin, hollow sheets or tubes, stagger your tool and crampon placements one above the other to lessen the risk of fracturing the ice horizontally between two placements. Sometimes a thin, flat ice pillar on a steep rock wall will have small pockets behind it, which you can hook with your tools. These may provide the most security you can find. On this kind of ice an even better technique than chipping holds for your crampons is one I call *pressing*. Simply push your frontpoints into the ice and then, as you weight them (if they are sharp and your butt is well away from the ice), the points will penetrate. Hollow ice can sometimes be quite easy to climb. You can punch right through the ice with your tools, forming handholds that can later be used for your feet. When these conditions prevail, the difficulty is more of a psychological nature—there may be a real risk of falling through into a hollow tube. A tool (or tools) with a downward-sloping adze gives you another option for climbing thin, rotten ice; the tool's larger surface area can resist the tendency to slice through the ice.

Thick but rotten ice is often easier to deal with

using two long-shafted axes. These tools give more options for placements, and more force can be generated when they are swung to penetrate through surface layers. Rotten ice may be on the verge of collapsing, so beware.

Class 7 Ice

Very few pure ice climbs reach this level of difficulty. On alpine ice you may find an extremely overhanging pitch on a serac or ice cliff that merits this rating. On water ice there are situations where a curtain of overlapping icicles has formed a long, steeply overhanging, difficult-to-protect stalactite, pillar, curtain, or wall that could potentially warrant the classification. Keep in mind that tools with classical curves lock into the ice when you pull out on the shafts, and therefore become more secure on extreme overhangs. In contrast, pulling out on the shafts of reverse-curve picks on such terrain tends to disengage the tools.

Backstepping and *turnout* are two techniques that reduce the amount of strength required to reach high on overhanging terrain and plant your tools. On horizontal roofs of less than a body length, there are several choices for clearing the lip. In extreme cases, *heel hooking* one of your tools can take some weight off your arms for a short rest. *Stacking* tools is often useful, and occasionally a *figure 4* will allow a high reach to solid pick placement.

After making the high placement, a good way to clear the lip is to disentangle yourself from the figure 4, throw the foot opposite your high placement above the lip of the overhang, and plant the frontpoint, letting the other foot dangle for a minute as you roll up the arm that has the high placement. This creates a cross-body lock from which you can bring the dangling foot up in a quick movement, popping the frontpoint in above the lip. Then sit on that heel, flagging the other foot up and out for balance. From this position you can remove the lower tool and replace it higher, which establishes you above the roof. Call it the *gorilla grunt!*

Text continues on page 167

A gymnastic sport-climbing technique that can be used for clearing overhangs is the figure 4. Getting into position is difficult as you must cross the opposite leg up and over the crook of your arm (below left). . . . Then you hook your toe under the ice or against the rock, which allows you to lever your body into a high and stable position from which to swing your other tool (below center). . . . Finally, stacking tools will let you pull over the roof (below right) . . . and squat on one frontpoint, flagging the opposite foot high for balance (right), positioning yourself for climbing above the roof. In this case, you have made only four axe placements to clear the roof—a minimal number.
(Photos: Brad Johnson)

The gorilla grunt is a term I have coined to describe an efficient sequence of moves for clearing roofs. Here (opposite page) **I have my first good pick placement in the ice above the roof with my left tool, and I am preparing to hook my right tool over the head of the left tool, thus avoiding the need to get a stick with the right tool and making the next placement much quicker, since I don't have to remove the tool from the ice first.** . . . **Turning my body into my left arm shifts my right shoulder higher and allows me to get a high stick with my right tool without having to strenuously hold myself up by a crooked arm. I am also getting a heel-toe jam under the roof to take some weight off my arms and maximize the reach** (above, lower left). . . . **Shifting to the right, I have reversed the move to replace my left tool higher** (upper left). . . . **Again reversing the move, I get a final high stick with my right tool. My left foot is flagged out under the roof for balance** (right). *(Photos: Brad Johnson)*

Above: **There is now enough room for me to take a quick high step onto my right monopoint. At this point I can roll into my right arm again and place my left pick higher (not shown) . . . which allows me to bring my left foot up to the lip of the roof, and I'm now in a monkey hang, ready to continue above the roof.** *(Photos: Brad Johnson)*

A sequence of movements I call the orangutan hang is designed for climbing onto free-hanging curtains of ice from overhanging rock behind and spiraling onto the front faces of the curtains so the climb can be continued.

Opposite page: **A backhand swing is necessary** (below left) **to get a first stick in the curtain.** **(Practice it in advance of using it on a climb.)** . . . **Your arm will be in a crucifixion position** (below center). . . . **Then drop your feet from the rock, turn to face the curtain, plant your frontpoints high in the curtain and, with the tool that had been on the rock, get a high stick near the corner of the curtain** (below right).

Right: **This allows you to pull around the corner and get a new stick on the outer face of the curtain, in good position to continue up the climb.**

(Photos: Brad Johnson)

Above: **As in rock climbing, flagging one foot or the other off to the side is a useful technique for maintaining balance in awkward situations.**

Left: **Heel and toe hooks are a key to stabilizing yourself on pillars and in convoluted ice. Modifying your heel clamp with the addition of a one-inch bolt with the end left sticking out makes heel hooking much more secure. The bolt may be slightly sharpened, but this is not really necessary and can be a pain in the buttock when squatting on your heels to rest! Above: Stacking tools, one pick hooked over the other, is quite often an energy-saving and useful technique.**

(Photos: Brad Johnson)

Climbing Mixed Ice and Rock

Ice climbing, as defined in this book, includes climbing on rock and ice simultaneously, climbing snowed-up rock with crampons and/or hand tools, and making the occasional move or series of moves on dry rock that may be necessary to connect bits of ice.

Mixed climbing tends to defy analysis. Virtually every move is different, and you are, in fact, inventing the best techniques as you go. This sort of climbing provides the greatest challenge and intrigue. I have a few suggestions.

Crampons on Rock

On rock holds, frontpoints often provide the most secure foot placements; but whether you have placed the front- or sidepoints on a hold, any movement of your foot will tend to make dual frontpoints "walk" off the hold. Monopoints eliminate this problem. On very low-angle, smooth slabs, keeping all crampon points in contact with the rock will yield better results than trying to edge or frontpoint. On slightly steeper slabs the opposite is true, and a single point on a tiny crystal may provide all the purchase you are going to get.

Dry Tooling

All the moves that you make in free climbing on rock without tools—liebacks, mantels, crack jams, and so on—you can also make with tools. You have the additional choice of using any hold with your hand or your tool. Planning moves in advance is a complex exercise, but crucial for smooth movement on the hardest routes.

You can *hook* small or large edges with your tools. This requires a proper, steeply hooked pick configuration. Ice axes or hammers with steeply drooped picks hook well on rock holds, but if they are too steeply drooped, you will have difficulty getting them into corner cracks to torque them. A moderate droop or curve with a sharp hook configuration at the very tip of the pick permits the best torqueing, slotting, and camming in cracks, and still hooks well.

Torqueing is an art in itself. Any part of the axe can be used. The pick fits blade cracks well and, with pressure to the side of the shaft, can be used in slightly wider cracks. The adze takes over where the pick leaves off. Sometimes the thick part of the head at the junction of the pick can be used in a constriction, like a nut. The adze may also be used for these maneuvers, which are often combined with liebacking technique to move upward. Especially if the shaft is rubber-coated, it may provide a good hold in a constriction or when liebacking a wide, vertical crack. Because of its oval cross section, the shaft in its narrow profile can be inserted into cracks of roughly the same size, then cammed by pulling sideways on the pick. In wider cracks, you can lieback off a shaft that is inserted deeply into the crack.

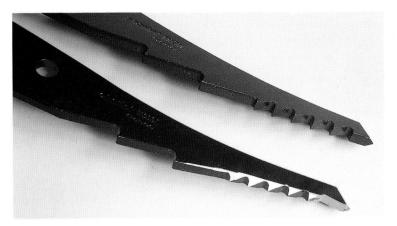

Most picks from the factory (top) need modification. Properly modified picks (bottom) have a very steep hooking angle at the first tooth, and the teeth are beveled on the sides, allowing positive hooking and easier removal. *(Photo: Ian Tomlinson)*

In the area of Vail's classic Rigid Designator, we could work on advanced technique for mixed climbing and thin ice. In the higher levels of difficulty (classes 6, 7, and 8), the climbing is most often mixed, thin, or both. *(Photo: Ian Tomlinson)*

Sometimes it is necessary to climb from under an overhang onto the back side of a hanging curtain and, once there, turn the corner out onto the front face. In this specialized situation use the *orangutan hang*, which requires skill in a *backhand tool swing*. You must practice this technique before you use it if you want to be able to get reasonably good sticks with your tools. The sequence begins with the *backhand swing;* then hang with arms outstretched, turn to face the ice curtain and scrunch up onto your frontpoints; place your other tool near the corner and, with the aid of a high heel hook around the side of the curtain, lever your body up into a position where you can plant a tool out on the face of the curtain and turn the corner.

Above us, gray rock showed here and there, with only thin streaks of ice. Time for gloves off and a bit of the bare-knuckle stuff, groping for rock holds in the powder and under verglas. It was painfully slow, with the hot aches to be endured, and it was an hour before I could traverse 'round a little corner back to where the gully reasserted itself. Here there was a cave of sorts and a bulging section beyond, where a chockstone barred the way. We had arrived at the famous crux pitch. A crack over on the right seemed to offer the best hope. One crampon scraped its way up this whilst the other scratched at a slab on the left as a mittened hand fumbled for rock holds. Sometimes a mittened handjam worked best, at other times a quick lob of the pick into a dribble of ice or a frozen sod. It was a style of climbing typical of the cliff's harder routes.

—Paul Nunn, describing Britain's Western Gully in
Cold Climbs, Diadem Press

Text continues on page 179

Above: **Dry-tooling techniques include using different parts of the head, anvil, or adze of the axe as nuts or in torqueing mode in cracks of various sizes.** *(Photo: Brad Johnson)*

Below: **We started out on a climb called the Little Thang, behind the famous free-standing pillar of the Fang—which was unformed. . . . The climb begins with steep M6 dry tooling past three bolts to reach the ice. In these situations, a properly shaped hooking pick is crucial. . . . You always have a choice to make: whether to grab a hold with your fingers or hook it with your tool.** *(Photos: Ian Tomlinson)*

Clipping protection requires dexterity in your glove system (above). After clipping the bolt I hung back on straight arms and took a short rest before continuing. The rest was just enough to allow me to climb the thin ice with the precision tool placements and monopoint delicacy required. Most often I would place my monopoints in the holes left by my picks (bottom right). As the ice thickened I followed the path of least resistance, staying directly in balance over my feet by cross-through frontpointing (upper right).

(Photos: Ian Tomlinson)

The Little Thang is on the right. A direct start to the larger flow of ice on the left is called the Seventh Tentacle.
For climbs like these that end under a roof on thick ice, a V-thread is a clean, easy, and appropriate rappel anchor. *(Photo: Ian Tomlinson)*

Clockwise from lower right: **Even steeper and more difficult dry tooling and heel hooking a block lead to hanging ice on the Seventh Tentacle—M6+ in the conditions we found.** *(Photo: Ian Tomlinson)*

Squatting on the block and locking a knee behind an icicle (lower left) **. . . took the weight off my arms . . . and allowed me to make a controlled and careful pick placement in the ice above the overhang** (upper left) **. . . at which point I stemmed out to an icicle with my left foot, replanted my right tool higher, and stemmed with my right frontpoint as well** (above right)**, which allowed me to establish myself above the overhang.**

(Photos: Ian Tomlinson)

Bird marveled at the precision and utility of crampons and picks in dry tooling and took to this style of climbing as an extension of rock climbing, employing her tools as extensions of her hands and feet. *(Photo: Ian Tomlinson)*

Bird used a different, probably less-efficient rest to clear the overhang when she scummed a shoulder up under the ice. She managed to pull over, but with more effort than absolutely necessary. Although the following day would be her graduation, she had already finessed beautiful and hard climbs that many people have trouble with after years of climbing ice. *(Photo: Ian Tomlinson)*

Opposite page and above, from lower left: **On our last day we climbed Secret Probation, a short but intensely strenuous and technical M7 roof, corner, and face climb. . . . Bouldering moves off the ground allow access to clipping the fixed protection at the roof, which is climbed by a series of crack hooking and torqueing moves . . . into a corner above the roof. . . . Strenuous liebacks off the picks allow a precision stick with the right tool in very thin ice on the corner's right wall. . . . Once established on the little tongue of ice the climbing eases to WI5, but the protection is scant and the lead is serious.** *(Photos: Ian Tomlinson)*

Bird struggled on the crux corner moves, attempting to climb too straight-on, rather than liebacking far enough to the right, which caused her picks to continually slip down the edge of rock. We called it a day. *(Photo: Ian Tomlinson)*

Class 8 Climbing

Although only one climb I know of (Octopussy) has class 8 technical moves, this situation will surely change in the coming years. It is very hard to conceive of a climb on pure ice that would offer class 8 moves, though it could be a horizontal roof formed by a broken pillar, or a long, extremely overhanging pitch on an alpine ice cliff. More certainly, these test pieces will be found on mixed rock and ice terrain. The techniques already outlined should be sufficient to climb these routes; you will simply encounter longer series of extreme moves. As with the *upside-down heel-toe jams* of Octopussy, these climbs will require creative solutions in addition to standard technique. There is no question that soon someone will do a class 9 climb.

Descending Extreme Ice

It is a good idea to practice *down-climbing* even very steep pitches. The ability to climb down out of dangerous terrain will save you from potentially serious falls. It is possible to descend simply by placing your tools at shoulder level and climbing straight down below. When you can, however, try placing your tools about shoulder level but diagonally out to the side, and doing a sort of side-to-side series of liebacks down the ice. There will come a point on overhangs and in other cases where the climbing is so committing you won't be able to reverse the moves. At these times an arsenal of techniques for quick protection and rappeling off is essential.

Protection and Belays

It would be difficult to describe every possible way of dealing with all the potential protection challenges and belay situations you will encounter as you climb ice, but a few basics will give you the tools to begin to safely acquire your own experience. Eventually there may be times when you will make a belay off one screw only or even just two tools, but you will not understand enough of the

variables and forces involved to do this sort of thing safely in the beginning.

Clean Protection

Many waterfall climbs are festooned with features that can be slung with webbing to provide natural runners for lead protection or belays. Look for these opportunities—small solid pillars, tunnels in the ice, slots between pillars that can take a large nut or a screw slotted as a T-anchor, mushrooms or cauliflowers, and so on. Large Tri Cams between rock and ice can sometimes be quite secure if the fulcrum point is set fairly deeply in the ice to begin with. If there is no natural T-slot, in thin, hollow ice you can cut a vertical slot in the ice that will accept the screw with a

A sling around a pillar often provides good protection. In more complex situations, multiple holes can be threaded with a long sling and clipped with a carabiner in such a way as to equalize the force among all points of support. *(Photo: Ian Tomlinson)*

sling around the middle. In hollow ice you can also punch two holes some distance apart and thread them with a runner. Bollards, or ice mushrooms, are harder to cut in water ice than in alpine ice, but are still useful. In water ice, a more efficient technique is the *V-thread technique* of intersecting screw holes threaded with either the rope or a runner.

Placing a Piton or Screw

Whether you are placing a piton or a screw, the angle at which it should be driven varies between perpendicular to the surface and a 45° upward angle. This angle is affected primarily by the type and quality of the ice, but the angle of the slope and other factors are also important.

Generally speaking, on solid, cold, vertical water ice, you would drive a Snarg directly in at nearly 90°. On soft glacier ice, on the other hand, you would want to chop a step and place a screw vertically down into the ice at the back of the step. In any case, remove all poor surface material before placing a screw or piton. As the device is driven or screwed in, more surface ice will be disturbed. This, too, must be removed so that the screw or piton can be inserted until its eye is flush against good, unfractured ice.

Ice screws can be placed one-handed, especially the new ultrasharp stainless steel or chrome-moly versions with very aggressive cutting teeth. But, particularly on the lead, tapping out a deep, narrow starting hole with your pick will make placement easier and keep surface fracturing to a minimum. Make the hole as deep as possible while maintaining a diameter that is slightly less than that of the screw or piton. A properly placed screw or piton in good ice will stand any force you are likely to subject it to.

Thin ice is difficult to protect, but *screws placed in series* can make the best of a bad situation.

Hook-type Pitons

Hook-type pitons offer quick but often questionable protection on difficult leads. They can be jammed

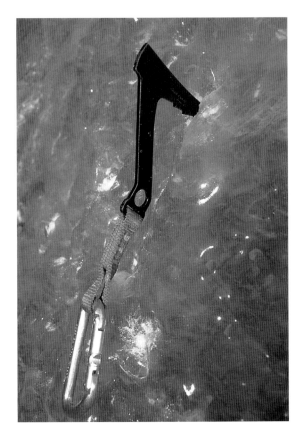

Although the best protection for ice climbing is usually a well-placed screw or natural runner, there are several hook-type pitons that offer quick intermediate drive-in protection for passing a crux. These pitons work best in chandelier-type ice or soft ice.
(Photo: Ian Tomlinson)

into a pick hole and pounded in or can be pounded directly into a crease between icicles or chandeliers. Their security depends on how badly the ice is fractured as they are driven in. Look for aerated or bubbly ice for best results with these. Occasionally your third tool can be left as a point of hook-type protection for a running belay.

Rock Gear

Mixed climbing can make use of all the standard types of rock climbing protection available. Often even pure waterfall climbs can have rock belays, so an ice climber should be thoroughly familiar with the use of this equipment.

Placing Ice Screws or Pitons on the Lead

The only pure free climbing technique for placing screws and pitons on the lead follows this sequence: hang straight-armed from one well-placed tool; make a good, deep, narrow starting hole, about hip-level for screws or overhead for pitons; then screw or pound the protection into the ice, clearing any surface-fractured ice until the eye is flush against solid material.

You can arrange temporary protection for placing the screw or piton—if you have a third tool—by placing your second tool high and securely and clipping a carabiner through either the hole in the spike or the wrist loop and clipping the climbing rope through that carabiner. This is not meant to take your weight, but to serve as a backup in case of a slip. Some people have recommended draping the climbing rope over the head of the tool, which is a very dangerous practice since the sharp edges of the pick could easily cut the rope under tension.

If you need to use both hands to place a screw, try sliding your arm up to the elbow through your wrist loop. You can then use that hand to support the screw as you turn it with the other hand.

Although it feels like aid climbing to me, a common and useful technique that frees both hands for placing a screw on steep ice is to clip into one or both hand tools with a carabiner or a skyhook attached to a cow's tail tied to your harness. This technique is also useful in certain emergency situations, such as when the pick of one tool breaks or a crampon goes askew on a boot. This technique is considered aid (A0).

Aid on Ice

Piolet traction, skill, and boldness will eliminate the need for aid climbing on ice 99.9 percent of the time. Once in a while, however, an overhanging serac wall or some other horror will humble you into using aid.

Hanging by a fifi hook, or cliffhanger, attached to a daisy chain and your harness, which is hooked into the hole in the spike of your tool, is a simple aid technique for freeing your hands to place protection. In this photo I have also clipped the climbing rope through my second tool as a backup belay. This technique is considered A0. *(Photo: Brad Johnson)*

The fastest way is to clip étriers into small loops of cord that are tied through the holes in the spikes of your tools. Simply place the tool and stand in the sling. You can also place ice screws or pitons and climb *étriers* (four- or five-step webbing ladders) that have been clipped into them, but this is much slower and usually unnecessary.

A Standard Belay Setup

One of the safest and most logical belays, the one I use at least 90 percent of the time on technical ground, is arranged like this:

1. Chop a step wide enough to accept both feet. Stand in the step.

Ice bouldering a short distance off the ground is the perfect way to push technique, test strength, and try new moves.
(Photo: Jeff Lowe)

2. At a comfortable arm's reach above the step, on the side on which the second will follow the lead, place a drive-in or screw and clip into it with a clove hitch. (You may now give the off-belay call to your belayer.) This anchor will become the first point of protection for the second as he or she leads through onto the next pitch.

3. On the opposite side of the step, place a second anchor below the first. Clip into this anchor with a clove hitch, adjusting the slack as necessary.

4. Clip the rope that leads to the second through the higher anchor with a separate carabiner and set up a body belay or rig your belay device in the normal fashion. Running the tail of the rope around your body and through a carabiner at your harness tie-in point will ensure control of the belay. This procedure works smoothly even with an iced-up rope. Let your second know he or she is on belay.

Following the Lead

The rope directly in front of you is often at risk when you are following an ice pitch. If there is any question that you may have to place a pick close to where the rope lies, use the pick of one tool to hook the rope to the side of the tool that is in the ice, keeping it out of harm's way. Ice screws can be removed just as they were placed. Removing drive-in, screw-out ice pitons, however, usually requires some initial chopping to clear the eye for spinning. This protection is more difficult for the second than for the leader. Removing hook-type pitons is sometimes simply a matter of pulling up and out on the carabiner; at other times you can tap directly up on the shaft to free them, and sometimes they must be chopped most of the way out.

Beyond Technique

The techniques described here will do the job, yet mastering these methods need not be the final goal. With these as your basic repertoire, you can go further, modifying and expanding them according to your own instincts. Rather than carving the ice to suit a particular vision, the creative ice climber is a sculptor whose vision is shaped by the medium as it exists.

Suggested Exercises

Crampon Practice

◆ Good crampon technique comes as a result of confidence. Confidence is gained through experience. Slow movement allows time for fear. Fear interferes with pure experience. So, to maximize experience, short-circuit fear, and foster good crampon technique, set up a toprope on low-angle ice. Then, with an alert belayer, run as fast as you can up and down the slope. Try this with an upright posture, and again from a light crouch with your back straight and knees bent, and yet again any way you want. Now consider what you have experienced.

Top: **Classic flat foot or French crampon technique requires that all points under the boot be equally embedded in the ice.**
Center: **Crampons with parallel side rails allow hedging, with the upper row of points embedded in the ice and the lower row resting on the surface.**
Bottom: **Edging the uphill row of crampon points is a dangerous practice as the ice can break out and you can lose your footing.**
(Photos: Ian Tomlinson)

Accurate and powerful swings are best accomplished with the axe head and shaft in alignment with the wrist, arm, elbow, and shoulder. *(Photo: Ian Tomlinson)*

♦ When cramponing with one or both feet sideways, *pied à plat*, it is important that all sidepoints be equally weighted and penetrate the ice to an equal depth. It is also important that the points of the trailing foot remain equally weighted as you step up. If you try to edge the upper points or if you allow your lower foot to torque in the ice as you move up, you may fracture the ice in a dinner plate, losing your purchase. To illustrate this effect, try it out on hard ice. Experiment with different angles of ankle bend and slope steepness.

Assuming you are cramponing flat-footed on a 30° slope, close your eyes and back off 15° on your ankle bend; then allow your points to drop down again into the proper position. Concentrate on the information traveling from the ice up through your crampons, boots, feet, ankles, and legs to your brain. Feel what is happening to your foothold as you torque the points. Be alert for this feeling as you climb, and seek to avoid it.

♦ Think of your frontpoints (all your crampon points, for that matter) as your claws, rooted deep in your feet. Obviously you will not want to slam, wedge, or otherwise abuse your appendages any more than necessary. Even on very hard ice, a good climber will gently tap the frontpoints in on ice up to 60° or 70°, preferring to stand upright in balance and with heels low to let gravity pull the points deeper into the ice. On even steeper ice, finesse is still possible, as slight wrinkles nearly always exist in the ice surface, and these can be used as small but adequate footholds. Try toproping pitches of various angles using frontpoints only and no hand tools. Search for footholds, and use as little force as possible while kicking in. Try pressing and weighting your points on 50° ice, with no kicking. What happens when you point your toes down a little and try to kick the points in? Also on a toprope try a very steep pitch of waterfall ice using natural handholds only. Finally, climb a pitch of 60° to 70° ice blindfolded. As you climb, quantify the degree of tension in your calves: fully tensed, 50 percent, 10 percent, and so on. At what level of tension do you feel you are getting the most security from your frontpoints?

Planting Tools

♦ Regarding tool placement, it is important to recognize exactly what is meant by the statement "when forces are properly aligned." Hold your ice axe vertically at arm's length in front of you. Point the pick directly forward. Put the tip of the pick against the ice (or the wall). Any force traveling from your shoulder and arm through the shaft and pick will be aligned on one plane and will therefore cause the greatest possible penetration of the pick. Now turn the pick 10° out of the alignment; it is easy to visualize the confusion of forces that results in shattered ice. Again holding your axe in front of you, allow the pick to rest on the surface of the ice (or the wall), pick pointing directly into the ice, and hold the shaft roughly parallel to the surface. All forces are now converging closely on the pick. They will converge exactly if you are using a tool with a pick curved to match the arc of the swing, but will be slightly conflicting on very steeply drooped picks. This accounts for the need for a downward flick of the wrist at the end of the swing when using the old Terrordactyls, for instance. Keep the pick against the ice and pull the spike away. Note the glancing blow that would result. Try this information out on the ice. Identify exactly the degree of misorientation with each swing that is less than perfect. Pick the spot you want to hit and keep your eyes on it as you swing. (Wear glasses or goggles to avoid injury from ice chips.) Again pick the spot and, holding it in your mind, close your eyes and swing. Try concentrating on a spot a couple inches under the surface of the ice where you want your pick to end up.

- On a toprope, climb the same pitch twice using hand tools and crampons. The first time up, attack the ice with all the rage you can muster, and allow yourself to be lowered down. The second time climb with as much style and finesse as you have at your command, and climb back down. Note how you feel after each ascent. Climb the same pitch blindfolded.
- Climb a pure rock pitch (an obscure and ugly one), and experiment with all your tools. Try various combinations of tools in different conditions.

Mind Games

- Mentally climb a route you have just done, re-creating it in as much detail as possible. Concentrate especially on the things you felt as you climbed. Try not to watch yourself do the climb, but do it in your head. Before starting up a new climb, imagine yourself in as much detail as possible making the ascent. After you have made the climb, think back. Was your imagination equal to the challenge, or are there gaps in your mental abilities? Work on those gaps—they are the only true limits of what is possible for you.
- When you are out with climbers who are more skilled than you are, turn off your analytical mind when you watch them climb. Let the performance flow directly into your subconscious. Do not reduce what you are seeing into words. Rather, like a young child, just let yourself learn by good example.

Breakthrough Experiences

We have all known those times when a skill we have been working very hard, but with no success, to master suddenly comes to us, often when we were not even trying. If we do not recognize such breakthroughs immediately and allow the lesson to sink in at the very moment it occurs, we are in danger of losing much of what has been gained. An example all novice ice climbers can appreciate is the first experience of a properly swung and planted ice axe. The first several swings will most likely cause more shattering of the ice than penetration, with a wobbly hold resulting. But that first swing when forces are properly aligned through shoulder, arm, shaft, and pick, and the resulting "thunk" provide an unmistakable feeling of security and satisfaction. Such feelings, once recognized, are available for later use, precipitating the correct sequence and execution of actions that will yield the desired results again and again.

Going Solo

Alone on ice is a wonderful place to be. At times, soloing exposes the climber to greater danger, but very often the experienced person is safer when alone. The soloist leaves behind doubt, fear, and competitive urges, and strikes out on a journey of self-discovery, vulnerable to new insight and experience. Every move takes on added significance, as, in climber/philosopher Willi Unsoeld's words, you are "walking the edge of imminent dissolution."

Without question the most dangerous situation for a single climber is traversing snow-covered glaciers with hidden crevasses. Most people smartly avoid this circumstance, which leaves a little too much to chance. On the other hand, the solo climber's speed can turn many rockfall- and avalanche-prone alpine routes into reasonable ventures. Even the steepest frozen waterfalls can be safely ascended by the experienced soloist who treats each axe placement as a portable belay, never making a move until it is certain the hold is absolutely reliable.

Opposite page: **John Cunningham alone on Ben Nevis**
(Photo: Jeff Lowe)

Right: **In the winter of 1995 I made the first solo ascent of the Adirondack classic, Positive Thinking (WI5-) on Poke-O-Moonshine. For an experienced, confident, and careful climber, who treats each tool placement as a portable belay, soloing on good ice can be safer than belayed roped climbing is for the novice or incautious climber.**
(Photo: Tom McCarthy)

Special Techniques

Anchor Technique Using a V-Thread

Since the mid-1970s I've been using an anchor technique called a V-thread, primarily for rappeling to avoid having to leave behind screws or sections of conduit. A V-thread is faster and easier than cutting a bollard, which is also a clean technique. A V-thread is made by placing two screws about six inches apart and angling them so that the holes will meet as far

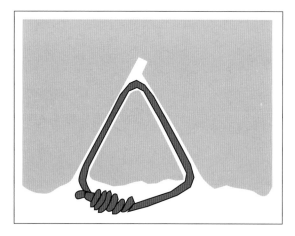

A V-thread anchor

back in the ice as possible. After placing the first screw, back it out most of the way and use it as a sight for placing your second screw. You will feel the second screw turn more easily when it intersects the first screw hole. Remove both screws and poke a sling into one hole, using a tool fashioned from a 12-inch length of hanger wire with a carabiner eye in one end and a quarter-inch hook at the other. Then reach into the other hole and hook the end of the sling through.

Clip a carabiner into the two ends of the sling, and you have a very solid anchor for lead protection, belays, or rappels. In solid ice, the V-thread tests to well over 2,000 pounds. A flat sling spreads the force over a larger surface area than a cord would and takes longer to melt through, which is the typical mode of failure. An 8mm or 9mm rope can be passed directly through the V for absolutely clean rappeling, but if there is any melting, freezing, or running water near the hole, use a sling to avoid the rope freezing into the ice.

Pulling the sling through the V *(Photo: Ian Tomlinson)*

A carabiner clipped into the two ends of the sling *(Photo: Ian Tomlinson)*

Thin-ice Protection Using Screws in Series

Reliable thin-ice protection can be had by placing screws in series. This is a technique I borrowed from the multiple-stake set-ups used to anchor circus tents in soft, shallow ground. Place two screws, one directly above the other, about 18 inches apart. As soon as the screws bottom out against the rock, stop turning. Back off a partial turn on the lower screw, so the eye is pointing directly up. I carry a five-foot length of 7mm static cord with a six-inch loop tied in one end. Tie off the upper screw using the loop. Run the cord down through a carabiner in the eye of the lower screw and back up through the bottom of the tie-off loop. This achieves a mechanical advantage for pulling tension between the upper and lower screws. Pull quite hard and lock the cord off with a series of trucker's hitches below the tie-off loop. When properly done you will be able to strum the cord like a bass fiddle string. Finally, with a separate sling, tie off the lower screw flush to the ice and clip your climbing rope through a carabiner here.

Since ice screws fail by successively fracturing surface layers of the ice under tension until a shear force is converted primarily to a direct outward pull, screws in series provide a unique advantage. The tension from the upper screw keeps the lower screw from flexing downward and, since the upper screw can withstand a force of several times that which is applied to the eye of the lower screw through its lever arm, in most cases the tip of the lower screw must shear through the ice for this arrangement to fail. Even weak, thin ice is very strong in resisting a shear force. In tests, screws in series resist several times the force of two screws tied off and equalized. The security of the arrangement can be even greater if a force-limiting Air Voyager or Screamer sling is applied between the lower screw and the rope.

Screws placed in series *(Photo: Brad Johnson)*

Because longer screws work best in this technique, I seldom carry any screws less than seven or eight inches in length.

Kangtega, Khumbu, Nepal
(Photo: Jeff Lowe)

The Hard Water Guide

▼ ▼ ▼ ▼

AN OVERVIEW OF WORLD ICE, WITH SIXTEEN SELECTED CLIMBS

Good ice can be found around the world, often in the most unlikely places. In a cold year excellent and challenging (though often short-lived) ice climbing turns up in a number of unexpected places—for example, Georgia in the United States, a locale more normally associated with warm Southern charm than with icy cliffs. The Caucasus Mountains in Russia contain huge mixed routes and pure ice climbs. Circling the globe, the high mountains of equatorial Africa, South America, and New Guinea contain very fine ice. The Himalaya, the greatest range on earth, offers the greatest ice climbs. At either pole the mountains are literally buried in glacier ice. The possibilities for discovery are endless for anyone committing the time, energy, and money to research and travel to these places. In this overview of world ice I will touch only lightly on these out-of-the-mainstream or very exotic locations, and deal primarily with the popular, easily accessible, and reasonably economical areas.

The Western Hemisphere

Alaska

Alaska has immense potential for both alpine-type and frozen waterfall climbing. Most of the ice climbing that has been done in the high mountains of the state has occurred in the Alaska Range, home of Denali, North America's highest peak. Denali is like an oversized version of Mont Blanc—a range unto itself, replete with its own versions of the Peuterey Ridge, Brenva Face, and Chamonix Aiguilles. Any climb on Denali is a high-altitude expedition or super-alpine problem. The lower surrounding peaks, however, offer wonderful high-caliber routes from 2,100 to 5,000 feet high on the many facets of Mount Hunter, Mount Huntington, the Rooster Comb, and others.

The Alaska Range, Denali in particular, has some of the worst weather in the world. Approaches are either by foot, dog sled, or skis, all of which take several days, or by ski plane, which takes half an hour from the ramshackle village of Talkeetna, reachable by car or train from Anchorage.

In winter very accessible frozen waterfall climbing is available around Valdez.

Since 1975 local and visiting climbers have established hundreds of excellent routes of all grades, from low-angle, one-pitch introductory climbs, to 600-foot ascents of grade IV, WI5 and 6, such as the cauliflowered pillars of Wowie Zowie. In December and January the days are very cold and extremely short (five hours of daylight at the turn of the year), so the best months for climbing are February and March.

Baffin Island and Greenland

Rock climbers have enjoyed the opportunities available on both Baffin Island and Greenland, but each has obvious potential for good ice climbing as well. Summer temperatures are often too warm for good conditions to exist in the couloirs that slash the huge granite walls, and there is not much in the way of steep alpine ice slopes on either of these giant islands. Most likely, however, winter would provide a host of possibilities on frozen waterfalls. This remains to be proven by a crew of climbers determined enough to brave the extreme cold and the logistical barriers of climbing in such a remote locale. Since both islands discharge chunks of their ice caps into the sea, an artful expedition might be arranged to climb elegant, never-to-be-repeated routes on the icebergs.

Canada

The entire western half of Canada contains range after range of wilderness peaks, starting with the great massifs of Mount Logan and Mount St. Elias in the north, with their Denali-like climbing and scale, and extending south to the Coast Range and Mount Waddington, five hundred miles north of Vancouver. All of these remote ranges are heavily glaciated and offer major wilderness ice adventures to those willing to make the discovery on their own. In the winter months the mountains of Vancouver Island provide more accessible but still very exciting and little-known Scottish-type climbing on the rimed-up, 3,000-foot cliffs of Mount Colonel Foster and other peaks.

North America's major ice climbing center is the Canadian Rockies. Here are found the Canadian equivalents of the Eiger or the Matterhorn, with correspondingly more problematic faces and ridges. Summer and autumn offer innumerable couloir, gully, and face climbs of hard alpine ice. The Columbia Icefields Campground in particular, on the highway about halfway between Banff and Jasper, is adjacent to a number of excellent ice routes, from the relatively mild north faces of Athabasca and Andromeda, to the great routes of Slipstream and the Grand Central Couloir. In the harsher conditions of winter, the climbs around the Icefields take on added dimensions of difficulty and seriousness. Large frozen waterfalls form below the high peaks and are often climbable from late November through March.

Although winter temperatures in the northern Rockies can be very low (40° to 50° below zero at times) and avalanche hazard is often extremely high, some of the

world's best frozen waterfall climbing is found in these locales. The climber may develop his or her skills on such routes as Cascade Falls and Professor's Gully, then progress through Takkakkaw Falls or Bourgeau Lefthand, and move on to the likes of the Terminator on Mount Rundle or Gimme Shelter on Mount Quadra. These last two are among the hardest frozen waterfalls of their length ever climbed. Hundreds of climbs have been made of all grades, but the most amazing chunks of ice on the big faces are yet to be explored.

In Quebec, the adventurous climber can find new route possibilities at Baie Eternite or the Malbaie Valley, with thousand-foot waterfall climbs such as L'Equerre and La Pomme d'Or, and in Parc Jacques Cartier, where locals opt for helicopter approaches.

The United States South of the Canadian Border

The northeastern United States is well known for the wide variety of winter ice on such crags as Cathedral Ledge in North Conway, New Hampshire, which harbors dozens of ice climbs, including the famous four-pitch Repentence and its harder neighbor, Remission. Not far away, Frankenstein Cliff offers routes in all grades up to 300 feet, while 600-foot climbs on Cannon Mountain, such as the Black Dike and Fafnir, have a more serious air. The gullies in Huntington Ravine (the birthplace of winter ice climbing in the United States in the 1920s) are exposed to the renowned Mount Washington winds, which have been measured at over two hundred miles per hour!

Lake Willowby in Vermont has a wide, 400-foot-high cliff that sports a number of hard climbs, including the Promenade, a climb on good New England ice similar in length and difficulty to Colorado's Bridalveil Falls. Katahdin in Maine gives some of the hardest, longest, and most alpinelike climbing in the region on the walls of its several steep "basins" that lead to the 5,100-foot summit. However, the approach is long (fifteen miles) and the weather generally bad, so Katahdin is not as popular as some other areas.

Good summer gully climbing is available in the mountains of Wyoming and Montana, including the Tetons' Black Ice Couloir, the most famous. The Tetons have also yielded a number of high-quality off-season climbs. The Big Horns and Wind River Range hide some fine climbs for the person not afraid to explore with no certainty of finding anything. Both states also have good but little-publicized winter waterfall climbing. The waterfall climbs near Cody, Wyoming, are some of the best in the West.

Colorado and Utah are essentially void of alpine ice, but good off-season water ice can be found in the high mountains of Colorado, and winter provides opportunities for much frozen waterfall climbing. Some of the best concentrations of climbs rise above a highway in Provo Canyon, Utah, with more than a dozen fine lines up to 850 feet. Farther south, in Zion Canyon, several long routes have,

Mike Weis beginning the crux second pitch on the first ascent of Bridalveil Falls, Colorado. (Photo: Jeff Lowe)

in cold winters, formed on the sandstone walls. In the Ouray/Silverton/Telluride area in the San Juan Mountains of southwestern Colorado are Bridalveil Falls and Ames Falls, the two best climbs in the state, each having a distinct character. Rocky Mountain National Park, not far from Denver and Boulder, has relatively little ice to offer the many climbers who live in the area; but what there is has been fully exploited, and the term "mixed climbing" has been extended to include radical techniques on some short but very hard, iced-up rocks.

The Sierra Nevada of California are home to some of the most enjoyable gullies in the country. The V-Notch, the U-Notch, and the Mendel Couloir are justly popular climbs that are reached by pleasant hikes through John Muir's "Range of Light." Ice Nine, to the left of the Mendel Couloir, is a challenging mixed route. In cold winters Yosemite Valley offers the 1,000-foot Widow's Tears, which may be America's most beautiful ice climb. Further north, in Washington, are Mount Rainier and other peaks of the Cascade Mountains. Rainier has been the training ground for generations of Pacific Northwest expedition climbers, the many glaciers on its flanks closely simulating conditions in the greater ranges. Other Cascade peaks, such as the north faces of Mount Maude and Mount Redoubt, though still glaciated, are considerably steeper than Rainier and contain some good, moderate, alpine-type routes. In some winters, off-season-type ice forms excellent climbs like the Northwest Face of Mount Stuart and the Eve Dearborn Memorial Route on Mount Index.

South America

Between the southern Rocky Mountains and the northern Andes in Columbia few opportunities exist for the ice climber, with the exception of the high volcanoes near Mexico City. But from Columbia to Patagonia, the entire Andean chain is icy in its higher elevations. Peru's Cordillera Blanca is the most popular and accessible of the areas. Routes of all grades, on ice that varies from porridge to good water ice, can be found at altitudes between 18,000 and 22,000 feet. Huaraz, the main jumping-off point for the Blanca, is a Spanish-speaking Chamonix in June and July, the best climbing months. Even farther south, the Vinson Massif in Antarctica is 16,000 feet high with 7,000-foot faces.

The Eastern Hemisphere

The British Isles

The Scottish winter hills are the best training ground imaginable for the climber who eventually plans to go to the Alps, Andes, or Himalaya. They are also rewarding in their own right! Spending a day on one of the fine gully or buttress routes of Ben Nevis, occasionally being engulfed in spindrift or buffeted by the storm while grappling with a bulge of snow-ice, or trying to delicately frontpoint up a rock slab that is thinly veneered in verglas, you get a sense of being in bigger, more remote, and serious mountains. In the evening at the pub in Fort William, the day's lessons on the hill are rehashed over a pint, and plans for even greater things on the morrow are made. No place in the world is more conducive to absorbing the essence of the ice experience than Scotland, with its long history, adventurous traditions, resident masters, and beautifully harsh winter weather.

The huge variety of Scottish winter ice climbing includes the traverse of the Cuillin Ridge on the Isle of Skye, the big walls in remote corries of the Northern Highlands, and the superb climbs of Craig Maigheadh, such as Smith's Gully, South Post, and North Post. Among other gems, the Cairngorms boast Shelter Stone Crag, looking like a mini-Dru from below and giving hard, 1,000-foot mixed climbs such as Sticil Face, Citadel, and Needle. But beware the Cairngorm blizzards; they have proved lethal for several parties. Lochnagar, on the east side of Scotland, gives climbs from grade I to IV in gullies and buttresses, and harbors the famous chimney of Parallel Gully B.

If Scotland has more than its share of fantastic winter climbing, in a good season England can lay claim to a smaller number of equally fine itineraries in the Lake District on Scafell Crag and others, and in North Wales on Craig yr Ysfa, Snowdon, Craig y Rhaeadr, the Black Ladders, Cwm Idwal, Lliwedd, and Clogwyn du'r Arddu. The Black Cleft, Central Gully, Devil's Appendix, Western Gully, and the Somme are names attached to climbs of excellent character. Furthermore, as English climber Rob Collister said, "The essence of Welsh winter climbing is glinting frozen water against a backdrop of blue sky; axes wobbling in improbable pockets on booming icicles.... It's too bad winter here is so short and inconsistent!"

The Irish winter scene, compared with Scotland, Wales, and the Lakes, is very limited. However, there are routes up to WI4+, mainly on fleetingly frozen waterfalls. The Mourne Mountains provide some of the most consistent conditions, along with the Wicklow Hills.

Norway and Sweden

Although Norway has no alpine ice, it does have some of the best frozen waterfall climbing in the world. The most famous of these *fossen* are the Vettisfossen and Mardalsfossen in the Romsdal region. Local and visiting climbers continue to discover wonderful new frozen secrets each season, and a trip to Norway must rank high on the list of priorities for waterfall ice specialists. Norway also has some of the longest, best, and hardest Scottish-type winter climbs yet done. For instance, the 6,000-foot East Pillar of the Trollwall provides a multiday route at a technical standard similar to the Orion Face of Ben Nevis.

Norway has so much excellent waterfall ice on a large scale that up to now less emphasis has been placed on mixed routes. After all, with climbs the quality of the

Bridalveil-like Vettisfossen, the 600-foot-high and 400-foot-wide Hydnefossen, and the twenty pitches of high-standard climbing on Dontefossen (with other major *fossen* still unclimbed), climbers in Norway have little motivation to make the move onto mixed terrain.

The Alpine Countries and the Caucasus

It is hard to say enough here about the Alps, and since hundreds of books have been written with the Alps as their subject, what follows is only a superficial survey of what is available.

The Mont Blanc massif is perhaps the finest mountaineering playground on the planet. Ice climbs of all types and levels of difficulty are available here, usually not too far from a *téléphérique* station or hut. Year-round it is possible to ascend elegant snow arêtes or climb classic snow and ice faces. During winter or in cold spring and fall conditions, great frozen "cascades" form on the Brouillard and Freney Faces; in cold summers, the northeast couloir of the Dru and the Super Couloir on Mont Blanc du Tacul are modern grade V classics.

The limestone peaks of the Eastern Alps offer scope for any type of ice climbing, from serious, classic "Welzenbach" north faces, such as the Fiescherwand, to 1,200-foot frozen waterfalls in Salzburg and near Vienna. Good waterfalls are found throughout the Alps, and in recent years, the valleys below the peaks in Italy, as well as in France, Austria, and Germany, have seen intense development.

Perhaps the densest concentration of high-standard, high-quality frozen waterfalls in Europe is found in the Cirque de Gavarnie in the Pyrenees, which has dozens of routes ranging in height from 500 feet to Dominique Julien's 1,500-foot Voie de l'Overdose.

The Caucasus of Eastern Europe have a long history of ice climbing. In 1868 and 1874 the long snow slopes and glaciers of 18,000-foot twin-summited Mount Elbrus were first climbed by mixed parties of English, Russian, Swiss, and French climbers. In 1946 a Russian party climbed the North Face of Ullu Tau, a classic ice route comparable to the great climbs of the Swiss Oberland, such as the Lauper Route on the Northeast Face of the Eiger. The state-of-the-art in Caucasus ice climbing is represented by the direct route on the Northwest Face of the North Peak of Ushba. This climb, made in 1986 by the English team of Mick Fowler and Victor Saunders, is, according to the first ascensionists, comparable in difficulty to the Cecchinel/Nomine Route on Mont Blanc's Grand Pilier d'Angle. Long classic pure ice and mixed routes, arêtes, and faces of all levels of difficulty are available in these wonderful mountains.

New Zealand

New Zealand provides ice climbers with a variety of challenges. As Mont Blanc is to the Alps and Denali is to Alaska, so is Mount Cook to New Zealand. Mount Cook presents classic snow ridges, ice arêtes and faces, and mixed climbs.

Extensively glaciated, the mountain has provided generations of climbers with alpine-type climbs and excellent experience for tackling the greater ranges in other parts of the world. On the surrounding lower (under 11,000 feet) peaks of Mount Tasman and Mount Hicks, routes of a very high standard are available, some of the best being the Balfour Face, the Yankee/Kiwi Couloir, and Heaven's Door—all first-rate mixed climbs of about 2,000 feet. In the Haast Range, the South Face of Mount Aspiring is one of the great modern ice climbs.

The Darren Mountains are the site of some of the best frozen waterfall climbing in New Zealand. In recent antipodean winters, climbs have been made on some startling ice pillars.

Other Areas

In addition to the locations described above, there are a number of good routes on Africa's Mount Kenya, put up over the last twenty years by a small group of local and visiting climbers. The Koreans and Japanese have begun to develop waterfall climbing in their mountains, where they have been doing snowy winter climbs for years.

The Himalaya

It is impossible to do justice to the ice-climbing potential of the great mountains that are collectively called the Himalaya. The alpine ice potential was first tapped in a nonexpeditionary style by Peter Habeler and Reinhold Messner in 1975, when they climbed the Northwest Face of Pakistan's 26,000-foot Hidden Peak in three days up and down. In the 1980s and '90s, it has become increasingly common for small parties of two or three to tackle very difficult ice climbs in pure alpine style. The best technical climbs, such as the North Face of Cholatse in Nepal, have been made on peaks between 20,000 and 23,000 feet.

The Himalayan winter season is an untapped resource of frozen waterfalls. Although a few have been climbed, such as the 2,000-foot cascade across the valley from the Sherpa village of Namche Bazaar, climbers have until now been reluctant to travel so far for what is essentially crag climbing, when the great peaks loom above.

Without a doubt, some of the greatest ice climbs of the future will take place in these huge ranges.

WORLD CLASSICS

Selecting a few ice climbs as extreme classics from what must now be twenty thousand routes around the world is not an easy task. For the purposes of this book, I have chosen only from among those routes that I have personally been on (although in a few cases I haven't succeeded), which, at this point, number roughly a thousand. About three hundred of these were first ascents. This criterion means that the information is firsthand and that the relative grading of the climbs is consistent. I have tried to choose examples of highly technical climbs on vastly different types of ice in a wide range of geographical locations—climbs with a singular character that, though it changes somewhat with different conditions, always provides the climber with a lasting experience. If you make an ascent of any one of these great climbs, you will come away richer than when you began the climb.

The Northwest Spur of Mount Hunter, Alaska

The Northwest Spur is a regular magical mystery tour, with all sorts of fine problems, from snow arêtes to cornices to ice cliffs to mixed climbing on the Triangle Face. Although it is not particularly difficult in modern terms, it is the steepest of the major ridges on the north and west sides of Mount Hunter, rising directly above the "Kahiltna International" glacier landing strip, the jumping-off point for south-side Denali expeditions. It has been an obvious challenge for a couple of generations of climbers. A very fit twosome traveling without bivouac gear could make the round trip climb up and down from base camp to summit in a long Alaskan day, which would be a way to keep the commitment level on this climb very high. Most people will choose the more conservative compromise, however, of bringing adequate bivouac gear and food; this will cause them to move slower and force them to make at least one or two bivouacs. In any case, the Northwest Spur offers thousands of feet of enjoyable, rapid movement on varied angles of ice and snow, with a few more difficult pitches to break up the rhythm.

Location: Mount Hunter rises out of the southeast fork of the Kahiltna Glacier (the normal landing site for west- and south-side Denali climbs) in the Alaska Range.

First Ascent: George Lowe III and Mike Kennedy, July 1976

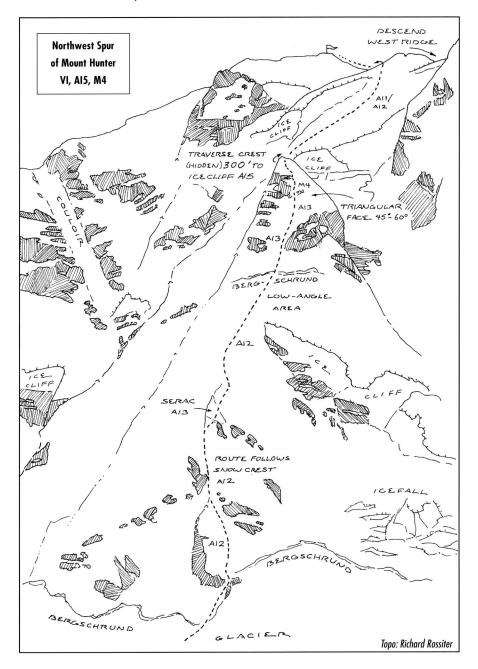

Northwest Spur
of Mount Hunter
VI, AI5, M4

DESCEND
WEST RIDGE

AI1/
AI2

ICE
CLIFF

TRAVERSE CREST
(HIDDEN) 300' TO
ICE CLIFF AI5

ICE
CLIFF

M4

AI3

TRIANGULAR
FACE 45°-60°

AI3

COULOIR

BERG- SCHRUND

LOW-ANGLE
AREA

ICE
CLIFF

AI2

ICE
CLIFF

SERAC
AI3

ROUTE FOLLOWS
SNOW CREST
AI2

ICEFALL

AI2

BERGSCHRUND

BERGSCHRUND

GLACIER

Topo: Richard Rossiter

Elevation Gain: About 7,000 feet

Difficulty: Grade VI, AI5, M4

Time: 3 to 4 days round trip from base camp at the "Kahiltna International" landing strip

George Lowe III and Mike Kennedy on the Triangle Face of Mount Hunter
(Photo: Jeff Lowe)

Equipment: Eight or ten ice screws, a handful of rock pitons and nuts, a couple of deadmen, snow shovel, full bivi gear (optional), map, and compass

Season: May to August (has been climbed in winter)

Comments: The Northwest Spur of Mount Hunter is technically the easiest of the climbs highlighted in this book. It is still a big Alaskan route, though, with all the attendant hazards of avalanches, cornices, storms, and route finding, which maintain the climbing interest and challenge. If you want a state-of-the-art modern climb, do the North Buttress, or the slightly easier Moonflower Buttress variation, on the rocky pillar three-quarters of a mile further to the left of the Northwest Spur.

Approach: Fly from Talkeetna (50 miles away; flying time, 30 minutes), or drive to Petersville and ski or snowshoe up the Kahiltna Glacier for 5 or 6 days to reach the southeast fork.

Route: Cross the bergschrund to the left of the toe of the spur. (This minimizes exposure to ice cliffs that hang on the right side of the spur.) After 300 or 400 feet, skirt a rock band by way of a short gully on the right, then angle back up and left until the crest of the spur is met. Follow this until you encounter a seraclike obstacle at about the 1,500-foot level. A pitch or two of steep climbing (AI3) on the right side leads to easier cruising for 1,000 feet up a trough between seracs on the crest of the spur, which is now quite broad and ill-defined. This section ends at the 2,500-foot level in a large, very low-angle area below the Triangle Face. A good camp or bivouac could be made here. Climb directly up 45° to 60° (AI3) ice for about twelve pitches to the top of the Triangle Face (there are two or three pitches of mixed climbing near the top, M4). At this point a heavily corniced and extremely steep-sided ridge leads 300 feet horizontally back from the top of the face to the base of the ice cliff that bars access to the summit snow slopes. This is the crux of the climb (AI4–5) and involves several intricate pitches of weaving in and out among the cornices and sometimes traversing the very hard 80° ice on one side of the ridge or the other. (A shovel is useful for removing some of the smaller cornices.) From this point the first ascent party discovered a moderate ramp leading through the ice cliff, above which there is 2,000 feet of snow slogging to the base of the final summit pyramid. The summit is climbed via a prominent ridge on the southwest side. (The route here corresponds with the West Ridge climb.)

Descent: Follow the West Ridge route down to the Kahiltna Glacier and walk the 3 or 4 miles around to the landing site on the southeast fork. The trickiest route finding on this descent occurs after you have come down from about 14,000 feet to the point where the summit ice cap meets the West Ridge. (This is a narrow spot with huge ice cliffs on either side and is very hard to locate in a whiteout. Therefore it might be worth taking bearings and distances from a map at the summit before descending.) At any rate, once you have gotten onto the ridge, follow it all the long way down to the glacier. This main ridge runs almost due west; care should be taken not to accidentally follow one of the sub-ridges in another direction. The descent is extremely long and requires considerable moderate down-climbing and care in dealing with cornices.

Keystone Green Steps
(Photo: Jeff Lowe)

Keystone Green Steps, Valdez, Alaska

Keystone Canyon is a waterfall ice climber's paradise, with numerous climbs on both walls of the canyon accessible in minutes from the Richardson Highway,

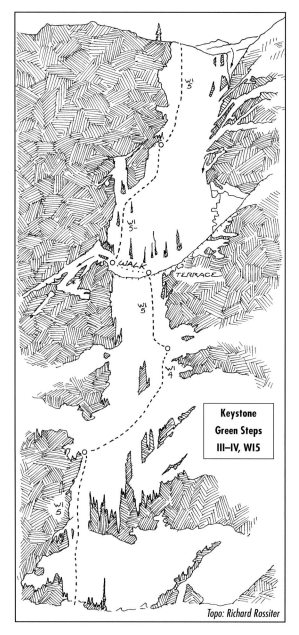

Keystone
Green Steps
III–IV, WI5

Topo: Richard Rossiter

the main artery into the town of Valdez. Before the winter of 1975–76, there had been no ice climbing in the area. That winter my friend John Weiland and my girlfriend, Christie Northrop, were working in Valdez, the former as a carpenter and the latter as a tugboat cook in Prince William Sound. In late December I drove from Colorado to visit them. John had recommended I bring my ice-climbing gear, as "there's a lot of water ice around here, better than anything in Colorado." Although that statement is not necessarily true, Alaskan ice climbing is different and the climbs are often more massive.

When I arrived, I found that there *is* an incredible amount of water ice in the region. With the short days, John and I ended up retreating in the dark from Bridalveil Falls, our first attempted climb, from just below the top of the crux fourth pitch. A few days later, accompanied by our friend Scott Etherington, we climbed the first pitch of the more difficult Keystone Green Steps. After I had led the pitch and John and Scott had followed it, it became obvious that, as a party of three, we were climbing too slowly. Scott generously offered to let John and me finish the route as a twosome. It was already near 3:00 P.M. and almost dark, so we came back the next day and climbed three pitches to the big ledge, hauling a pack full of bivi gear. We then made an eighteen-hour, brandy-assisted bivouac on a flat floor of ice in the cave behind the upper curtain. We finished the climb in three short pitches the next day. Altogether we had made six leads, but the climb is normally done in five pitches with 165-foot ropes. We had spent a total of about eight hours climbing.

The combination of dramatic line, massive blue and green ice, and easy access guarantees that the Keystone Green Steps will always be a sought-after route, even though it is no longer at the cutting edge of difficulty. It was the first major climb in one of North America's premiere waterfall climbing regions.

Location: Keystone Canyon is about 15 miles north of Valdez, Alaska. On the east side of the highway two main falls are visible: the Green Steps is on the right; on the left is Bridalveil Falls (there seems to be a Bridalveil Falls in every Western state!).

First Ascent: Jeff Lowe and John Weiland, December 1975

Elevation Gain: About 600 feet

Difficulty: Grade III–IV, WI5

Time: 4 to 6 hours on the climb

Equipment: Eight to ten ice screws, 165-foot ropes, head lamps (if you are climbing in December or January)

Season: November to April

Comments: The waterfall ice climbs of the Valdez area could easily keep the most voracious climber busy for an entire season. A special trip to Alaska just to climb there is entirely justified.

Approach: Simply park your car and walk or ski across the ice of the Lowe River to the base of the falls, a 5-minute approach.

Route: The long (140-foot) first pitch takes the left side of the falls to a belay at a low-angle area (WI5). The second pitch diagonals up and right to a belay partway up the next steep section (WI4). The third pitch climbs a long, steep pillar to a huge "halfway" ledge (WI5) with a good bivouac cave behind the curtain of ice, then walks left on the ledge behind the icy curtain. The next pitch again goes up the left edge of the ice for 75 feet to a belay ledge (WI5). The sixth pitch is long and leads (WI4) past a low-angle area at the base of the final 60-foot wall. The final wall brings you directly to the top (WI5).

Descent: Two long rappels from trees down the south margin of the ice deposit you onto the halfway ledge. Walk north along the ledge and down into a gully. Down-climb or rappel the gully. Alternatively, you can make three rappels from the halfway ledge to avoid the down-climbing.

Grand Central Couloir of Mount Kitchener, Canadian Rockies

The Northeast Face of Mount Kitchener is one of the great roadside crags of the Canadian Rockies. Kitchener is really just a rolling high point on the eastern edge of the Columbia Icefields, sloping gently to the west. On the north and east, however, it is as if half of the mountain has been shoveled away by the bite of a giant spade, leaving a mile-wide concavity of ice-festooned, rotten limestone. The Grand Central Couloir allows passage through this shattered rock almost completely on ice with one or two very difficult mixed pitches. The awesome prominence of the climb, when seen from the highway below Sunwapta Pass, is hard for a climber to ignore, and it engenders a reluctant desire to experience the mysteries of that incredible gash.

Although not the first or the last route to be done on the face, the Grand Central Couloir is, by far, the most obvious and classic line. Mike Weis and I made

Grand Central Couloir, Mount Kitchener *(Photo: Jeff Lowe)*

the first ascent in August 1974, the summer after we had climbed Bridalveil Falls in Telluride, Colorado. We climbed at night to avoid the rockfall that accompanies warm summer days, but later ascents have found better conditions in late summer or autumn.

The Grand Central Couloir was done about the same time as the Super Couloir on Mont Blanc du Tacul and the MacIntyre/Colton Route on the Walker Spur of the Grand Jorasses in the Alps. Together these climbs represented a high-mountain extension of skills gained on steep waterfall ice using curved picks that had, by then, been in use for five or six years.

Location: Three miles west of the Icefields Highway and a few miles north of Athabasca Pass, Mount Kitchener is one of the peaks that border the Columbia Icefields. The Northeast Face can be seen perfectly from a turnout in the road about a third of the way down from the top of the steep grade descending from the pass.

First Ascent: Mike Weis and Jeff Lowe, August 1974

Elevation Gain: 4,000 feet (approximately)

Difficulty: Grade V, AI4, M6 VS

Time: 8 to 16 hours on the climb

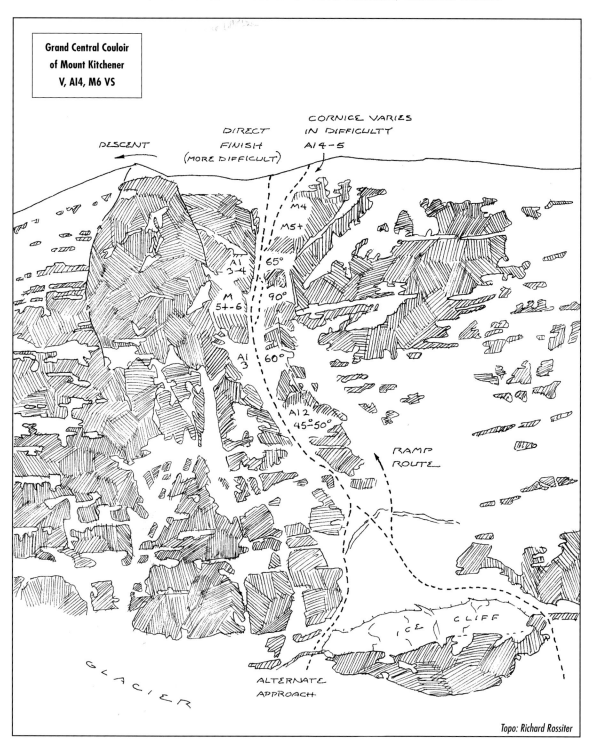

Grand Central Couloir
of Mount Kitchener
V, AI4, M6 VS

CORNICE VARIES
IN DIFFICULTY
AI4-5

DIRECT
FINISH
(MORE DIFFICULT)

DESCENT

M4

M5+

AI
3-4   65°

M
5+-6   90°

AI
3   60°

AI 2
45°-50°

RAMP
ROUTE

ICE CLIFF

GLACIER

ALTERNATE
APPROACH

Topo: Richard Rossiter

Equipment: Six or eight ice screws, six or eight pitons (including several knife-blades), a half set each of Stoppers and Friends, bivouac gear (optional)

Season: August to November

Comments: This is a big, objectively hazardous alpine climb that can be safely done by waiting until the cornice has fallen and for cold weather (or by climbing at night) to avoid rockfall. The upper gully contains some very difficult and serious climbing. Bivouac sites are extremely scarce.

Approach: Sign out for your climb at the information center at Athabasca Pass, then drive 3 miles north to a point at the end of a long, flat stretch of highway. Park at the point where the road ascends a short distance before commencing the final long, steep descent from the pass. Hike down to the Athabasca River west of the road and cross it via a log that spans the narrow gorge into which the water funnels at the end of the flat stretch. After crossing the river, follow the south edge of the trees and ascend west up and over the ridge in front of you (this ridge hides the face of Kitchener from view until you have topped it). Contour along barren scree slopes into the basin below the face. To get to the head of the basin, traverse the dying glacier at its base. It should take about 3 hours to reach the face from the highway.

Route: Climb easy snow (some ice at times) up slopes to the right of the hanging glacier in the bottom of the wall and cross over left onto the glacier. At this point you have two alternatives: (1) go directly up the center to the upper bergschrund, then cross it on the left by way of a very steep pitch; or (2) if the huge crevasse is impassable, cross over to the left side of the glacier, negotiate the bergschrund there, and diagonal up and right to the point where the two variations meet at the base of the couloir proper. From this point, about 1,500 feet of 50° ice, steepening to 60°, will bring you to the narrow upper couloir (AI3). The final section begins with a hard, probably mixed, pitch in the back of the couloir, which, at this point, is almost a dihedral. This pitch is the crux of the climb and is poorly protected (M5). The belay is semi-hanging from pitons in the left wall. One-half of the next lead is also mixed, and then steep, 65° ice leads to a rather broad section of ice below the upper rock section of the couloir. Two pitches up and right on ice of slightly lesser angle lead to a narrow, chimneylike gully that, in turn, is followed for a pitch up and right to a notch in the rib that borders the main couloir. Short rock steps (the first, 5.9) interspersed with snow and ice slopes lead up the crest of the couloir for two pitches to a belay at the base of the summit ice cap. One easy ice pitch and one very difficult pitch through the cornice bring you to Kitchener's broad summit.

Descent: Walk southeast about one-third to one-half mile to where the East Ridge meets the summit ice cap. Immediately you are faced with a deep gash. One 60-foot rappel deposits you into the gash, and a short but loose bit of 4th-classing brings you out the other side. From here, follow a long, relatively gentle snow or ice slope down the ridge crest to the saddle between Kitchener and the small peak known as K2. Contour down and left on snow and scree, heading toward a glacial tarn below the North Face of K2. A moderately steep slope through a cliff band must be negotiated just above the lake. Wander down to the ridge top you crossed on your approach to the face, and continue down the way you came. Sign out at the information center.

Gimme Shelter, Mount Quadra, Canadian Rockies

I first saw this line in October 1980, when I went into the Valley of the Ten Peaks to solo the Supercouloir on Mount Deltaform. On the drive in to the parking

area at Moraine Lake, I noticed the impressive streak of ice plastered to the 1,000-foot rock band below the hanging glacier on the East Face of Mount Quadra. Although it was only two-thirds formed at the time, I vowed to come back in a future winter to check it out.

In January 1983 I made the long ski approach to camp below this singular route. My partner was Alex Lowe, a climber from Montana who was little known at that time, though he was one of the best ice climbers and all-around American mountaineers. He has since become famous for guiding Everest several times and authoring numerous extreme new routes on rock and ice. On our attempt, Alex and I disagreed as to the relative security and wisdom of climbing under the seracs of Quadra's hanging glacier. In the end we retreated, after several pitches of excellent, bold thin ice. This was not due to the difficulty of the climbing, but rather to my uneasiness with the seracs. In April of that same year, Kevin Doyle and Tim Friesen, a couple of the best Canadian climbers, made the first ascent. However, they stopped at the top of the water ice, leaving the upper seracs to the hanging glacier unclimbed.

Alex Lowe leads the introductory pitch on an unsuccessful attempt on Gimme Shelter
(Photo: Jeff Lowe)

Then in 1992, a parallel line formed to the right of Gimme Shelter. Called Arctic Dream, it was climbed by Joe Josephson and Joe McKay, who also stopped below the seracs. Finally, in April of 1992, the Québecois climber Serge Angellucci and Frenchman François Damilano completed Arctic Dream (grade V, WI6) through the ice cliff to the hanging glacier, making, in my mind, the first full ascent.

Gimme Shelter is the more impressive of the two lines, however, and the ultimate climb would be to ascend Gimme Shelter and the ice cliff above to the hanging glacier, then finish on one of the little couloirs leading to the actual summit of Mount Quadra above the glacier shelf. This would yield an incredibly varied grade VI route with about 3,000 feet of elevation gain, combining thin waterfall ice difficulties with an alpine ice cruise.

To date even the original pitches of Gimme Shelter have not had a second ascent.

Location: The North Face of Mount Quadra rises above the Consolation Lakes, southeast of Moraine Lake. Gimme Shelter is in the center of the wall below the hanging glacier on the left side of a large rock buttress.

First Ascent: Kevin Doyle and Tim Friesen, April 1983

Elevation Gain: 1,000 feet to the bottom of the ice cliff of the hanging glacier

Difficulty: Grade V, WI7 (unconfirmed)

Time: The first ascent involved one bivouac on the prominent ledge two-thirds of the way up. See Comments below.

Equipment: Eight or ten ice screws, two or three blade pitons, one or two small angle pitons, a few small to medium Stoppers, half a set of Friends; head lamps, to avoid a possible bivouac; skis and/or snowshoes to speed the approach

Season: November through April, depending on the particular season

Comments: Without question the ice cliffs and seracs of Quadra's hanging glacier present a real objective hazard on this climb. If you decide to take the risk, prepare yourself mentally to move quickly. It should be possible for a fast party of two to do the climb in 6 or 8 hours, which would be far preferable to making a bivouac on the route. If you are climbing this well, it should also be possible to continue through the ice cliff in two or three pitches and solo up the couloir to the peak in another 3 or 4 hours. This would be one of North America's finest days on ice.

Approach: From Lake Louise follow the road toward Moraine Lake, which, in winter, is gated after a very short distance. From here ski to Moraine Lake and continue south to Consolation Valley, a total distance of about 15 miles that requires 5 or 6 hours. Make a camp here and prepare for an early start.

Route: An introductory pitch (WI4) climbs from the top of the snowfield below the face to a snow ledge at the bottom of the main falls. From here six or seven pitches follow the line of thickest ice to the bowl at the bottom of the ice cliffs. All of these pitches will be WI5, 6, or possibly 7, with very sparse protection.

Descent: If you climb only the original route, rappel from pitons and V-threads back down the climb. If you continue to the hanging glacier, or even the summit, you have the option of walking east on the glacial shelf and descending the large snow couloir that borders the left side of the North Face.

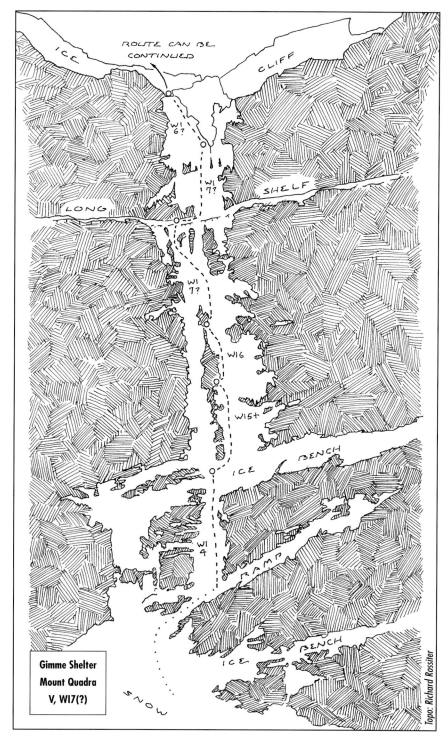

ROUTE CAN BE CONTINUED

ICE

CLIFF

WI 6?

WI 7?

SHELF

LONG

WI 7?

WI 6

WI 5+

ICE BENCH

RAMP

WI 4

ICE BENCH

**Gimme Shelter
Mount Quadra
V, WI7(?)**

SNOW

Topo: Richard Rossiter

Bridalveil Falls

(Photo: Greg Lowe)

Bridalveil Falls, Telluride, Colorado

Time doesn't just flow. It leaps tall lives in a single bound, creeping along like a stalking cat, then pouncing when you look away. It is hard to believe that over twenty years have surged by since the first ascent of this classic waterfall.

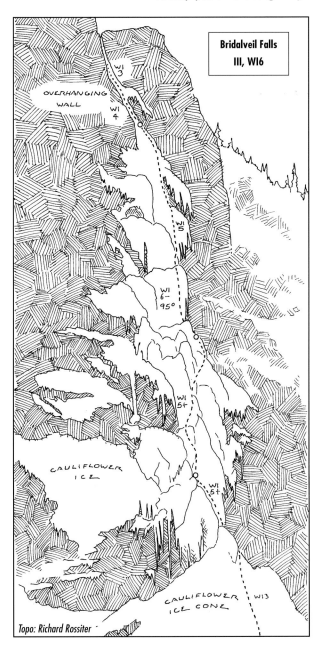

**Bridalveil Falls
III, WI6**

CAULIFLOWER
ICE

CAULIFLOWER
ICE CONE WI3

Topo: Richard Rossiter

Bridalveil doesn't just flow either. In summer it crashes, pounds, plunges so gracefully from a distance, so thunderously amid the giant conglomerate boulders in its basin below. As you look up at the roaring column, face dripping with spray, it is difficult to imagine any force formidable enough to still such awesome power.

But a Telluride winter is cold enough to freeze hell itself (To-HELL-you-ride!). In late autumn, the edges of the main fall sprout delicate white wings of ice. By December the whole cascade has hardened into a brittle pillar, narrow and spotty, with many cauliflowers and chandeliered sections in early season, much fuller and smoother by late February and March.

In 1974, waterfall ice climbing was in its infancy. While we waited for our Yosemite informants to let us know when the Widow's Tears had frozen (which never occurred that year), Mike Weis and I heard about an unclimbed challenge closer to home. We drove to Telluride from Lake City, where we were based as Outward Bound winter instructors, to take a look.

It was love at first sight. From the parking lot of the Idarado Mine we gazed in wonder at the beautiful, convoluted shaft of ice that rose 400 feet to an antique power station standing castlelike at the top of the cliff. Totally entranced, we made the one-hour ski approach, all the while vulnerable to the surrounding avalanche chutes.

The climb itself proved to be a landmark for Mike and me, and for the history of the sport. Although the Canadian Rockies classic, Nemesis, was climbed around the same time, it was ascended primarily with aid and fixed ropes. Using 70cm bamboo-shafted Chouinard axes and prototype Snargs my brother Greg had made specially for us, Mike and I free-climbed through the brittle bulges, insubstantial pillars, and numerous overhangs. In the conditions of the first ascent, and climbed free, the route was WI6+. More than twenty years later there are still very few climbs of greater difficulty; the top end of the scale is now only about 7 on pure ice.

Later that year Mike and I went back to Bridalveil with Greg, who wanted to film the climb. Although still of excellent quality, we found the climbing to be much easier—about 5+—in the conditions prevailing that March. The third ascent was not made until several years later, when Scotsman Gordon Smith and Aspenite Steve Shea confirmed the quality and difficulty of the route. In 1978, ABC filmed Mike, Henry Barber, and me for a broadcast, and later that year *Sports Illustrated* featured my first solo of Bridalveil as a cover story. The climb became the one to do for aspiring hard-people.

Location: Bridalveil Falls is located 2 miles east of the town of Telluride, Colorado, at the end of the box canyon.

First Ascent: Mike Weis and Jeff Lowe, January 1, 1974

Elevation Gain: About 400 feet

Difficulty: Grade III, WI6

Time: 4 to 6 hours

Equipment: Eight to ten ice screws, several long runners for slinging pillars

Season: December to March

Comments: The approach is threatened by huge avalanches from the bowls and gullies of Ajax Mountain. Immediately after storms and at other times of high avalanche hazard, consult with knowledgeable locals before heading up to Bridalveil.

Approach: Drive east on Telluride's main street approximately 2 miles to a parking area just outside the gates of the Idarado Mine. (Do not block access to the mine.) Don skis and follow the snow-covered jeep road a mile and a half to the base of Bridalveil, which is easily seen from the parking lot.

Route: Start in the middle, below the initial 75° to 85° apron. The first pitch ascends the apron and, usually, an overhang above, often using natural handholds on cauliflowers and pillars rather than tool placements. After 120 feet there is usually a cave to belay in. The next short pitch goes up and right over more overhangs (in early season) to belay on a prominent ice ledge halfway up the climb on the right. The third pitch is a long and continuously vertical pillar up the right side of the falls, ending in a spacious cave belay. Above is a final moderate face, which leads into the exit chimney.

Descent: Either rappel the route from V-threads, which is a good idea in sensitive avalanche conditions, or walk off left on the road behind the power station, then down the gully below the rock wall over which Bridalveil spills, and back to your starting point.

Birdbrain Boulevard, Ouray, Colorado

Birdbrain Boulevard
(Photo: Jeff Lowe)

By 1980 I had become somewhat jaded with climbing good, thick waterfall ice. It seemed that no matter how long or steep the climb was, so long as the ice was thick, a way could always be found to get up it. Although I now know better than this, at the time I turned my attention to ice and mixed climbs in the Andes, Alps, and Himalaya. But in February 1985, several friends and I were in Ouray, Colorado, to shoot a catalog for my old climbing equipment company, Latok, so we took the opportunity to combine work with a little fun. Mark Wilford and Charlie Fowler, two of America's best ice climbers, and I made the first ascent of a 1,000-foot mixed route that I had first spotted many years earlier.

Birdbrain Boulevard slashes through black conglomerate rock in the high cliff band to the right of the classic moderate ice route called The Ribbon. It is mainly a chimney line, varying in width from 1 to 10 feet, sometimes coated with good thick ice. But the line seemingly ends in a hopeless overhang 200 feet below the top. Although the second or third pitches can sometimes be more difficult, the key to the route is the lead that climbs out the right side of the cave below the overhang, ascends a difficult icy crack, then traverses back into the main line above the roof. Each pitch of Birdbrain has a character of its own, unusual for a chimney climb.

Oh, about the name. The climb is located across the road that leads to Camp Bird Mine, which has been in operation since the late 1800s, and when we first looked at it seriously with the idea of climbing it, we felt we must all have birdbrains.

Location: Birdbrain Boulevard is located a few miles west of Ouray, Colorado, off the Camp Bird Mine road, in the San Juan Mountains.
First Ascent: Charlie Fowler, Mark Wilford, and Jeff Lowe, February 1985
Elevation Gain: 1,000 feet
Difficulty: Grade IV, WI5, M6 S
Time: 8 to 12 hours round trip from the car
Equipment: 180-foot ropes, four or five ice screws, several knifeblade and angle pitons, a half set each of Stoppers and Friends; skis and skins, or snowshoes
Season: February to early May
Comments: The area where Birdbrain Boulevard is located is especially subject to

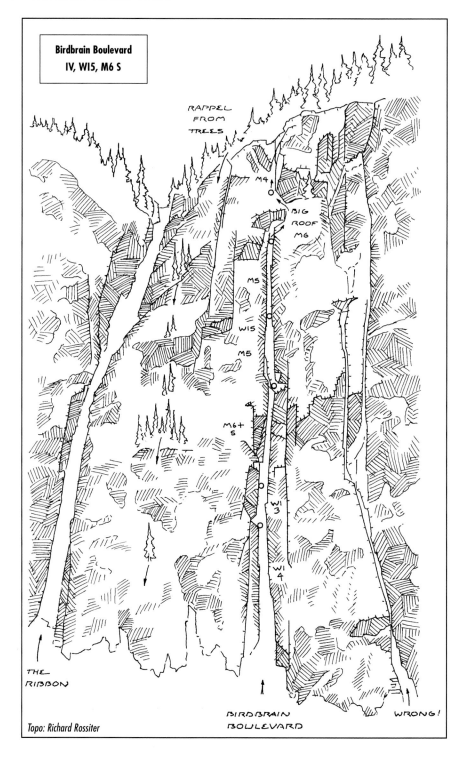

Birdbrain Boulevard
IV, WI5, M6 S

RAPPEL FROM TREES

M4

BIG ROOF M6

M5

WI5

M5

M6+ S

WI 3

WI 4

THE RIBBON

BIRDBRAIN BOULEVARD

WRONG!

Topo: Richard Rossiter

avalanche hazard, both on the approach slope leading to the climb, and from massive avalanche drainages that flank the cliffs bordering the climb. Once on the climb, however, it is quite safe.

Approach: From Ouray take U.S. 550 south out of town to the first right-hand turnoff, County Road 361, or the Camp Bird Mine road. Follow this over a bridge across the Uncompahgre Gorge and go several miles further to a parking spot (usually plowed) at the base of a series of switchbacks up the right side of the canyon at a point where it narrows considerably. Ski down a short road leading to Cascade Creek, cross the creek, and zigzag up the slope to the climb. The approach should take about an hour, depending upon snow conditions.

Route: The first pitch is steepening snow and ice that leads to a vertical 2-foot-wide chimney with ice at the back (WI4). Belay from ice screws where the chimney opens onto a wide sheet of ice. A short pitch climbs good 75° to 80° ice to a belay from knifeblades in a cave on the left (WI3). The long (about 160-foot) third pitch begins on a little vertical ice and continues with poorly protected mixed chimney climbing (M6+ S). Pitch four has more mixed chimney climbing (M5), ending with a steep (90°) wall of ice (WI5). At this point the chimney widens into a thinly iced face that leads to a belay in the cave below the big roof (M5). The crux pitch climbs vertical ice out the right side of the cave and a wide crack via mixed climbing above, then makes a hard snowy and icy rock traverse back left into a belay in the chimney, which is at that point narrow and deep (M6 S). The seventh and final pitch climbs the snow-filled chimney to the top (M4).

Descent: Six or seven rappels from trees down the rib to the left of the climb bring you back to your starting point.

Jeff Lowe on the Seventh Tentacle. Octopussy can be seen in the upper left corner.
(Photo: Brad Johnson)

Octopussy, Vail, Colorado

Octopussy is by far the shortest route designated as a classic in this book, but it is historically significant for the new level of technical difficulty that it introduces. The climb is at least a full technical grade more difficult than anything else I have managed to climb. The route may prove to be at the upper end of the M8 class, comparable to 5.13 rock climbing. It is also located in a very accessible area near other short high-end test pieces.

At the beginning of the 1994–95 ice season, with very little ice, I was completely unsuccessful in my attempts to repeat the climb. This was no doubt due, in part, to the extra ten pounds I was carrying around my waist at the time. However, the figure-4 moves at the lip of the roof, with the minuscule hook placements and the upside-down acrobatics required to execute them, will undoubtedly impress the most skilled climbers. Perhaps you will be able to find a less convoluted method to ascend this incredible test piece.

Octopussy II, WI5+, M8
(Photo: Brad Johnson)

Location: You will find Octopussy in the Rigid Designator amphitheater in East Vail, Colorado.

First Ascent: Jeff Lowe, April 1994

Elevation Gain: About 120 feet, including the Seventh Tentacle

Difficulty: Grade II, WI5+, M8

Time: Two hours (?)

Equipment: Four ice screws, half a dozen quickdraws, Friends to #3

Season: December through the end of March

Comments: Although the Seventh Tentacle varies greatly in difficulty (from M6+ to M7+) depending on how far down the ice hangs, Octopussy itself will probably always be M8—only slightly easier when the curtain hangs down more than a few feet below the roof. From a safety standpoint, it is a good idea to refrain from placing a screw in the ice curtain until you are well above the roof line. This eliminates the risk of the curtain breaking with you on it, attached by the screw to a ton of falling ice.

Approach: Driving west from Vail Pass on Interstate 70, take the East Vail exit and follow the frontage road west until it passes under the freeway. Turn left toward a fancy housing development and immediately left again into a parking area. From the parking area walk east, then take the first right and go south through the cul-de-sac to a bridge that crosses Gore Creek. You are now on a maintained cross-country ski trail. Follow this east for several hundred yards until the Rigid Designator and the Fang (if it is formed) come into view on the right. The Seventh Tentacle is directly behind the Fang, to the left of the smear of ice called the Little Thang. Octopussy is the clump of ice hanging from the left end of the roof above and left of the Seventh Tentacle. Follow the climbers' trail (or posthole) across the meadow, through the aspen grove, and up the drainage to the climb.

Route: Although it is possible to begin with the Little Thang (M6), you might as well start with the Seventh Tentacle (M6+ to M7+ S), which is just to the left of the three bolts that begin the former route. If you are unable to make the moves on the Seventh Tentacle, there is no point in attempting Octopussy. The Seventh Tentacle can be identified by a fixed angle piton 8 feet off the ground in a block, with a single bolt 4 feet higher. Belay from bolts underneath the roof at the top of the ice about 80 feet up. Octopussy begins with a moderate rock traverse (M4) left under the roof for about 25 feet. Soon you will see two fixed pitons at the junction of the roof and the wall, and two more out underneath the roof. Very technical hooking moves and extreme acrobatics lead out the 10-foot roof to the ice. Be gentle with the hook placements, as they could be destroyed by flailing. Once you are on the face of the ice, it is only 10 feet more to the top.

The crux headwall of Trapecio's South Face. *(Photo: Jeff Lowe)*

Descent: Rappel from a V-thread, removing your protection as you go, or, if your second is going to follow, climb up into the trees and traverse left to the fixed rappel point at the top of the Rigid Designator.

The South Face of Trapecio, Cordillera Huayhuash, Peru

The trek around Peru's Cordillera Huayhuash is among the most engaging I have ever done. It is one of the world's classic walks. Beginning in Chiquan on the northwest side of the range, the complete 100-mile circumnavigation can be done in an extremely comfortable ten to fifteen days. There is fantastic fishing in lakes Mitucocha, Carhuacocha, Jahuacocha, and Viconga, and the views of Yerupajá, Siulá, Rasac, Rondoy, and Jirishanca are ever-changing and inspirational.

I have made two circuits of the Huayhuash, each time less for the climbing than for the trek itself; but each time a pack of climbing gear somehow managed to find its way onto the burro. On the first trip in 1983, the North Buttress of Puscanturpa Norte caught my eye, and there I made one of the best free rock climbing solos I have ever done. I also fell under the spell of the the South Face of

Trapecio, which didn't look very difficult in the lower and upper regions, but the veil-like middle section was at once horrifying and ultimately attractive. The thought of climbing it was like contemplating an affair with the seductive wife of an ayatollah.

In 1985, the burro was again overburdened with a climbing pack, this time containing ice gear. After doing the most difficult and insecure solo ice climbing of my life, I quit my climb above the crux rock band. Although the 500 feet of

climbing from there to the summit looked easy, I had no more stomach for risk, and I rappelled and down-climbed from that point. So far as I know, the route awaits a first complete ascent.

Location: The South Face of Trapecio is near the southern end of the Cordillera Huayhuash, Peru.

First Ascent: Jeff Lowe, July 1985 (incomplete)

Elevation Gain: About 2,000 feet, from approximately 16,500 feet to the summit at 18,500 feet

Difficulty: Grade V, WI6+ VS

Time: Probably a full day for a fast party, with a bivouac possible on the descent

Equipment: Six or eight ice screws, two or three hook-type ice pitons, six or eight rock pitons (including several knifeblades), one or two deadmen, bivouac gear or not—at your discretion

Season: June to August

Comments: In the 1980s there were a number of problems between trekkers and members of the *Sendero Luminoso* (Shining Path). These Marxist rebels robbed and shot several tourists, not to mention massacring many locals in the guise of "liberating" the country from the "capitalists." However, since their ideological leader was captured and jailed in 1992, the situation seems to have settled down, and it now appears quite safe to travel in the area.

Trapecio *(Photo: Jeff Lowe)*

Approach: Travel by bus from Lima to Huaraz, then by truck to Chiquian, where it is possible to hire an *arriero* (guide) and burro(s). The *arriero* can guide you to a campsite in a beautiful meadow at 15,000 feet, below the South Face of Trapecio. It involves approximately six days of walking—time well spent.

Route: Begin up a couloir/ramp system of bulging white ice in the middle of the face. About 300 or 400 feet of AI3 to 4 climbing leads to 40° to 45° snowfields, which are followed for probably 500 feet to the base of the crux headwall. The first rope-length is AI3 and 4 climbing in an open corner. The next pitch begins with a very difficult series of mixed moves, which are followed by easier going on thick, but quite steep, 85° blue water ice. The last pitch of the headwall is completely vertical for a full rope-length, a 10-foot-wide stripe of snow ice only 1 to 3 inches thick. The still-unclimbed slopes above the headwall are fairly uniform, at an average angle of 50° to 55° and mostly névé. However, there appear to be one or two steeper pitches (class 4 to 5?) through the upper rock bands.

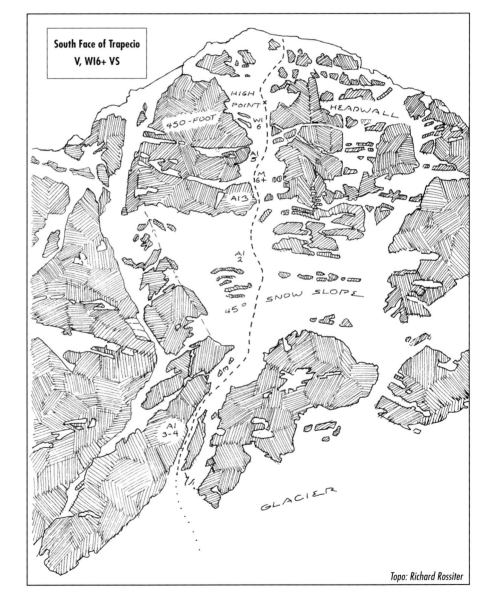

Topo: Richard Rossiter

Descent: My plan for the descent was to down-climb and rappel the East Ridge, which is mainly snow with some apparent serac and cliff obstacles, but nothing that appears too unreasonable. In fact, I made three rappels from the top of the headwall from rock pitons and down-climbed the remainder of the face. My descent required about two and a half hours.

The Southwest Buttress of Taulliraju, Cordillera Blanca, Peru

Taulliraju *(Photo: Jeff Lowe)*

Translated from the native Quechuan, *taulliraju* means "flower of ice." It is an apt description of a peak straight out of a climber's flight of fancy. Hovering over the ancient Incan pass of Punta Union like a crystal hummingbird, the mountain is at its most alluring and mystical in late afternoon light, with clouds swirling around its twin granite pillars. The south pillar was the scene of Nicolas Jaeger's inspired solo climb in 1979. The southwest pillar is even more attractive, with its comet tail of a couloir at the bottom and the intricate arabesques of its upper ice arête.

When I first saw a photo of this pillar taken by my brother Mike in the early 1970s, I knew I would someday have to come and climb it. Three years before Alex Lowe and I made our climb, the first ascent was done by an Italian expedition with six members using fixed ropes and siege tactics. Alex and I made the climb and traversed the peak in a four-day, alpine-style round trip. Other routes have been done on this side of the mountain, at least one of which is a more difficult mixed rock and ice climb; but none tugs the strings of the climber's heart with greater force than the Southwest Buttress.

Location: The Southwest Buttress of Taulliraju is above 16,000-foot Punta Union pass, at the head of the Santa Cruz valley in the Cordillera Blanca of Peru.

First Ascent: Gianni Calcagno, Piero Perona, Ugo Vialardi, Costantino Piazzo, Tullio Vidoni, and Stefano DeBenedetti, August 1980; first alpine-style ascent: Alex Lowe and Jeff Lowe, July 1983

Elevation Gain: About 3,200 feet, from approximately 16,000 feet to 19,128 feet

Difficulty: Grade VI, WI6, M6 (one point of aid)

Time: 2 or 3 days in ascent, 1 day for the descent

Equipment: Six or eight ice screws, two or three hook-type ice pitons, six or eight rock pitons (including several knifeblades), one or two deadmen, bivouac gear

Season: June to August

Comments: The Santa Cruz valley gives access to an exemplary array of peaks, including the ice pyramids of Alpamayo, Artesonraju, and Pirámide, and therefore serves as a convenient base for an extended period of climbing. Acclimatizing with hikes up to Punta Union pass inspires awe and respect for the Incans who carved and laid the stones that lead upward like a staircase to the clouds. The Incans seem to have thought about stone and ice and the

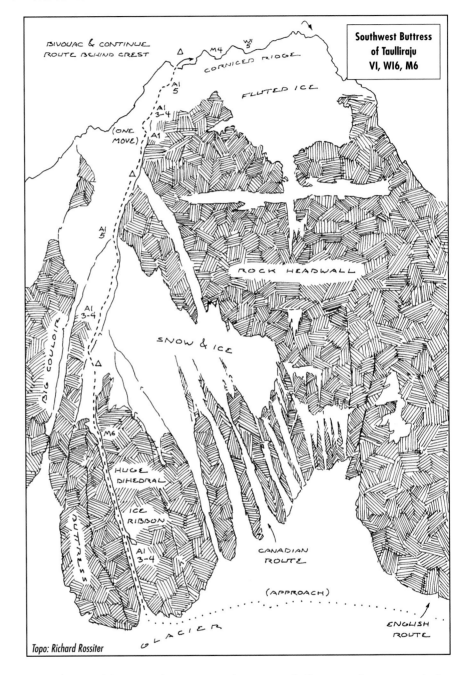

BIVOUAC & CONTINUE ROUTE BEHIND CREST

CORNICED RIDGE

M4 WI 5

FLUTED ICE

Southwest Buttress of Taulliraju VI, WI6, M6

AI 5

AI 3-4

AI (ONE MOVE)

AI 5

ROCK HEADWALL

AI 3-4

SNOW & ICE

BIG COULOIR

M6

HUGE DIHEDRAL

ICE RIBBON

BUTTRESS

AI 3-4

CANADIAN ROUTE

(APPROACH)

ENGLISH ROUTE

GLACIER

Topo: Richard Rossiter

natural world in ways that we can only guess at. In Peru it is always a good idea to retain your *arriero* for the duration of your stay in the mountains to prevent thievery.

Approach: Travel by bus from Lima to Huaraz, then by bus from Huaraz to the village of Cashapampa, where you can hire an *arriero* and burros. A 2-day walk will bring you to good camping in meadows below Taulliraju and Punta Union.

Alex Lowe leading hard mixed ground in the lower couloir on Taulliraju.
(Photo: Jeff Lowe)

Route: The first third of the buttress is climbed by way of the major gash between walls of El Capitan–quality granite. Follow this for about a dozen pitches of steepening WI3, 4, and 5, which gradually thins into some very difficult mixed climbing (M6) in a sort of chimney and eventually leads to the crest of the icy ridge. Snow ledges provide a place for the first bivouac. Then follow the fluted ice arête for about fifteen pitches by the line of least resistance. The climbing is WI3 to 5+ among cornices, towers, arêtes, and couloirs weaving back and forth across the crest of the ridge. A bivouac cave with a flat floor is located a pitch or so below the rock band that bisects the arête several hundred feet below the summit ridge. On a short, overhanging rock step through the band, you can place one piton for aid to pull onto the steep, whipped-cream rolls that lead to the summit ridge. Several increasingly nerve-wracking leads on extremely steep Andean cheese ice lead to the horribly corniced crest of the summit ridge. Rather than follow the crest, drop down half a rope-length on the east side of the mountain. Here you can make a third bivouac in an ice cave. Following more or less the junction of rock and ice at the top of the east face, traverse for several pitches toward the summit of the mountain. Finally, a difficult (WI5) waterfall-ice pitch takes you directly back onto the crest of the summit ridge. A gentle stroll up easy snow leads to the summit.

Descent: Climb a short way (about 100 feet) down the south buttress, then make a series of five or six rappels, mostly from rock anchors, down the Southeast Face. This will bring you to the high glacial shelf on this side of the mountain. Cross the glacier in a southeasterly direction for about one-half mile, then look over the edge for the top of the Southeast Pillar, which drops down to meet the slopes on the east side of Punta Union. Another ten rappels or so down this rocky ridge deposit you on these eastern slopes, a short distance from the Inca Trail. Hike back over Punta Union to your base camp.

Citadel/Sticil Face, Shelter Stone Crag, Scotland

Shelter Stone Crag is a granite prominence in a remote corrie in the Cairngorms. With 1,000 feet of excellent steep rock, it is one of Scotland's highest cliffs, home to a number of challenging summer climbs. In good winters, the features of the escarpment are delicately etched with ice.

Gordon Smith on the lower slabs of the Citadel route, Shelter Stone Crag
(Photo: Jeff Lowe)

Citadel takes a line up the center of the face, following grooves and chimneys to a crux corner and wall to reach a large snow ledge at two-thirds height. The summer line continues through steep rock directly above the right-hand corner of the ledge. Although it has been climbed in winter by Murray Hamilton and Ken Spence, it is rarely in icy condition. By traversing left on the ledge, however, the bottom two-thirds of Citadel can be linked with the upper chimney line of Sticil Face, making a very challenging natural winter link-up. This combination was first climbed by Al Rouse and Brian Hall in the winter of 1973. I repeated the route with the Scotsman Gordon Smith the next winter. Like Rouse and Hall, we pulled on a piton on the crux pitch below the ledge (M6, A1). Later, the first completely free ascent was made by Rab Anderson and Graeme Nicol. The rating given here is my estimate, based on a twenty-year-old memory and reports from the free-climbing team.

Location: Shelter Stone Crag is located in the northern Cairngorms alongside Cairn Etchachan.

First Ascent: Alan Rouse and Brian Hall, winter 1973; first free ascent: Rab Anderson and Graeme Nicol, 1987

Elevation Gain: About 1,000 feet

Difficulty: Grade IV, M7 (unconfirmed)

Time: 6 to 8 hours

Equipment: One or two ice screws, two or three blade pitons, one or two small angle pitons, a few small to medium Stoppers, half a set of Friends; head lamps, to avoid a possible bivouac; skis and/or snowshoes to speed up the approach when there is deep snow

Season: December through March, depending on the particular season

Comments: The Cairngorms are subject to whiteouts and severe winds and storm. Be expert with map and compass and be ready to use them on the approach/

retreat from the climb. Stop at the Aviemore Lodge, one of the homes of the Scottish National Mountaineering School, near the Cairngorm ski area for information on conditions and approach.

Approach: From the top of the Cairngorm ski area, cross the Cairngorm plateau and drop down into the corrie with a little lake below the crag (2 hours).

Route: Beginning on iced-up slabs near the toe of the rock, follow the line of Citadel for two pitches of WI3 climbing. A more difficult chimney pitch (M4+) leads to a belay below the crux. The crux is a difficult series of moves over some bulges and past a short wall with fixed pitons to easier ground

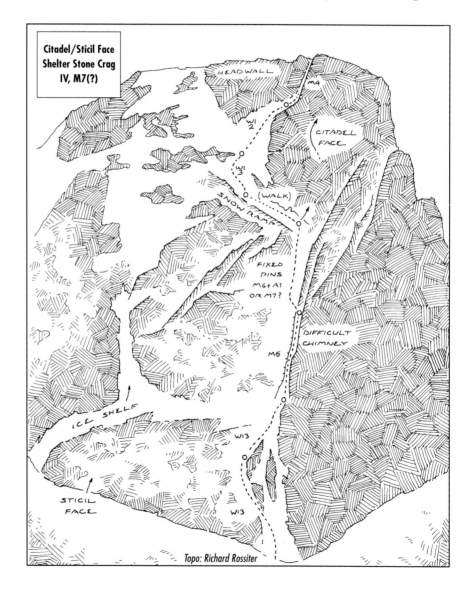

Citadel/Sticil Face
Shelter Stone Crag
IV, M7(?)

Topo: Richard Rossiter

(M7?). An easier pitch (M2 or 3) leads to the large snow ledge. Walk left on the ledge, then diagonal up and left at its end to a junction with the Sticil Face chimney (easy climbing). One easy and one moderate (M4) pitch follow the chimney to the top.

Descent: Since the top of Shelter Stone Crag is really just the edge of the Cairngorm plateau, you can simply walk back around the top of the corrie and rejoin your approach track.

The Landmark Routes of the Northeast Face of Ben Nevis, Scotland

The Northeast Face of Ben Nevis, under full winter armor, is a savage and impressive place. Alpine in nature, with 2,000-foot buttresses and 1,500-foot faces seamed by impressive gullies and chimneys, this was the scene of a number of premonitory ascents between 1957 and 1960 by Jimmy Marshall, Tom Patey, Robin Smith, Dougall Haston, Hamish MacInnes, Ian Clough, and others. These routes were ten years ahead of their time and technically more difficult than any contemporaneous ice climbs in the Alps. To my mind, the most classic, the Orion Face Direct, which had its second ascent in 1971, is roughly comparable to routes done in the high mountains during the 1970s, such as the climbs on the Grand Pilier d'Angle, the Balfour Face of Mount Tasman in New Zealand, Route Canal on the Northeast Face of the Grand Teton, or New Hampshire's Black Dike. When you consider that all of the Ben Nevis routes were made using step-cutting techniques with straight-pick ice axes, in five to twelve hours, with only the occasional rock piton or runner around a spike for protection, they become all the more remarkable. Collectively, these climbs represent the high-water mark of the old classic style of ice climbing. With curved picks, rigid boots, tube screws, fleece and waterproof/breathable shell clothing, and the like, Ben Nevis has lost some of its mythical qualities, but any ice climber interested in the history of the sport should make a pilgrimage there in honor of the old masters.

In 1974, in the company of John Cunningham, Hamish MacInnes, Tut Braithewaite, Henry Barber, Alex MacIntyre, Yvon Chouinard, and others, I spent

Ben Nevis *(Photo: Jeff Lowe)*

a month in Scotland working on a never-released film for the National Geographic Society. Ferried by helicopter each day to the top of the Ben from our base at the Clachaig Inn in Glencoe, I had the occasional opportunity to sneak away (with others and alone) during lulls in the filming and experience a number of these great routes. Nevis blizzards, styrofoam ice plastering all the exposed rock, nightly samplings of the great Scottish brews in the pub, trading tales with some of the era's greatest climbers—these remain some of the most fulsome memories of my ice-climbing career.

Here I have listed a number of the important climbs made from 1957 to 1960. Rather than describing them in great detail, I have only indicated the length, the grade, the first ascent parties, and the date for each.

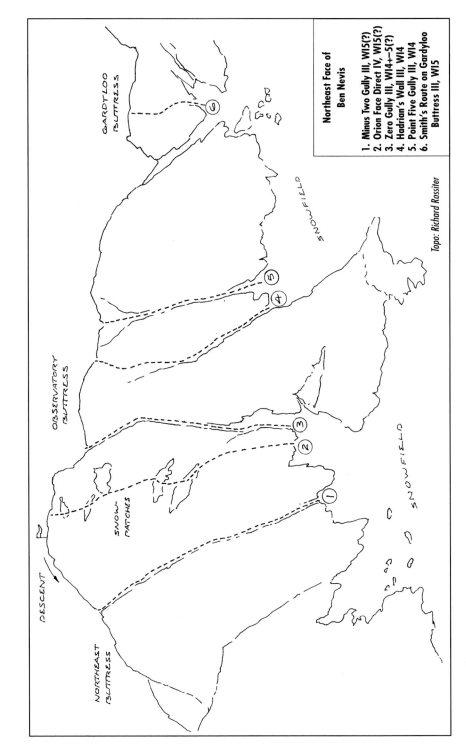

Northeast Face of Ben Nevis

1. Minus Two Gully III, WI5(?)
2. Orion Face Direct IV, WI5(?)
3. Zero Gully III, WI4→5(?)
4. Hadrian's Wall III, WI4
5. Point Five Gully III, WI4
6. Smith's Route on Gardyloo Buttress III, WI5

Topo: Richard Rossiter

Top: **Typical climbing on Ben Nevis snow-ice**
Bottom: **A rare perfect day on the Ben. John Cunningham belays Yvon Chouinard to the top.**

(Photos: Jeff Lowe)

Location: Ben Nevis (4,408 feet) is located in western Scotland, a few miles east of Fort William.

Minus Two Gully: 900 feet, grade III, WI5(?). First ascent: Jimmy Marshall, J. Stenhouse, Dougall Haston, February 1959. This is probably the hardest technical climb of the classic Nevis gullies.

Orion Face Direct: 1,500 feet, grade IV, WI5(?). First ascent: Robin Smith and Jimmy Marshall, February 1960. This beautiful direct but natural line follows steep ice grooves to the basin and continues to follow the line of least resistance quite directly to the summit.

Zero Gully: 1,500 feet, grade III, WI4+ to 5(?). First ascent: Hamish MacInnes, Tom Patey, and Graeme Nicol, February 1957. In thin-ice conditions the climbing can border on M6.

Hadrian's Wall: 800 feet, grade III, WI4. First ascent: W. D. Brooker, Jimmy Marshall, and Tom Patey, February 1959. Probably the easiest of the routes listed here, it is still a fine climb.

Point Five Gully: 1,000 feet, grade III, WI4. First ascent: J. M. Alexander, Ian Clough, D. Pipes, and R. Shaw, in hard conditions over 5 days in January 1959. The second ascent, by Robin Smith and Jimmy Marshall in good conditions, took only 7 hours.

Smith's Route on Gardyloo Buttress: 400 feet, grade III, WI5. First ascent: Robin Smith and Jimmy Marshall, February 1960. A short but technical and extremely aesthetic route, it uses the prominent slanting grooves that drain the upper funnel of the buttress.

Approach: The approach to all of the routes passes the distillery on the highway leading northeast out of Fort William and continues up the Allt a Mhulinn on foot to the CIC Hut (open only to members of the Scottish Mountaineering Club), usually a journey of 2 to 3 hours. From the hut, it is another 30 to 45 minutes up to the climbs.

Descent: Contour around to the south and east to the Carn Mor Dearg Arête, and from there into the Coire Leis. From the Carn Mor Dearg Arête there may be a line of rappel posts leading down into the Coire Leis.

MacIntyre/Colton Route, Grandes Jorasses, France

The MacIntyre/Colton route follows ice fields, gullies, and chimneys on the right flank of the famous Walker Spur of the Grandes Jorasses. Whereas the classic climb on the crest of the granite spur is perhaps the most elegant of the three "last great challenges" of the 1920s and '30s—the other two being the north faces of the Matterhorn and the Eiger—the MacIntyre/Colton is a bit terrifying to contemplate. One can easily imagine the heavy rockfall of summer funneling down the line of ascent. Still, the logic of the route is undeniable: a thin white slash through dark boilerplate slabs in the heart of the quintessential north wall. And in the cold

of autumn or winter the rockfall is stilled, so it is reasonably safe. When this climb was first done in 1975, it marked the beginning of an era of climbers looking for difficult seasonal ice on the great Alpine faces. It remains one of the most challenging routes of this nature, the enduring signature of two great English climbers—Alex MacIntyre and Nick Colton.

Mike Kennedy and I climbed the first two-thirds of the route in winter conditions in October 1986, then traversed left to the upper part of the Walker Spur, where we found the climbing quite challenging on snow-covered rock. In honor of the first ascensionists, the original finish is described below.

Location: The MacIntyre/Colton Route rises on the French (north) side of the Grandes Jorasses—which is part of the massif of Mont Blanc—at the head of the Lescheaux Glacier.

First Ascent: Alex MacIntyre and Nick Colton, July 1975

Elevation Gain: About 3,500 feet, from the bergschrund to the summit of the Walker Spur

Difficulty: Grade V, WI6, AI3, M6, A3 S

Time: 12 to 16 hours

Equipment: Six or seven ice screws, a dozen assorted knifeblades, standard and small angle pitons, a half set of Stoppers and Friends, head lamps, bivi gear (optional)

Season: October through April, depending on the particular year

Comments: To my knowledge, the MacIntyre/Colton has not been climbed completely free. The pitch above the small ice field that bisects the two runnels in the middle of the route is usually pure rock and has required some aid from pitons. Perhaps, in good conditions, you can climb thin ice on the face to the left. Another option might be to follow an ice-filled, foot-wide crack that rises from an upper-right-hand corner of the central ice field and connects with the upper ice field. This crack has been climbed by Jean-Marc Boivin as part of a route called Extreme Dream and is probably about M5 or harder.

Approach: Take the train from Chamonix to Montenvers and walk or ski up the Mer de Glace to the Lescheaux Hut on the left bank of the Lescheaux Glacier. Alternatively, you can take the *téléphérique* to the Aiguille du Midi and ski down the Mer de Glace to its junction with the Lescheaux Glacier. In either case, the Lescheaux Hut is your base for the climb, and reaching it will take several hours. In the morning it is another hour or so up the glacier to the base of the climb.

Route: Depending on conditions, cross the bergschrund either on the right or left side of the base of the central ice field. Many times this will entail a pitch or more of difficult climbing—up to AI5. Follow the 50° to 60° slope (AI2) above for about 1,000 feet to the bottom of the steep ice runnel that constitutes the middle portion of the climb. Several pitches of WI4 and 5 and M5 up to 90° lead to the small central ice field. The original route crosses this 50° ice field

Grandes Jorasses
(Photo: René Robert)

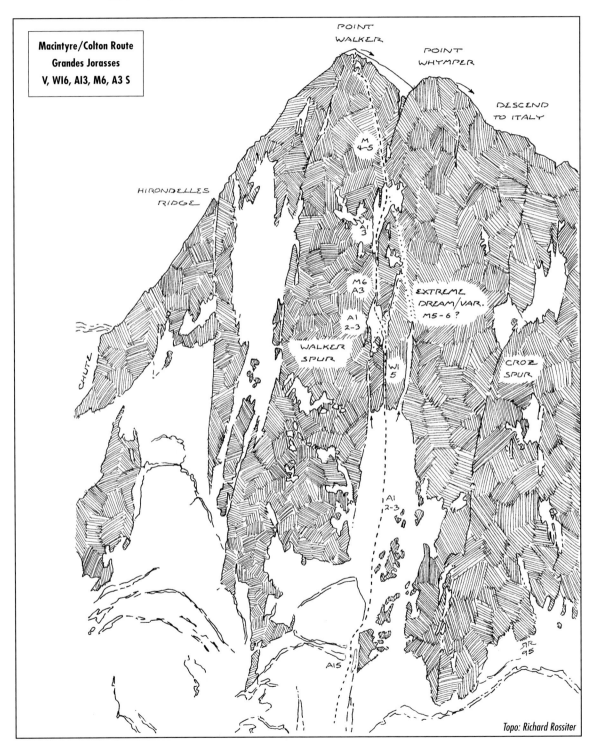

Macintyre/Colton Route
Grandes Jorasses
V, WI6, AI3, M6, A3 S

POINT
WALKER

POINT
WHYMPER

DESCEND
TO ITALY

M
4-5

HIRONDELLES
RIDGE

IV
A3

M6
A3

EXTREME
DREAM/VAR.
M5-6 ?

AI
2-3

WALKER
SPUR

CROZ
SPUR

CHUTE

WI
5

AI
2-3

RR
95

AI5

Topo: Richard Rossiter

up and left. An intricate rock pitch with some aid and a tension traverse left (AI2 or 3, M5) lead to a belay at the very bottom right side of the upper gully coming down from the left side of the highest ice field. Another moderately difficult pitch on rather steep ice (WI4) leads to four or five pitches of lower-angle climbing (50° to 55°, AI2), which brings you to the rim of the upper ice field below the central chimneylike depression in the final rock headwall. Eight pitches of M4 to 5 mixed climbing follow this depression to a junction with the last pitch of the Walker Spur (M5 in winter conditions), and then you top out on the very summit.

Descent: The long descent from the Walker Spur is down the south (Italian) side of the mountain. Begin by walking to Point Whymper, the slightly lower point several hundred feet west of Point Walker. Follow a rib of broken rock and ice directly south until you can cross the bergschrund on the South Face ice field onto a glacier shelf. Cross the shelf to the right (facing the valley), underneath some ice cliffs. At the far end of the shelf is another rocky rib. Ascend it a short distance above the shelf to a fairly prominent notch. From there a rappel deposits you in a narrow, glacier-filled basin. Cross it down and right to a rocky prominence, which you descend until you find rappel anchors. Make a rappel or two and then continue down as directly as possible. Eventually you will connect with a trail leading to the little Italian village above Courmayeur, where it is possible to buy a well-deserved meal and a bottle of wine at one of several cozy restaurants. (Don't forget your passport and some money!) From here you can catch a bus back through the tunnel to Chamonix.

Super Couloir Direct, Mont Blanc du Tacul, France

Mont Blanc du Tacul is a veritable ice-climbing university. This one mountain, which is accessible in an hour or so from the *téléphérique* of the Aiguille du Midi (on the French side) or Courmayeur (on the Italian side), harbors more than a dozen classic ice climbs and several excellent mixed routes. These range in difficulty from the 45° Gervasutti Couloir (grade III, AI2, 3,000 feet) to the Super Couloir Direct (grade V, WI5-, M6, 2,800 feet), one of the most compelling high-mountain ice climbs I have ever seen.

For several years after it was first climbed, the Super Couloir was considered perhaps the hardest ice climb in the Alps; early ascents all required one or two bivouacs, although now it is almost always climbed in a day. However, most parties avoid the Direct start by climbing the first rock pitches of the Gervasutti Pillar, which forms the right-hand border of the couloir. The Direct start is often said to be out of condition because of too little ice. However, that is never the case; it is very good mixed climbing, torqueing, hooking, and liebacking in thin-to-wide vertical cracks, even in the leanest conditions.

Regrettably, many people who climb the Super Couloir also stop at the end of the crux water-ice pitch, which is still 1,000 feet from the top. Since this is a mountain route, I think that last section of easy snow and ice is an integral part of the climb and shouldn't be missed. Having said that, I have to admit that on my own solo climb in March 1993, I followed the fixed rappels from the end of the difficult climbing, my only excuse being that I had to make the 4:30 P.M. train from Montenvers at the bottom of the Mer de Glace. Considering that I had begun the climb at 11:30 A.M. and it was only 1:30 P.M. when I finished the difficulties, I still felt it was a good day on the hill.

Super Couloir Direct, Mont Blanc du Tacul
(Photo: Jeff Lowe)

Location: Mont Blanc du Tacul is a satellite peak of Mont Blanc, sitting at the head of the Vallée Blanche on the French side. The Super Couloir is located on the Northeast Face and leads directly to the 12,947-foot summit. Good topographical maps of the range can be found in any bookstore in Chamonix.

First Ascent: Patrick Gabarrou and Jean-Marc Boivin, 1976

Elevation Gain: 2,800 feet, from 10,147 feet to 12,947 feet at the summit

Difficulty: Grade V, WI5-, M6

Time: 8 to 14 hours on the climb

Equipment: Six or eight ice screws, two or three blade pitons, one or two small angle pitons, a few small to medium Stoppers, half a set of Friends; head lamps, to avoid a possible bivouac; skis and/or snowshoes to speed up the approach

Season: October through June

Comments: The Super Couloir is a very popular climb, and, if you don't want to be clobbered by ice from climbers above, you will have to get a very early start. The best way to do this is to take the *téléphérique* the night before your climb and stay at the Torino Hut.

Approach: From either the Aiguille du Midi or the Torino Hut it is about an hour and a half by ski and foot across the Mer de Glace of the Vallée Blanche to the bottom of the Super Couloir, depending on the snow conditions.

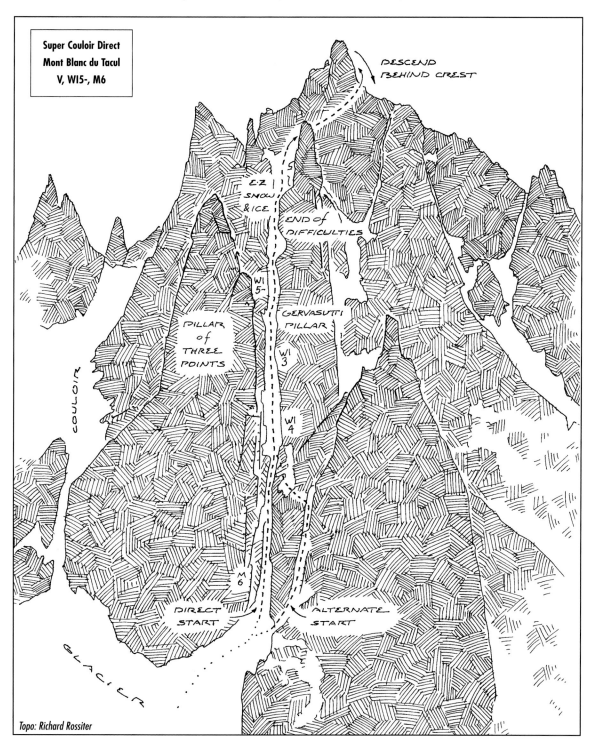

Super Couloir Direct
Mont Blanc du Tacul
V, WI5-, M6

DESCEND BEHIND CREST

EZ SNOW & ICE

END of DIFFICULTIES

WI 5-

GERVASUTTI PILLAR

PILLAR of THREE POINTS

WI 3

WI 4

COULOIR

M 6

DIRECT START

ALTERNATE START

GLACIER

Topo: Richard Rossiter

Route: Two pitches of difficult mixed climbing follow the direct fall line from the upper couloir. Each of these pitches has some M6 climbing when done completely free, which is uncommon. Once in the couloir, 200 feet of easy snow leads to the bottom of the water ice. The first pitch is WI4, and this is followed by six pitches of rolling WI3 ice to a final crux pitch (WI5-). Above this point the angle recedes dramatically, and 1,000 feet of easy snow and possibly some mixed climbing lead to the summit.

Descent: Descend the regular route down the west flank of the mountain, usually following a well-trodden trail in the snow. In a whiteout you will be glad to have a map and compass to help you find the correct way off the mountain and back across the glacier to the *téléphérique* or down the Mer de Glace, if you are continuing on skis.

Blind Faith, Tête de Gramusat, France

The Tête de Gramusat is the location of several of the longest and most difficult waterfall climbs in Europe. A 1,400-foot-high limestone ziggurat draped in fangs and curtains of ice, its main face was first ascended in January 1991 by Frenchman François Damilano and Scotsman Robin Clothier. They called their route Gramusat Direct. Although the climb does go up the center of the face, it is not actually direct in that it diagonals from left to right to avoid a huge roof 500 feet above the ground. After following the first two and a half leads of Gramusat Direct, Blind Faith tackles the roof directly, then climbs an impressive two-tiered pillar higher up.

The name of the route comes from the fact that I blindly followed Thierry Renault to the base of a climb I had never seen. Looking up from the bottom at the icy daggers suspended from the big roof, I could see none of the wall above and had no idea how big it was or what the climbing would be like. I had to go on blind faith that Thierry knew what he was getting us into. This climb was responsible for rewhetting my appetite for waterfall ice climbing, which had been somewhat dormant for over a decade.

Location: The Tête de Gramusat is located in the Vallée de Freissinières in the Briançonnais region of France. From the town of Briançon take the N94 highway in the direction of Gap. Three miles before the village of Roche de Rame turn right on the D38 highway toward Freissinieres. Continue to the village of Viollins, where you will find a small parking lot. In early season you may be able to drive further up the road, thus avoiding a good portion of the approach on foot.

First Ascent: Thierry Renault and Jeff Lowe, January 1992
Elevation Gain: 1,400 feet
Difficulty: Grade V, WI6+, A2 (M7+ if climbed free?)
Time: 8 to 12 hours on the climb

Tête de Gramusat
(Photo: Thierry Renault)

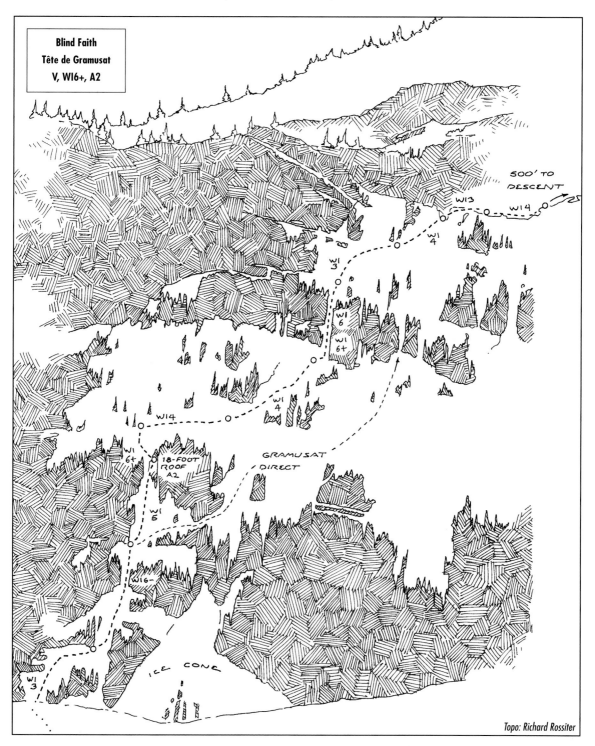

Blind Faith
Tête de Gramusat
V, WI6+, A2

500' TO DESCENT

WI3

WI4

WI4

WI6

WI6+

WI4

WI4

WI6+

18-FOOT ROOF A2

GRAMUSAT DIRECT

WI5

WI6-

WI3

ICE CONE

Topo: Richard Rossiter

Thierry Renault spears the icicle at the end of the roof on Blind Faith. *(Photo: Jeff Lowe)*

Equipment: Eight to ten ice screws, two or three blade pitons, one or two small angle pitons, a few small to medium Stoppers; head lamps, to avoid a possible bivouac

Season: January to February

Comments: Although Blind Faith is relatively safe from the standpoint of objective hazard, the approach slopes directly below the Tête de Gramusat have snow overlaying an ice slab—potential avalanche conditions. In addition, the climb is quite long, so you must move quickly to complete it in a day. Although the descent can be made by head lamp (as on the first ascent), it would be much more pleasant to come down in daylight.

Approach: From the parking lot walk up the road until you are beyond the main face of Tête de Gramusat. Find a gully coming down below the rappel descent and follow a trail or post hole up this gully to the cliff. Total approach time: 1 hour 15 minutes to 2 hours 30 minutes, depending on where you park your car.

Route: Blind Faith shares the first two pitches of Gramusat Direct, the first pitch being quite easy (WI3) and the second being quite difficult (WI6-). Where Gramusat Direct makes a long traverse right to avoid the roof, Blind Faith continues directly up the steep pillar (WI5) that ends under the roof. The fourth pitch turns the roof by way of cracks on the overhanging left wall of a large hanging dihedral about 10 or 15 feet below the junction with the actual horizontal roof. On the first ascent, three points of aid were used to cross the roof (A2), but it could be done completely free at about M7 or 7+. The pitch finishes on hanging spikes of ice leading up and left through another dihedral, through a much smaller overhang, and reaching good ice for a belay (WI6+). Above the roof a long rightward traverse (WI4) ends at a belay on good ledges somewhat left of the fall line from the upper pillar. A moderate (WI4) pitch diagonals up and right to a belay on the left-hand side of the base of the impressive pillar. The pillar itself is actually two parts, the first half being vertical and overhanging (WI6+ S) to a stance behind the pillar on a good ledge. The pitch continues for the rest of the rope-length up the still vertical and difficult upper half of the pillar to its top (WI6-). Three more moderate (WI3–4) pitches lead up and slightly right to a huge, ice-filled bowl. Two final pitches of WI3 and 4 traverse right in the bowl and up at the end to finish the climb in common with Gramusat Direct.

Descent: Follow a snow ledge through the trees to the right above the top of the cliff for 500 feet or so to a point overlooking the descent buttress. Six or seven rappels down the buttress lead you to the approach gully. You should be able to find fixed anchors.

The Hungo Face of Kwangde, Khumbu, Nepal

Hungo Face of Kwangde
(Photo: Jeff Lowe)

From November 28 to December 3, 1982, David Breashears and I made the first ascent of the North Face of Kwangde (20,323 feet) above the village of Hungo in the Khumbu region of Nepal. The face is 4,500 feet high and composed of tongues and smears of thin white ice over boilerplate granite slabs. The average angle (taken from the Schneider map) is 65°, exceptionally steep for an ice route. In the morning we would peek out of our BAT tents to see the sun rise over Makalu's pink granite. During the day we could trace the trade route over the Nangpa La into Tibet. In the afternoon, fingers of cloud crept up the valleys toward Cho Oyu, Everest, and Lhotse. Supper was accompanied by alpine glow on the top of Ama Dablam. We spent the fourth night hacking a cave from the hard ice of an old cornice just below the summit. Inside the coffin-sized hole we wondered if the wind would rip our home off the mountain, but we arrived on the summit early the next morning, convinced that we had completed what would become a hard modern classic climb. We descended in two days via the South Face, over a notch in the Southeast Ridge, down its East Face, and finally around the toe of the Northeast Ridge to Hungo. The weather was good during the climb, with temperatures of 15°F during the day and -5° to -10°F at night. Moderately high winds and spindrift early in the climb made us feel like salmon swimming upstream.

A unique climb with a character all its own, our route on the Hungo Face is, overall, the finest pure ice climb I have ever done. Although a Spanish team succeeded in climbing a less direct and easier line on the right side of the wall in the mid-1980s, so far as I know, our central route remains unrepeated—although there have been several attempts.

The climb is characterized by reptilian tongues of white ice that flicker down over compact granite slabs on the lower 2,000 feet of the face. These tongues are not present in the warmer months, generally appearing in December and lasting into March. In many places the wall presents long, poorly protected pitches of thin, porcelainlike ice over steep rock.

We spent four days and nights on the 4,500-foot-high face during the first ascent, and another day and a half on the descent back to the tiny village of Hungo, which serves as a base camp below the North Face. A well-acclimated team of two might be able to cut that time by 30 percent to 50 percent by traveling extremely light and fast.

Location: The Hungo Face of Kwangde is located above the village of Hungo, Khumbu Himal, Nepal (Schneider map "Khumbu Himal," available in Kathmandu).

First Ascent: David Breashears and Jeff Lowe, November 28 to December 2, 1982

Elevation Gain: About 4,500 feet, from approximately 16,000 feet to the summit at 20,323 feet

Difficulty: Grade VII, WI6 VS

Time: 4 to 6 days round trip from Hungo

Equipment: Extra-long rope(s) (100m double ropes are best); a dozen or so rock pitons from thin blades to a 1" angle; one set of wired nuts; one set of Friends or TriCams; eight or ten ice screws; bivi gear (including single-point suspension enclosed hammocks)

Season: December to March

Comments: Kwangde is (mis)classified as a "Trekking Peak" by His Majesty's Government of Nepal, so you must get a permit in Kathmandu before you can climb. Although Kwangde is not high by Himalayan standards, climbers should take all the precautions to acclimatize and avoid altitude illness.

Approach: Travel by air or foot from Kathmandu to Lukla. Porters or yaks can be arranged in Lukla to carry your gear and food to Namche Bazaar and on to Hungo, a 2- or 3-day walk.

Route: From the village of Hungo there is an elevation gain of around 5,000 feet through rhododendron forests and grassy hillsides to the crest of the moraine at the base of Kwangde's face. With full loads, expect it to take 5 to 7 hours—if you are already acclimatized. It is probably worth establishing an advanced camp below the face and making a few carries from Hungo to the advanced camp for purposes of acclimatization. There are four major tongues of ice in the lower wall in a more or less direct line beneath the summit. The route takes the second tongue from the left. The first 1,800 feet is often very thin, squeaky,

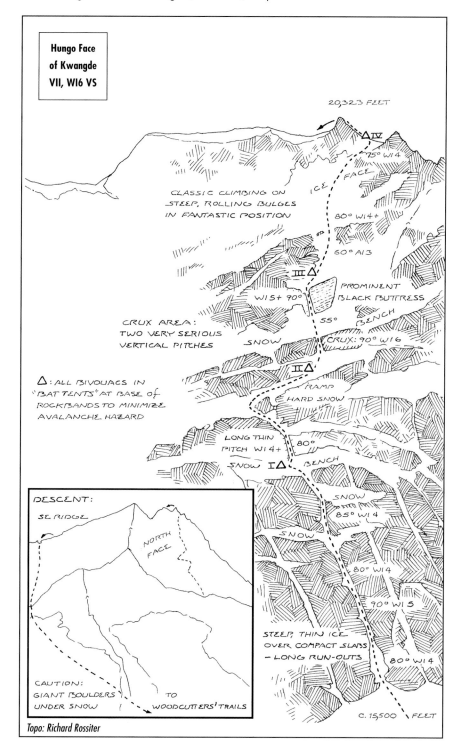

**Hungo Face
of Kwangde
VII, WI6 VS**

20,323 FEET

△ IV

75° WI4

ICE FACE

CLASSIC CLIMBING ON
STEEP, ROLLING BULGES
IN FANTASTIC POSITION

80° WI4+

60° AI3

III △

WI5+ 90°

PROMINENT
BLACK BUTTRESS

55°

BENCH

CRUX AREA:
TWO VERY SERIOUS
VERTICAL PITCHES

SNOW

CRUX: 90° WI6

II △

RAMP

HARD SNOW

△: ALL BIVOUACS IN
"BAT TENTS" AT BASE OF
ROCKBANDS TO MINIMIZE
AVALANCHE HAZARD

LONG THIN
PITCH WI4+

80°

SNOW I △

BENCH

SNOW
85° WI4

SNOW

80° WI4

90° WI5

STEEP THIN ICE
OVER COMPACT SLABS
– LONG RUN-OUTS

80° WI4

DESCENT:

SE RIDGE

NORTH
FACE

CAUTION:
GIANT BOULDERS
UNDER SNOW

TO
WOODCUTTERS' TRAILS

C. 15,500 FEET

Topo: Richard Rossiter

**Jeff Lowe at the top of the
thin, rotten-ice crux of the
Hungo Face of Kwangde**
(Photo: David Breashears)

friable ice over crackless rock. In several places you will need to run out the lead more than 200 feet to find a belay. This section up to the site of the first bivouac for the first ascent has ice to 90° (WI5). Above the first bivouac site is somewhat lower-angle, but very thin and poorly protected, ice. This leads to a snow ledge that jogs left around the lower part of the central rock band and then back right 300 or 400 feet to the only ice break in the upper part of the central band. The first ascent party bivouacked again here. Very thin, detached vertical ice provides a long pitch over the steepest part of the central rock band, and is the crux of the climb (WI6 VS). From here, ascend a narrow and increasingly steep gully/chimney to the left of a black rock prow in the upper left center of the face to yet another hammock bivouac at the top of a lower-angle slope. The final section of the face consists of WI3 to WI5 climbing on 50° to 85° ice diagonally up and right to a junction with the Northeast Ridge a few hundred feet below the summit. A fourth bivouac is possible here. From this point, easy 5th-class rock climbing up the Northeast Ridge leads to the highest point.

Descent: From the summit, drop off the South Face in a slightly easterly diagonal direction, making rappels and down-climbing the ice face for 1,000 to 1,500 feet to arrive at an almost-flat hanging glacier. Follow the hanging glacier east to the notch between Kwangde and Kwangde Nup. A few rappels and a lot of down-climbing on the East Face below the notch bring you to the basin between the peaks. From here it is an arduous and intricate route-finding job down around the toe of the northeast ridge of Kwangde and through the bush-choked slopes above Hungo. Eventually you will connect with woodcutters' trails that will take you back to the village.

The Northwest Face of Kangtega, Khumbu, Nepal

Twin-summited Kangtega towers like a glacier-capped fortress above Thyang-boche Monastery, the heart of the spiritual lives of the Sherpas. Whereas its more famous neighbor to the north, Ama Dablam, represents the epitome of mountain elegance with its clean spire and sweeping ridges, Kangtega is complex, blocky, and forcefully inaccessible from the northwest vantage. Its sheer West Face falls for thousands of feet from the summit plateau, threatened by ice cliffs several hundred feet high. The Northwest Ridge, dividing the steep, icy Northeast Face from the West Face, soars an impressive 6,000 feet to a fore-summit that is separated by a deep and worrisome gash from the edge of the summit plateau. The Northwest Peak, which is slightly lower than the Southeast Peak, rises directly out of the plateau glacier. To reach the main peak from the northwest, the summit plateau must be crossed by passing below the Northwest Peak, and another 1,000-foot, fluted ice face is confronted on the west side of the summit pyramid.

On our summit day in April 1986, I was feeling sick, so our foursome split into two ropes of two, with Marc Twight and Alison Hargreaves making the more arduous climb to the Southeast Peak, while Tom Frost and I contented ourselves with an easier, uproped climb to the virgin Northwest Peak.

This route is long and varied, with surprises at every turn, a lot of moderate climbing, and a truly difficult mixed-climbing crux. There are bivouacs in self-dug snow caves, as well as in an immense natural ice cavern, which we found on the left edge of the summit ice cap, above the headwall crux.

Kangtega *(Photo: Jeff Lowe)*

Location: The Northwest Face of Kangtega is located in Khumbu, Nepal, south of Mount Everest, above Thyangboche Monastery (Schneider map "Solo Khumbu" available in bookstores in Kathmandu).

First Ascent: To Northwest Peak: Tom Frost and Jeff Lowe, April 1986; to Southeast Peak: Marc Twight and Alison Hargreaves, April 1986

Elevation Gain: About 7,000 feet

Difficulty: Grade VII, AI4+, WI4, M6

Time: The first ascent required 10 days round trip from base camp to base camp. A fast, well-acclimatized team of two should be able to cut at least 3 or 4 days from that time.

Equipment: Eight or ten ice screws, a dozen rock pitons, a set of Stoppers and a set of Friends, one deadman, full bivi gear

Season: March to May (premonsoon) or September to November (postmonsoon)

Comments: Kangtega is high enough that careful acclimatization is a prerequisite to a successful and safe alpine-style climb. A permit is necessary to climb Kangtega. You can obtain the application from the American Alpine Club Expedition Committee, 710 Tenth Street, Golden, Colorado, 80401, USA, or from the American Mountain Foundation, 1520 Alamo Avenue, Colorado Springs, Colorado, 80907, USA.

Approach: You will meet your liaison officer and *sirdar* (head Sherpa), in Kathmandu. They will help with the purchase of food, the arranging of porters, and so forth. From Kathmandu fly—or take the bus to Jiri and walk— to Lukla. From Lukla it is a 3-day walk to Thyangboche (13,500 feet), a good place to spend a couple nights acclimatizing. From Thyangboche take the trail north toward Pangboche; but just after passing the convent at the bottom of the hill below Thyangboche, take a trail to the right that leads up into a broad valley and a very comfortable base camp in a boulder-strewn meadow at 14,000 feet (about 4 hours from Thyangboche).

Route: From base camp walk up to the toe of the Northwest Ridge and follow the glacier diagonally up and right along the base of the Northwest Face. You will gain several thousand feet of elevation on this glacier, with two or three steeper

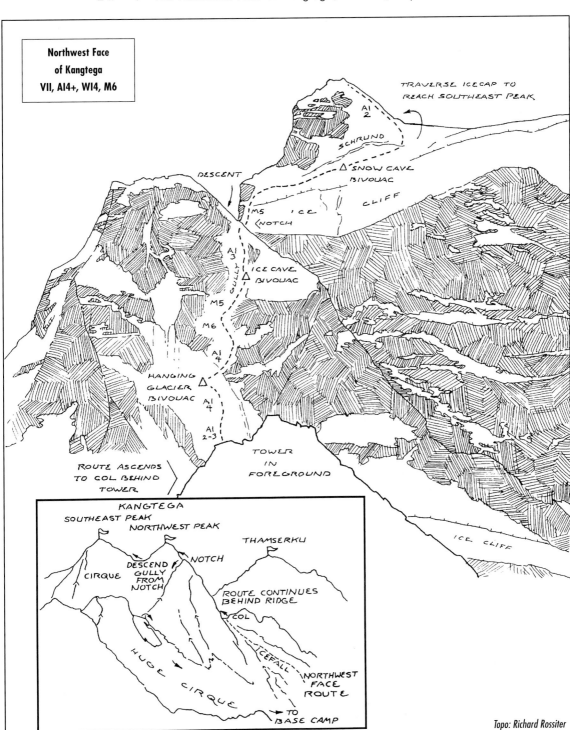

Northwest Face
of Kangtega
VII, AI4+, WI4, M6

TRAVERSE ICECAP TO
REACH SOUTHEAST PEAK

AI 2

SCHRUND

SNOW CAVE
BIVOUAC

ICE CLIFF

DESCENT

M5 ICE
(NOTCH

AI 3

GULLY

ICE CAVE
BIVOUAC

M5

M6

AI 4

HANGING
GLACIER
BIVOUAC

AI 4

AI 2-3

ROUTE ASCENDS
TO COL BEHIND
TOWER

TOWER
IN
FOREGROUND

ICE CLIFF

KANGTEGA
SOUTHEAST PEAK
NORTHWEST PEAK

THAMSERKU

DESCEND
GULLY
FROM
NOTCH

NOTCH

CIRQUE

ROUTE CONTINUES
BEHIND RIDGE

COL

HUGE CIRQUE

ICEFALL

NORTHWEST
FACE
ROUTE

TO
BASE CAMP

Topo: Richard Rossiter

Left: **In the area between the col at the top of the approach glacier and the Great Notch on the Northwest Ridge, the Northwest Face route follows a glacier tongue and the headwall above—in about 25 pitches of climbing.**
Right: **Marc Twight on the first pitch of the headwall**

(Photos: Jeff Lowe)

steps and a final short headwall. The headwall leads to a saddle between a little point sticking out from the bottom of a huge tongue of ice that drops from a tiny hanging glacier perched on the side of the Northwest Face. A dozen pitches of AI3 to 4 climbing take you to the hanging glacier. Five difficult pitches of steep ice and mixed climbing (varying from WI4 to M6) ascend the headwall up and right from the hanging glacier into the trough on the left side of the summit ice cap. Another five or six easier pitches (AI3) lead to the major notch in the Northwest Ridge. The pitch out of the notch onto the ice cap is quite difficult (M5), but it deposits you on the huge shelf below the Northwest Peak. Contour around the shelf and some moderate slopes below the Northwest Peak until you can see the ice face on the main peak. From here it is a 400-foot ascent on 45° to 60° snow to the Northwest Peak (AI2). To continue on to the main summit, you must lose some elevation as you walk down and across the glacier to the base of the face. Ten pitches of AI3 to 4 ice bring you to the summit.

Descent: Rappel and down-climb back to the notch in the Northwest Ridge. It might be preferable to continue down the route of ascent, but we descended the couloir on the east side of the notch in a dozen rappels to the glacial basin on the other side, then walked north and crossed over a notch in the Northeast Ridge, and finally made twenty or so rappels down the face at the head of the valley above base camp.

**Marc Twight walking across
the ice cap toward the final ice
face on Kangtega's main peak**
(Photo: Jeff Lowe)

AFTERWORD

Ice climbing is a path of approach to a world apart. It is a simpler, more dynamic world than the one we are used to. Death is close. Social concerns drop away as so many inconsistencies in a logical argument. The truth of an individual's nature begins to emerge as instinct shows its old, forgotten face.

There is a certain purity in engaging in what some would call a "useless activity." When the ice climber confronts the overhang, it is with the knowledge that no material gain will result from the completion of the task. Yet the climber's whole physical, mental, and spiritual being is committed to climbing the bulge, confident that when the climb is complete, the satisfaction will outweigh the effort.

However, the person with gravity tugging at his or her heels also senses the absurdity of the situation. In the face of great difficulty, the climber's mind may revolt against the challenge's apparent stupidity. But on second thought, the climber sees that no greater inherent meaning infuses the life left behind, except the meaning the climber invests in it. And so, as Don Juan says in Carlos Casteneda's *The Teachings of Don Juan*, the climber simply must "choose the path with heart."

Two people sit with their dreams in a cold room. Several candles illuminate the abandoned building that sheltered them the previous night. The flickering candle-light shows no affinity for the corners of the room, and the climbers find the darkness somehow oppressive. They waste no time in packing their gear for an escape from a space that has all the ambience of a tomb.

Later, they climb up to a hole in the ice with a ceiling of a hundred icicles and a floor of frozen motion. Superficially this cave resembles the room where they passed the night: it has an entrance, a floor, a ceiling. But the climbers feel the essential difference between this natural space and its manmade counterpart. The light showing through the translucent walls lends magnificence to the emotions of the pair. And whereas they had felt entombed in the confines of the building, discovering the cave is like finding a bright new home.

They are, purely and simply, climbing. *(Photo: John Krakauer)*

When they again find themselves out on the exposed face, there are no questions in their minds, and they are not looking for answers. They are, purely and simply, climbing.

INDEX

Founded in 1906, The Mountaineers is a Seattle-based non-profit outdoor activity and conservation club with 15,000 members, whose mission is "to explore, study, preserve, and enjoy the natural beauty of the outdoors . . . . " The club sponsors many classes and year-round outdoor activities in the Pacific Northwest, and supports environmental causes by sponsoring legislation and presenting educational programs. The Mountaineers Books supports the club's mission by publishing travel and natural history guides, instructional texts, and works on conservation and history. For information, call or write The Mountaineers, Club Headquarters, 300 Third Avenue West, Seattle, Washington, 98119; (206) 284-6310.

ABOUT THE AUTHOR

Jeff Lowe was skiing by the time he was four and at seven scaled the highest mountain in the Tetons. Ever since his first ascent of Colorado's Bridalveil Falls in 1974, he has been one of the world's premiere ice climbers, with a list of first ascents on ice that includes the Hungo Face of Kwangde in the Himalayas, Keystone Green Steps in Alaska, Asteroid Alley in Canada, and Birdbrain Boulevard in Colorado. In April 1994 he created Octopussy, currently the most difficult mixed climb in the world. In addition to designing innovative equipment and clothing for climbers, he has written numerous articles for such periodicals as *Sports Illustrated*, *Rock & Ice*, *Outside*, and *Climbing* and two books, *The Ice Experience* and *Climbing* (with Ron Fawcett, Paul Nunn, and Alan Rouse). He and his wife, Teri Ebel, and their two children live in Nederland, Colorado.

Also available from Arctic Wolf, P. O. Box 2035, Nederland, CO 80466 (800) 315-3932

Waterfall Ice: Jeff Lowe's Climbing Techniques
An Instructional Video with Bird Lew

Shot on location in Ouray, Vail, and Boulder Canyon in Colorado, and on Poke-o-Moonshine in the Adirondacks of New York, this comprehensive three-hour video includes thorough explanations and demonstrations of Lowe's innovative and little-known techniques as well as recommendations for choosing proper gear and clothing. $39.95

Alpine Ice: Jeff Lowe's Ice Climbing Techniques
An Instructional Video with Teri Ebel

Prepare yourself to climb the glaciers, seracs, couloirs, and ice faces of the alpine realm. This two-hour video outlines Lowe's methods for maximizing speed and conserving energy without sacrificing security. Also covered are the wide variety of ice and snow conditions encountered in the mountains and the essential skills needed for glacier travel, crevasse rescue, weather assessment, etc. $39.95